Religion
and Justice

in the War over Bosnia

Religion and Justice

in the War over Bosnia

edited by

G. Scott Davis

ROUTLEDGE
New York and London

Published in 1996 by

Routledge
29 West 35th Street
New York, NY 10001

Published in Great Britain by

Routledge
11 New Fetter Lane
London EC4P 4EE

Library of Congress Cataloging-in-Publication Data

Religion and justice in the war over Bosnia / edited by G. Scott Davis.
　　　　　p.　　　cm.
Includes bibliographical references and index.
ISBN 0-415-91519-8 (cloth). -- ISBN 0-415-91520-1 (pbk.)
1. Yugoslav War, 1991–, --Religious aspects. 2. Yugoslav War, 1991–, Moral
and ethical aspects. 3. Yugoslav War, 1991–, --Bosnia and Hercegovina.
4. Yugoslav War, 1991–, --Historiography. 5. Bosnia and Hercegovina--
History--1992– 6. Just war doctrine.
I. Davis, G. Scott, 1953–　.
DR1313.7.R45R45　　1996
949.702'4--dc20   96-25541
                                                                  CIP

Contents

Preface

This is an ambitious book. Any attempt to interpret events as they happen risks being misled by the limits of background knowledge, available information, and a general uncertainty about the impact of developing events on the future. When the events in question comprise war and mayhem, international recriminations, and mutually inconsistent accounts of what is happening and why, any interpretation can be certain only of offending some of the interested parties. Nonetheless, it seemed worthwhile, when confronted with the breakup of Yugoslavia and daily reports of atrocities in Bosnia and elsewhere, to make the effort to get beyond journalism and attempt some critical analysis of the moral issues involved in the war over Bosnia. This is not simply an academic exercise, but an experiment in citizenship, for at some point we cannot avoid taking responsibility for the acts and policies of the government that represents us, and understanding our own policies is inextricably tied to an understanding of the events that are presently shaping the international arena.

One of our goals is to be genuinely interdisciplinary. The division of academic labor often distances philosophers from political scientists, and both from historians. This is a bad thing. On the one hand, it encourages us to believe that events can be understood outside the narratives that have shaped and led up to them. On the other, it tempts us to think that justice and political judgment can be carried out with no thought for the practical give and take of life in the everyday world. If political life is the shared pursuit of the common good, then all the various goods must be taken seriously: goods of character and of material satisfaction, goods of international power and of internal solidarity. Even if we reject in the end some goods as legitimate objects of reasonable desire, we will remain accountable for our reasons why and why not.

Multidisciplinary aspirations do not, of course, insure a complete and comprehensive treatment of the subject. The essays that follow focus on particular issues, and are intended to be complete and self-contained. Consequently there are any number of issues that are not addressed or are considered only in passing. It is, therefore, only fitting that I let the reader in on how I put together the chronology and the introduction. Prior to embarking on this enterprise, I, like all too many Americans, had scant knowledge of the cultural and political history of Eastern Europe, much less of the Balkans. The region hovered on the edges of historical classics such as Barraclough's *Origins of Modern Germany* and Taylor's *Struggle for Mastery*, and there lingered a certain romantic association between Yugoslavian taverns and Homeric epic, traceable to Lord's *Singer of Tales*. I went first to the overview afforded by Singleton (1985). From there I moved to the available volumes of *A History of East Central Europe*, edited by Sugar and Treadgold for the University of Washington Press, supplemented by Barbara Jelavich's two-volume history of the Balkans. These pointed me to more specialized literature. Toward the end of my historical peregrinations I benefited from the appearance of Malcolm (1994) and Donia and Fine (1994). All of these sources contributed to the chronology that follows.

My goal in the chronology was to make the sorts of connections an informed reader might want to know for putting the Bosnian conflict in perspective. It strikes me as useful to be reminded that the southward movement of the Slavs was roughly contemporary with both the emergence of Islam and the entry of the Angles and Saxons into the British Isles. That the Ottoman conquest of Bosnia, the Spanish expulsion of the Jews, the decimation of the Americas, and the beginning of the Protestant Reformation happened within the span of a single lifetime should remind all parties of the tragic interconnectedness of war, religion, and cultural chauvinism which we have inherited from early modern Europe. No doubt I have left out important dates and events, though the advice of my colleague John Treadway, of the

University of Richmond's History Department, has improved the final version.

The editor's introduction is somewhat different. There I tried to bring out what I take to be the limits of journalism for providing an adequate grasp of the situation. We cannot do without the press and electronic media, but were we to rest content with the resources they provide it would be nigh on impossible to make morally informed judgments. After examining some examples of reporting from Serbia and Bosnia, I offer a brief introduction to the "just war" tradition in contemporary American thought. This is purely preparatory and in no way definitive, for while most of the contributors to this volume have written in and about that tradition, they are by no means uniform in their interpretations and applications. This is by design. Each essay stands on its own as an example of thoughtful scholarship directed toward understanding a complex ongoing set of political events. Seamless unanimity would almost certainly be a sign of intellectual flabbiness.

One concession to continuity, however, should not go unremarked. All but one of the essays in this volume were written and forwarded to me in July 1995. The last arrived shortly thereafter. The several stages of editing, even given the exceptional industry of my various editors at Routledge, could hardly keep up with developments on the ground in Bosnia. In this last run-through of the whole manuscript I have made an effort to bring the chronological stance in line with the current situation, usually by doing little more than changing tenses or excising a phrase that is no longer germane. While the individual contributors must, of course, take responsibility for the substance and argument of their essays, I deserve the lion's share for what awkwardnesses remain.

My editorial decisions do not reflect any consensus on the part of the contributors. I, of course, think everyone would be better off agreeing with me about most everything. I cannot guarantee that they will, so I should probably make clear where I stand on nationalism and the nation-state. I don't trust either. Between the first and final drafts of this preface I came upon Bogdan Denitch's *Ethnic Nationalism*, a very trenchant analysis of the background of and prospects for the current conflict and similar ones we may expect in the future. Although I have not changed anything in the body of the introduction or my contribution as a result of reading Denitch's book, it has deepened and clarified my thinking, and for the future I will stand markedly in his debt. In his own *caveat emptor*, Denitch writes that "the best of all alternatives, of course, would be the effective self-mobilization of democratic, egalitarian, and nonnationalist forces in Croatia, Serbia, and Bosnia." (1994: 21) I believe the same is true for the future political health of the United States. Though we are not likely to experience the murderous disintegration of Yugoslavia anytime in the near future, recent legislation against immigrants, calls for an official language, and assaults on the integrity of nonconforming minorities of all sorts are ominous and depressing. Books like this one, whatever else they aspire to, are invitations to the literate public to tackle the sort of thinking that helps us articulate the best of our own alternatives.

Acknowledgments

I mentioned above the exceptional help received from the Routledge editorial staff at every stage of this project. It's been a pleasure. So too has been my interaction with those colleagues who contributed to this volume. My family has suffered the usual enormities and I herewith tender the usual thanks. But I owe a special debt to the University of Richmond. My appointment as the first holder of the Lewis T. Booker Chair in Religion and Ethics provided the opportunity and the resources to undertake this project and bring it to fruition. I am grateful for the privilege.

Richmond, Virginia
January 28, 1996

A Note on Language

Of the peoples of what was Yugoslavia, all but the native Albanian speakers and a few ethnic minorities speak some dialect of the southern branch of the Slavic languages. The languages of the Serbs, Croats, and Bosnians bear each to the other a relation similar to those of Danes, Swedes, and Norwegians among the Germanic speakers. The Slovenes and Macedonians, to continue the analogy, would hold the positions of English and German. Albanian is also an Indo-European language, bearing to Slavic a relation analogous to that between English and French. Neither Hungarian nor Turkish, historically important to the Balkans, are Indo-European, though they bear an uncertain relation to each other.

Keeping these matters in mind is often important for assessing the claims and counterclaims of the various groups. When Orthodox Serbs refer to Bosnian Muslims, for example, it may sound like members of one long established ethnic group challenging the heirs of alien invaders. The fact is that Orthodox Serbs are the Serbo-Croatian-speaking children of Slav ancestors who moved south sometime around the sixth century and converted to Christianity sometime after the ninth, while Bosnian Muslims are the Serbo-Croatian-speaking children of the same Slav ancestors, who moved south at the same time but converted to Islam sometime after the fifteenth century. The proper analogy is that between an English Catholic and an English Protestant.

The relative homogeneity of ethnic and linguistic backgrounds is obscured by difference in alphabet. The Cyrillic alphabet is based on the Greek brought north by the missionaries Cyril and Methodius and modified over time to accommodate the phonemes common to Slavic. As it happened, early medieval rivalry between Rome and Constantinople for control of the Slav churches manifested itself in a competition between the Latin and Cyrillic alphabets. Croats inherited the Latin, while Serbs went with the Cyrillic, though it's but a day's diversion to learn to transliterate one to the other. Nonetheless, the rivalry remains an opportunity for one group to tweak the other, as in Franjo Tudjman's provocative and ill-conceived order to remove Cyrillic signs from Croatian streets in 1990.

For English readers it is obviously appropriate to stay with the Latin, but there remains the problem of how to represent Slavic names and phrases. Rebecca West, in *Black Lamb and Grey Falcon*, played it by ear, but she had a very good ear. The ancient memory of my introductory Russian is not a reliable guide. A fairly simple system of diacritical remarks has been developed for representing the most distinctive phonemes, but it can get in the way for some readers and is time-consuming to type without an altered keyboard. Even those who use the diacritics are occasionally inconsistent, as for example Glenny, who generally uses *s* for *sh* but regularly gives *Prishtina* for the capital of Kosovo, deviating thereby from the 1991 Michelin roadmap that I've kept ready to hand. I have followed Gutman and others in eliminating diacritics altogether. Still, for those interested, I provide the following rough guide:

c   Neither English *s* or *k*, it can range from the *ts* of *itsy-bitsy*, which is written with the simple *c*, to the *tch* of *batch*, written either *ć* or *č*.

dj The sort of *j* sound you get in a phrase like "he'd just better watch his backside."

h   The back-of-the-mouth sound that you're supposed to make for *Loch Ness*.

j   An English *y*. Yugoslavia and Jugoslavia are both Yugoslavia.

s   Is either an English *s* or *sh*, written *š*.

z   Is either an English *z* or *zh*, written *ž*.

Anyone with a passing acquaintance with Russian names will soon begin to recognize the familiar patronymics and diminutives. Thus

Karadjordje, Black George, is the father of Alexander Karadjordjevic, and so forth. The little weekend place, to take a loan word from English, becomes a *vikendica* on the model of the French *maison-maisonette*.

Yugoslavia, Croatia, Belgrade, and other place names are more familiar in their Latinized forms than *Jugoslavia, Hrvatska, Beograd,* and so on. I've retained the familiar. The same is true for *chetnik* as opposed to *cetnik*, and a few similar terms. *Krajina* poses an interesting problem. The word means "frontier" or "border area," but specifically refers to the military buffer zone established in Croatia by the Habsburgs, beginning in the sixteenth century. Serbs moved into the area to take advantage of special privileges extended to settlers, thus creating a band of Serbs between Croats and Bosnians (cf. Kann & David, 1884; Jelavich & Jelavich, 1977). *The Krajina* refers to this area, a part of Croatia. Finally, I use *South Slavs* and *Yugoslavs* interchangeably to refer to the Slavs inhabiting the lands that used to be Yugoslavia, whatever they are called today.

A Chronological Sketch

(early dates are sometimes approximate)

324 The Emperor Constantine consolidates rule over the Roman Empire, founding the city of Constantinople (Turkish Istanbul), which subsequently becomes the capitol of Byzantium, the earlier name for the Greek colony on the site

381 The Council of Nicaea promulgates a definitive creed for Christian Church

500 Migrating Slavs, originating probably in Belarus, begin to incorporate or eliminate prehistoric Thracian and Illyrian culture from the Balkan Peninsula

610–732 The career of Muhammad (d. 632) and the expansion of Islam through Arabia, the Fertile Crescent, North Africa, and Spain, culminating in the West with the defeat of Muslim armies by the Franks at Poitiers

650 Croats and Serbs, migrating from what is now Iran, establish presence in Balkans though ultimately assimilated by Slavs

800 Charlemagne the Frank crowned Emperor by the Pope at Rome

863–93 Mission of the Greek Christians Cyril (d. 869) and Methodius (d. 885) to the South Slavs; development of Cyrillic alphabet for representing the various Slavic languages

895–933 Magyars push east across modern Hungary to be stopped by Germans at Merseburg, on the border of Saxony

970 The Bulgarian priest Kozma writes against the followers of Bogomil, whose extreme ascetic movement spreads throughout the Balkans

1054 The Great Schism fractures Christendom into a "western" church, using a Latin liturgy, and an "eastern" church, using Greek and

Slavic liturgies, dividing East Central Europe into competing religious communities

1095 Pope Urban II proclaims the First Crusade to take Jerusalem from the Muslims

1204 Western armies of the Fourth Crusade capture and sack Constantinople, displacing the Byzantine rulers to Nicaea

1221–42 Tatar (Mongol) horsemen devastate Russia, Poland, Hungary, and other parts of East Central Europe

1261 Byzantine armies recapture Constantinople

1310–75 The House of Anjou established in Hungary; expulsion of non-Christians and systematic subjugation of Orthodox to Catholic

1338–49 Plague spreads west from Eurasian steppe to Constantinople and Alexandria (1347), Italy, France, and North Africa (1348), and Western Europe (1349), with mortality as high as forty percent in some areas

1345 Stephen Dusan of Serbia (d. 1355) claims the mantle of Emperor of the Serbs and Greeks

1366 Ottoman Turks achieve first major European gains at Adrianople (Edirne)

1377 Tvrtko of Bosnia (d. 1391) claims the kingship of Bosnia and Serbia

1382–86 Ottoman victories in Bulgaria, Albania (1385), and Serbia (1386)

1389 Battle of Kosovo Polje (Blackbird's Field); the Ottoman victory over the Serbs becomes the symbolic center of Serbian political history

1402–19 John Hus emerges as Czech voice for reform of Catholic Church; Hus is burned at the stake (1415); confrontation between Hussite and anti-Hussite factions leads to the Defenestration of Prague (1419)

1453 Constantinople falls to Ottoman armies; end of Eastern Roman (Byzantine) Empire

1459 King Stephen Tomas of Bosnia begins suppression of the Bosnian Christian Church in an attempt to enlist papal aid

1463 Bosnia and Herzegovina incorporated into the Ottoman Empire

1492 Expulsion of Spanish Jews following the reconquest of Muslim Spain leads to Jewish immigration to Ottoman lands, including Balkans

1509 Papal crusade proclaimed against non-Catholics in Poland and Lithuania

1517 Martin Luther's *Ninety-Five Theses* initiates the conflicts of the Protestant Reformation

1520 Accession of Suleyman I (d. 1566) as Sultan of Ottoman Empire

1526 Battle of Mohacs; Ottomans occupy Buda

1529 First Siege of Vienna, initiating three centuries of Ottoman/Habsburg conflict

1566 Death of Suleyman I in Ottoman victory at Szigetvar; battle becomes central theme in subsequent Croatian literature

1618 Beginning of the Thirty Years War; birth of Croatian writer Juraj Krizanic, early advocate of Slavic unification

1620 Battle of the White Mountain establishes Catholic ascendancy over Czech Protestants

1648 Peace of Westphalia ends Thirty Years War

1666 Jewish messianic movement associates Sabbatai Zwi and Nathan of Gaza; long-term impact on Jewish life in Ottoman and European lands

1677–81 First Ottoman/Russian War

1683 Death of Krizanic at Second Siege of Vienna

1699 Peace of Karlowitz; Habsburg incorporation of Hungary

1742 Birth of Serbian author Dositej Obradovic (d. 1811), advocate of Enlightenment ideals to the South Slavs

1787 Birth of Serbian scholar Vuk Karadzic (d. 1864), central figure in collecting and codifying Serbo-Croatian oral tradition

1789 French Revolution sets seed of independence movements in Europe and European dominions

1793 Birth of Jan Kollar (d. 1852), Slovak romantic and nationalist

1798 First campaigns of Napoleon Bonaparte (1769–1821)

1802 Birth of Lajos Kossuth (d. 1894), Hungarian leader and liberal advocate

1804 Serbian revolution under the leadership of Karadjordje Petrovic, founder of Serbian dynasty; Serbian autonomy recognized (1807); Ottoman reoccupation, Karadjordje flees to Habsburg territory (1812)

1815 Defeat of Napoleon; Congress of Vienna; second Serbian revolt, led by Milos Obrenovic, founder of Serbian dynasty; Karadjordje attempts return, assassinated by party of Milos (1817); Serbian autonomy reestablished

1829 Treaty of Adrianople grants Serbian independence under house of Obrenovic; Greek independence; autonomy of Romanian lands

1834 Mileta's Revolt forces Serbian constitution; Milos abdicates (1839); Alexander, son of Karadjordje, installed (1842)

1848 Revolutionary outbreaks spread from France to Germany, Austria, and the Balkans, seriously threatening the stability of all Europe

1858 Restoration of Milos Obrenovic as Prince of Serbia; death of Milos, installation of Michael Obrenovic (1860); assassination of Michael, installation of Milan Obrenovic (1868)

1875 Muslim/Christian conflicts in Bosnia fueled by Panslavic enthusiasm; rising rebellion throughout Ottoman Europe; intervention by Russia (1877)

1878 Congress of Berlin negotiates partition of Ottoman lands in Europe; Habsburg Austria given administration of Bosnia and Herzegovina

1889 Abdication of Milan in favor of son Alexander; Alexander abolishes constitution (1893); Alexander Obrenovic assassinated; Peter Karadjordjevic offered kingship, constitution restored (1903)

1908 Austrian annexation of Bosnia and Herzegovina

1912–13 First and Second Balkan Wars pit Slavs against Turks, Slavs against Slavs

1914 Assassination of Habsburg Archduke Franz Ferdinand in Sarajevo precipitates First World War

1918 End of First World War; revolution in Russia ends with establishment of Soviet constitution; emergence of independent Slavic states, including the Kingdom of the Serbs, Croats, and Slovenes, under King Alexander Karadjordjevic (1921)

1922 Mussolini and Italian Fascists seize power in Rome

1929 Kingdom of Serbs, Croats, and Slovenes becomes Yugoslavia; emergence of nationalist Ustashe in Croatia; stock-market crash signals worldwide financial collapse

1931 King Alexander proclaims parliamentary constitution for Yugoslavia; elections boycotted

1933 Adolf Hitler becomes Chancellor of Germany

1934–36 Hitler consolidates power in Germany; King Alexander assassinated; Germany invades Rhineland; beginning of Spanish Civil War

1938 *Anschluss* unites Nazi Germany with Austria

1939 Fascist victory in Spain under Franco; Germany invades Poland; Britain and France declare war, initiating Second World War

1941 Joseph Stalin becomes Soviet Prime Minister; Germans occupy Belgrade; *Ustashe* proclaim independent Croatia, allied with Germany; communist Partisans and anti-communist *chetniks* constitute Yugoslav resistance; Japanese bombing of Pearl Harbor brings United States into the war

1945 Yugoslav state organized under Partisan leader Josip Broz Tito; death of Hitler; bombing of Hiroshima and Nagasaki; end of Second World War; emergence of communist coalition in East Central Europe

1948 Friction between Tito and Stalin; Yugoslavia expelled from Communist Information Bureau (Cominform); beginnings of Yugoslavian self-management

1949 Establishment of People's Republic of China under Mao Zedong

1950 Korean War, Asia emerges as site of major confrontations of communist/anti-communist Cold War

1953 Death of Stalin; emergence of Khruschev as Soviet leader

1956 Soviet invasion of Hungary to put down reform movement; Janos Kadar installed as Hungarian prime minister

1964 Gulf of Tonkin incident propels United States toward war in Vietnam; Khruschev ousted in favor of Leonid Breshnev and Alexei Kosygin

1968 Soviet invasion of Czechoslovakia in support of socialism against liberalizing reforms

1979 Soviet invasion of Afghanistan

1980 Death of Tito in Yugoslavia; establishment of the Solidarity trade union in Poland; beginning of Iran/Iraq War

1984 Emergence of Mikhail Gorbachev as Soviet leader

1987 Slobodan Milosevic becomes Serbian leader amidst rising Serbian nationalist agitation

1988 Ethnic conflicts in Soviet Union; strikes in Poland; shake-up of leadership in Hungary and Czechoslovakia; protests by Albanians of Kosovo against Serbian rule

1989 Fall of Berlin Wall; widespread shake-up of leadership throughout East Central Europe

1990 Slovenia demands more independence for Yugoslav republics; dissolution of Czechoslovakia and reconstitution as Czech and Slovak Federative Republic; Serbians occupy Pristina, capital of Kosovo; Iraq invades Kuwait; Zagreb meeting to prepare for Croatian and Slovenian secession from Yugoslavia

1991 Macedonia, Slovenia, and Croatia secede from Yugoslavia; commanded from Belgrade, Yugoslav National Army attacks Croatia; UN arms embargo; formal dissolution of the Soviet Union

1992 Cease fire in Croatia; United Nations Protection Force (UNPRO-FOR) deployed; Bosnia and Herzegovina, led by Alija Izetbegovic, secedes; Radovan Karadzic leads Bosnian Serbs in conflict with government; European and American ambassadors withdrawn from Belgrade; UN economic embargo against Serbia; siege of Sarajevo

1993 Various attempts to secure agreement to Vance-Owen plan for "cantonization" of Bosnia

1994 Mortar attack on Sarajevo market generates international outrage, calls for NATO action against Serbs

1995 NATO airstrikes provoke taking of UNPROFOR hostages; Bosnian government forces attempt to break siege of Sarajevo; Croatian offensive retakes the Krajina region; systematic NATO airstrikes result in Serb calls for peace talks, with Slobodan Milosevic representing the Bosnian Serbs; U.S.-sponsored peace talks in Dayton, Ohio, lead to an accord calling for a unified Bosnia and Herzegovina, made up of a Bosnian-Croat Federation with control of 51 percent of the land and a Serb Republic with control of 49 percent of the land

1996 Peace-keeping forces under NATO command begin to enforce cease-fire and withdrawal to borders established by the Dayton Accord

Introduction

Interpreting Contemporary Conflicts

G. Scott Davis

In 1985, contemplating the prospects for Yugoslavia after Tito and more than aware of the "centrifugal forces" driving sections of the nation apart, Fred Singleton recorded that "my own inclinations are towards optimism and hope for the future." (Singleton, 1985: 285) Writing shortly after the elections of December 1990, Ivo Banac allowed that "the possibility of . . . civil war is great," while still holding out a chance for "peaceful, internationally supervised, negotiated dissolution, leading to at most a loose confederal arrangement." (1992: 186) His more pessimistic premonitions carried the day. From Vukovar to Mostar, Dubrovnik to Sarajevo, scenes of death and destruction of the civilian populations of Croatia and Bosnia are now commonplace. Slobodan Milosevic's rise to power in 1987–88, his call for a "Greater Serbia," and his suppression of Kosovo in the south and Vojvodina to the north, coupled with the worsening economic situation, led to increased tensions throughout 1989, which culminated in the fracas at the Communist Party congress in January 1990 that came to mark the symbolic end of Yugoslavia.

Beginning in June of 1991, out-and-out war moved from Slovenia to Croatia to Bosnia, with the Bosnians in particular having borne the brunt of the fighting. Cease-fires came and went; plans for the partition of Bosnia were embraced, and rejected, as it suited the aims of one party or another. The early summer of 1995 witnessed some gains by the Bosnian government, but the breakaway Serbs led by Radovan

Karadzic and his general, Ratko Mladic, responded in July by taking the safe haven of Srebrenica, amidst reports of massive atrocities. In August, as the United States and its allies wrangled over how to protect Bosnia, the reinvigorated Croatian army launched a campaign to retake the Krajina. Finally, as summer moved toward fall, NATO forces mounted a systematic air attack on Bosnian Serb installations. American diplomatic pressure, led by Assistant Secretary of State Richard Holbrooke, resulted in talks at Dayton, Ohio, which ultimately produced a peace accord promising a unified Bosnia and Herzegovina, made up of a Bosnian-Croat Federation and a Serbian Republic. As the new year rolled in, a NATO-led force to number some sixty thousand troops was being deployed in Bosnia. There was an uneasy peace, broken occasionally by snipers and anti-tank guns. Though at present the cease-fire is holding, few are willing to predict how long it will last.

But pessimism, however sober, does not absolve us from thought or action. Writing as the states of Communist Europe fell, and shortly before the buildup to Desert Storm and the Gulf War, Paul Kennedy insisted on the "clear need for the United States polity to understand much more about what is going on outside its borders." (Kennedy, 1991: 182) The interrelations of political, economic, and social change make it impossible to envision and plan for the future without some attempt to coordinate our political and social goals, and in lieu of a major cataclysm such coordination will have to be international as well as domestic. The ways that we do this will themselves command moral scrutiny, not simply from some "the bell tolls for thee" solidarity, but because of our complicity in events and their aftermath.

Consider Susan Strange's claim that "in Yugoslavia the fundamental imbalance of military force between Serbs and the Bosnians was indirectly the result of two ways in which the United States exercised its structural power in matters of security." (1995: 64) Her argument hinges on the leadership taken by the United States in making Yugoslavia a formidable Cold War army as a challenge to Soviet domination. Having watched that army be coopted in support of Milosevic's Serbia, the United States acquiesced in the embargo that kept arms from the Bosnian government. Strange concludes that "without leadership from Washington, it is doubtful whether this unevenhanded treatment of the civil conflict would have persisted for so long." (1995: 65)

My interest here is not in the justice of Strange's accusation, but in the way that any strategic policy implicates one country in the lives of others. If she is right in seeing the international community's treatment of Bosnia as "unevenhanded" then an injustice has been committed, and if our government engineered the situation then it shares in the blame. To recognize a blameworthy situation and do nothing about it compounds the offense. At least that's what we teach our children. Of course, if Strange is not right then it's another story, but either way it becomes a matter of conscience to bring whatever resources are available to bear on finding out where justice lies.

This is the point at which journalism become tremendously important. While it is a common trope of correspondents to portray themselves as cynical and hard-boiled, the detached coolness is part of a strategy to avoid being misled by the powers that be. Telling the truth is what journalists contribute to our attempts to be just. Worries about justice were responsible, in at least some measure, for the outrage felt by many journalists and their audience at the handling of the press during the Gulf War. Attempts to restrict reporting in the Gulf prompted a number of organizations and individuals to file suit against the government for its attempt to control the flow of information. (cf. Schanberg, 1991)

Just before the Gulf War broke out, Walter Cronkite wrote of the importance of a free press in time of conflict. He recounted the following story from his experience in the Second World War:

> Once in England the censors held up my report that the Eighth Air Force had bombed Germany through a solid cloud cover. This was politically sensitive; our air staff maintained we were practicing only precision bombing on military topics. But the censors released my story when I pointed out the obvious—Germans on the ground and the Luftwaffe attacking bombers knew the clouds were there. The truth was not being withheld from the Germans but from the Americans. (Cronkite, 1991: 382)

Indiscriminate bombing is an affront to justice, and keeping such information from the American public serves no legitimate war aim; it serves only the attempt of American strategy makers to avoid accountability. If our strategies are questionable, then as citizens we should hold our leaders to account. Cronkite tells the story in order to highlight the duplicity of the censors in the Gulf, closing with the healthy reminder that "any system that prevented the press from reporting freely on all aspects of the conflict could not have well served a democratic people." (1991: 383) Judgments of responsibility inevitably depend on findings of fact, and for this a free and independent journalism is indispensable. It is the beginning of any attempt to interpret the rights and wrongs of an ongoing war.

But it is not sufficient, a fact brought home with a vengeance by a cursory survey of the writing on the conflict in Bosnia. Take, by way of illustration, the Sunday *New York Times* for June 4, 1995. R. W. Apple's lead article for the "Week in Review" section provides a helpful summary of what constrains the major powers from acting decisively in Bosnia. Thomas Friedman's Op-Ed piece endorses lifting the arms embargo and attempting to contain the fighting within Bosnia. Among the letters to the editor, one advocates U.S. intervention of some sort on behalf of the Bosnian Muslims. Another takes A. M. Rosenthal to task for confusing Radovan Karadzic and his "murderous thugs" with Christian patriots, while Alex Dragnich reiterates the claim that "the Serbs want nothing more than the right recognized for the other ethnic groups that constituted Yugoslavia—self-determination." (Dragnich, 1995) Dragnich's contribution is interesting, connecting as it does the world of public debate with the halls of the academy. His earlier work is regularly cited in discussions of the origins of Yugoslavia, and the 1993 paperback edition of his *Serbs and Croats* offers the *Wall Street Journal*'s judgment that the "narrative has a clear and concise historical logic." (Dragnich, 1992) Singleton, however, while recommending Dragnich's earlier work, does so "despite its pro-Serbian orientation." (Singleton, 1985) How are we to distinguish among partisans?

This last question is crucial given the role of the media in shaping our understanding of events in Bosnia.[1] In a world of satellite hookups and on-site reporting, public sentiment, and with it political resolve, rides a rollercoaster built on dramatic coverage of breaking stories. It suffices to recall how quickly American sentiment turned against our involvement in Somalia as a result of television reporting. Our collective concern for the victims of ethnic cleansing has ebbed and flowed with the television tides as well. Print journalism remains a more sober way of sifting for the facts.

Of all the stories to come out of the Yugoslavian breakdown, none are more distinguished than those of Roy Gutman. His *Newsday* story of July 3, 1992, focused on the beginnings of "ethnic cleansing" in Bosnia, along with the attempts by Serb representatives to portray this as voluntary emigration on the part of the refugees. (Gutman, 1993: 21)[2] Through the fall, Gutman's stories chronicled the holding camps where survivors reported that prisoners "had their throats slit, their noses cut off and their genitals plucked out," (1993: 51) and reported that "members of Karadzic's inner circle" established a "transit facility" in Foca that, in the summer of 1992, "functioned as a rape camp, holding 74 people, including about 50 women." (1993: 157–158) Gutman has been particularly effective in deploying the Serbs's words against them, pressing his investigation until they become flustered in their evasions. In the case of the mayor of Prijedor, whom Serb spokesmen first reported dead, then charged with "resisting the armed forces," then said had "escaped," Gutman pursued Simo Drljaca, the newly installed police chief, until finally:

> A week later, on his home turf in Prijedor, he put it more bluntly. Cehajic, who was 53 at the time, had "disappeared." "You know how it is. You find they disappeared," said Drljaca. "There may be some who died in the process of disappearing." (Gutman, 1993: 111)

The Muslims of Bosnia, the story suggests, seem to have become remarkably adept at the "process of disappearing."

As compelling as Gutman's reporting is, skeptics remain. Misha Glenny notes the tendency of belligerents to inflate the numbers, remarking that the Omarska camp, which Gutman discusses in detail, held "between 3,000 and 5,000 according to figures released by international humanitarian agencies. The Bosnian government insisted that the number was 11,000." (Glenny, 1993: 203) The most common figure for casualties in the conflict is 200,000, though Glenny, writing in June of 1993 gives something over 100,000. (1993: 182) By February of 1995, Glenny was closer to the 200,000, (1995a: 60) but in April George Kenney, formerly of the State Department's Yugoslav desk, rejected the received figure in favor of "the range of 25,000 to 60,000 fatalities." (Kenney, 1995: 42) These disputes about the numbers may not be directly relevant to assessing justice or injustice, but they point up the difficulty of determining the facts, and this *is* important for assessing responsibility.

Determining responsibility is made harder by the predominantly anti-Serbian tenor of much of the journalism. There is the occasional piece inclined to blame all sides, seeing the recent swing in favor of Bosnia as the product of "newspapers and history books uniformly reflecting rosy images of prewar Bosnia peddled by the old communist regime." (Smajlovic, 1995: 113) In this particular case, though, it may be important to place Smajlovic's remarks in the context of her break with *Oslobodjenje*, the "Sarajevo Daily" of Tom Gjelten's recent volume. In the fall of 1992, according to Gjelten, Smajlovic left the Sarajevo paper "and moved with her nine-year-old son to Belgrade, where she went to work for *Vreme*, a weekly opposition news-magazine." Gjelten tells her story as that of a Serb from Bosnian Sarajevo who "can choose to stay out of this war and not take the side of my people," but who "cannot fight against them, and that's what staying at *Oslobodjenje* would have meant." (Gjelten, 1995: 50) Should this make us cautious in reading her most recent reflections?

Pro-Serbian writing can, however, be found. Florence Levinsohn sets out, in *Belgrade*:

> to try to set the record straight about the Serbs. . . . What had led to the terrible rupture of Yugoslavia, I wanted to know. Were the Serbs actually the murderous warriors described in the U.S.? . . . It didn't seem reasonable that the atrocities had all been on one side. That isn't normally in the nature of war. (1994: 3)

Through interviews with a broad spectrum of the Belgrade intelligentsia, Levinsohn becomes convinced that Serbia is more sinned against than sinning. Without denying the culpability of Slobodan Milosevic for raising the specter of nationalism and leading the nation into war, she conveys the impression that Serbia has been roundly mistreated by the United States and the Europeans. An informant early in her story traces the connections between Nazi Germany, the United States, and the United Nations's economic embargo on Serbia. "The day Bosnia was recognized," recalls her subject, "the 6th of April, was a date people here remember so well. It was the Nazi bombing of Belgrade in 1941." Having earlier heard claims of a German conspiracy in dismembering Yugoslavia, Levinsohn asks why the Germans of today would seek the destruction of Yugoslavia:

> "I don't know. It is very difficult to understand. But it is clear that in the very near future Germany is going to be so strong they will be able to do anything they want." It was the same theory I'd heard the night before from what I'd considered two mad zealots. This woman was clearly not a zealot. (Levinsohn, 1994: 34)

Since her informant is clearly sane, the inference seems to go, the conspiracy theory likely has a grain of truth. If so, then it is hardly surprising that the Serbian leader, Milosevic, would feel it necessary to take steps against the secessionists.

Following some reflection on Serbia's economic grievances under Tito's regime, Levinsohn's informant makes the connection between the Nazis and the Allies in the Second World War:

> "It was always a mystery. You know, Croatia was not bombed by the Allies, but Belgrade and other towns in Serbia were. On Easter Day in 1944. I recall the day very well. . . . And we were fighting on the side of the Allies! At this same time Croatia, a Nazi puppet, was never bombed. It was crazy. And no one knows why." (1994: 35)

Levinsohn lets this pass without comment, allowing her narrative to proceed to the war in Bosnia and the reports of rape and death camps. But the story returns later on, as Levinsohn interviews the press attaché at the American embassy. She reports their general agreement on the counterproductive nature of the UN embargo, though to his response that the United States is but "one of the parties involved" she retorts that "it was the U.S. that first adopted the formal position that Serbian aggression in Bosnia Herzegovina was the cause of the war there, and only then were sanctions imposed. Michael smiled weakly." When he instances the siege of Sarajevo and the destruction of Vukovar as direct consequences of Serbian support for the war in Bosnia, she counters with the firebombing of Dresden. "And," she presses on, "how about the Allies bombing Belgrade and other Serbian towns occupied by the Germans? 'Well,' Michael said, 'you have a point.'" (Levinsohn, 1994: 212)

There is a complex argument, really a net of interwoven arguments, being deployed here. First, there is the established fact that Belgrade was bombed, then invaded, by Nazi Germany beginning 6 April 1941, making the Serbs victims of manifest aggression. This victimization was repeated, so the argument goes, by the Allies at the end of the war, only to be perpetuated by the irrationalities of Tito's government. In the present war the process of victimization has been reenacted by the UN, under American impetus. Second, there is the memory of Nazi atrocities, for which many were tried as war criminals. But there is also the carpet bombing of the German interior, not to mention Belgrade, for which the Allies would surely have been tried had they lost the war. Thus even if Milosevic could be held unilaterally responsible for the war in Bosnia, he has only undertaken the sorts of strategy typical of modern leaders. Finally, the embargo depends on America's "formal position" that the Serbs are the aggressors. Levinsohn seems to contrast "formal" with "substantive," implying that there is no fact of the matter that justifies calling one side the aggressor as opposed to another. This makes the hardships imposed on Serbian noncombatants even more unfair, particularly since the embargo has failed to achieve its political ends.

To these arguments Levinsohn adds yet another. Since American intervention is perceived as crucial to separating themselves from the rump Yugoslavia, and since to "gain that intervention, it was crucially required that the Serbs be demonized," the governments of Bosnia, Croatia, and Kosovo "hired foreign propagandists to help them win their wars." This puts the Serbs at an unfair disadvantage, but worse, it raises the specter of an American public viciously duped into supporting the wrong side, since "most of us who are old enough have clear memories of U.S. victory stories coming out of Vietnam, most particularly the body counts that were later proven to be fabricated by the government." (Levinsohn, 1994: 312–313) Only by resisting "the disinformation trap" being laid for the American psyche will public opinion develop into "a more realistic picture of three peoples fighting each other on fairly equal terms." (Levinsohn, 1994: 318)

There's much to be said about each step here, but for the moment I want to focus on the way Levinsohn ties history to present conflicts. In the first strand of argument, it is crucial to make the link between the evil bombing of Belgrade by the Nazis and the "crazy," inexplicable bombing of Belgrade by the Allies. This provides the grounds for the Serbian claim to be advocates of democracy, inexplicably victimized by their supposed allies. But a little sleuthing in the history of the Second World War puts the situation in a different light. The Allies landed in Italy in the fall of 1943, and in the winter of 1943–44 the Russians were beginning their push into East Central Europe. By the end of March 1944, the Russians were preparing to liberate the Crimea and drive into Romania. "At the same time," writes Liddell Hart, "the Allied heavy bombers from Italy launched a series of blows at the main railway bottlenecks, beginning with attacks on Budapest, Bucharest, and Ploesti, in the first week of April." (1970: 574) Levinsohn's informant herself refers to the German anti-aircraft emplacements shooting at Allied planes. The bombings in and around

Belgrade would appear to have been part of the softening up of the German armies in the Balkans as a precursor to the liberation of Belgrade in October of 1944.

But why spare Zagreb? Although Tito was almost captured at Drvar, southwest of Banja Luka, in the German offensive of May, the Partisans did receive Allied air support. But this "was the last occasion on which German troops took a major initiative in the Balkans. From June 1944 until the final surrender, the Partisans, backed by an increasing weight of Allied support, gradually pushed the Germans back." (Singleton, 1985: 203) The last German armies in the Balkans fled north to the Danube and then pushed on into Hungary, pursued by the Red Army. In April of 1944 Belgrade was a Germany military command center closely linked to rail targets. That it came in for some heavy action is not in the least surprising. By the time Zagreb fell to Tito's Partisans in May of 1945, the Allied armies were long gone and there was no reason to target the Croatian capital.

Levinsohn's failure to follow up isn't just a worry for prissy academics; it reflects a critical and moral failure that has become all too common in the Bosnian conflict: invoking a partisan history to excuse contemporary barbarism. Essential to any responsible assessment of our political duties are history, politics and ethics. Understanding human actions generally requires placing them within a particular narrative, if only because the reasons we search for must connect the present to the past. People seek one thing over another because of what they believe about themselves, their family, and the community around them, and these beliefs refer inevitably to past events. If Levinsohn's informant genuinely believes that the Allied bombing of Belgrade was inexplicable, "crazy," then it is no wonder that she feels set upon. But the ease of rectifying the belief, particularly for the reporter, should make us wonder whether we are being intentionally left in the dark.

Without an adequate grasp of the history it is extremely difficult to assess competing political agendas. This is a problem that emerges early on in Levinsohn's book. At the outset she insists that:

> The rebellion in Yugoslavia ... was not a rebellion against communism; it was a rebellion by the nationalist Catholic Croatians and Slovenes and the Bosnian Muslims against the nationalist aspirations of the Eastern Orthodox Serb leaders. The wars in Bosnia Herzegovina and Croatia were religious-ethnic civil wars over disputed lands and control. (Levinsohn, 1994: 4)

To call the conflicts "rebellions" implies the revolt of subordinates against a legitimate sovereign. This claim in turn suggests that the interpretive work has already been done, that the recent history of Yugoslavia registered federal recognition of the Belgrade government by the separate republics, and that Belgrade had done nothing to forfeit that recognition. How we should treat these conclusions will detain us in a later chapter, but Levinsohn takes it upon herself to settle those questions and to pronounce the conflicts in Croatia and Bosnia the result of "a history of events between the Serbs and the Croats that made this war all but inevitable." (Levinsohn, 1994: 5) With the history done and the politics settled, the moral upshot is clear. The West should have worked harder to hold Yugoslavia together; having failed we are now visiting misery upon the citizens of Serbia; this is wrong and it should stop.

Would it were that simple, but it is not. Levinsohn's version of the story skillfully arranges material to insure that the reader focuses on a particular angle, in order to reinforce frequently unstated propositions. Nowhere is this clearer than in her treatment of the role of Islam in these conflicts. Slovenia and Croatia, for instance, may be viable entities, but Bosnia is "an ungovernable state. Its Muslim president had been jailed in the 1970s when he circulated a tract announcing his intention to convert Bosnia into a Muslim state." (1994: 14) This turns out to be important because, from the perspective of another of her informants, the Muslims of Bosnia "are the same Turks whose forefathers did all the terrible atrocities to the Serbs." (Levinsohn, 1994: 274) Here again history and politics reinforce one another.

Among the atrocities her subject cites is a tower "built entirely of the skulls of Serbs at Nis in 1809," and Levinsohn adds the further example, taken from an 1988 volume by Paul Pavlovich, of the Pasha of Nis ordering a pyramid of skulls as a monument during the Russo-Turkish war. Both references may be to the same famous story, in which Stevan Sindjelic, defeated at Nis, "set fire to the stores of gunpowder on which he himself sat, leaving to posterity the memory of a courageous deed of a caliber rare even in this heroic period." (Dedijer, et al., 1974: 273) Temperley's lively older history extolls Sindjelic as making for himself

> a name in song, like to that of Kiurtschia and Kara George, though his was a purer fame. Seventy years afterwards the Serbian troops entered Nish to find a Turkish tower garnished with the skulls of the Serbians

who had died in this great fight. A chapel hard by now contains the skulls. (1919: 191)

There is no reason to doubt that the vanquished were beheaded, given that "both sides customarily cut off the heads of the dead and carried them to their leaders as trophies. Not even the wounded were spared this final indignity." (Skrivanic, 1982: 330) What Levinsohn fails to point out is the political complexity of the first Serbian revolution, which had begun as a response to the depredations of renegade Janissaries, the Ottoman military elite, and bandit forces that could not be controlled by the capital. With the outbreak of revolt in 1804, the Sultan dispatched a new pasha to Belgrade to put down the renegades in support of the Serbs led by Karadjordje. After benefiting from the Sultan's aid, the Serbs continued to revolt. In 1805 the Pasha of Nis led an Ottoman army against a substantial Serbian army; the Serbs won. In a conflict that rose and fell over almost a decade, the destruction of the magazine was but one incident. After the Ottoman army retook Belgrade in 1813, Constantinople issued an amnesty, reinstated exiles, and undertook other measures of reconciliation, however short-lived. (Jelavich, 1983: I, 196–202) The story of Sindjelic occurs in the context of a war not unlike the American Revolution. But failure to place the story in its full historical context reinforces the equation of Bosnians with Turks and Turks with barbarians.

This demonization of the Bosnian Muslims is furthered by adding a sexual component to the savagery of war. Thus these "same Turks . . . would come into a Serb's house and take his wife," with the intention of humiliating the oppressed peasant. Not only do they rape the women, but "having been bisexual," Levinsohn's informant continues, "the Turks would also seduce the sons of the Serbs." The Muslims, it would seem, are civilization's worst nightmare: savage brutes give to barbarism and sexual perversion. Levinsohn signals some skepticism here, but closes with reflections on the Yugoslav novelist Ivo Andric, whose *Bridge on the Drina* reveals . . . a people mostly supine under the treacherous rule of the conquerors, living in friendly truce with the converted Muslims." (Levinsohn, 1994: 274) Broken by the First World War, violated by atrocities during the Second, this truce no longer holds and the Serbs, she implies, have risen with the goal of shaking off their victimhood.

To complete her picture of the situation, Levinsohn systematically minimizes accusations of Serb responsibility for assaults on their neighbors. Thus to accusations of genocidal activities during the Second World War, she responds that "there is simply no evidence for any such Serbian terrorism." (1994: 247) This is an odd remark when juxtaposed to Noel Malcolm's report that "Cetniks and other local Serb forces had killed many thousands of Muslims in the winter of 1941–42 and the summer of 1942. . . . At least 2000 Muslims were killed [in Foca-Cajnice] . . . and in February 1943 more than 9000 were massacred." (Malcolm, 1994: 187–188) That the numbers, which Malcolm takes from post-war Yugoslavian sources, may be inflated is true, but that there is "no evidence" does not seem to be borne out, and the claim is particularly jarring given that Malcolm's is one of the few sources cited by Levinsohn for background.

Minimizing the historical record makes it easier to dismiss accusations of Serb atrocities in the present conflict. Levinsohn tells several stories of rape and the abuse of Serbs by Croatians and Bosnians, from a report published in January of 1993 by the Serbian Council Information Center. The stories are analogous to those reported by Gutman, who notes that in July of 1992 he was present at the Bosnian Serb headquarters in Banja Luka while an army major "sat behind a portable typewriter churning out lurid diatribes. . . . Taken literally, it made no sense. I viewed the propaganda as a coded message for the army and the paramilitary bands operating under loose army supervision." When the major subsequently referred to these atrocities as the work of Janissaries, Gutman "tried to suppress a grin. 'Which century are you talking about?' I asked. He replied: 'It is a new and recent phenomenon. . . . " (Gutman, 1993: ix–x) The disinformation trap may work on both sides of the Drina.

Levinsohn's selective skepticism runs with a chill through her final pages, where she discounts the efforts of Gutman and others to locate and document rapes and other acts against noncombatants, asking rhetorically about the rape reports, "Where did the 50,000 figure come from? From the heads of the Bosnian Muslim leaders. How did they miraculously reach us in the United States and Europe? Through the good offices of [the public relations firm] Ruder Finn, which made no effort to check out such improbable numbers." (1994: 314) The language is almost indistinguishable from that of Karadzic's press officer in July of 1995, fielding questions about the fate of refugees following the Bosnian Serb taking of Srebrenica.

Levinsohn's *Belgrade* is a remarkable polemic, using the voices of contemporary Serbians to lay out a history designed to portray the citizens of Belgrade as the long-suffering victims of ignorance, duplicity, and malice. The goal is to sway the reader to the Serbian side, enlist support for lifting the economic embargo, and heighten the reader's supposed fear of Islamic fundamentalism establishing a beachhead on our European homelands. But I do not want to suggest that hers is the only perspective that incorporates an author's local sympathies and political animosities. The greatest of all such writing, Rebecca West's *Black Lamb and Grey Falcon*, is permeated by memories of ethnic strife and premonitions of impending war. Yugoslavia is a metaphor for Europe, caught between bouts of totalitarian oppression, represented by the Ottomans and the Nazis. She closes with a dramatic condemnation of the passivity of her own leaders:

> In the country it sometimes happens that the sleeper awakes to an unaccustomed stillness. It is as if silence stretched for miles above him, miles around him. . . . In England there was such a stillness, such a white winter of the spirit, and such a prolongation of it that death was threatened. It would have been expected, with fascist Italy and Nazi Germany crying out to kill, and England being what they both needed to kill, that there would be much bustling to and fro on the building of defences, that there would be shouts of warning, proclamations, calls to arms, debates on strategy. But there was silence, and no movement. (1941: 1114–15)

West and her husband traveled through Yugoslavia as Hitler assembled his troops for war; she collected her thoughts as Chamberlain shuffled toward Munich; and in her last pages West holds up Yugoslavia's resistence to Hitler as a lesson of hope. But for many, West's moral imperative has given way to ennui.

In *Balkan Ghosts*, the most self-consciously West-like of the recent reflections on Eastern Europe, Robert Kaplan portrays the world east of Vienna as a congeries of almost unimaginable malice, degeneracy, and corruption, but rarely relieved by a glimmer of insight or humanity. Kaplan reports a 1985 exchange with Milovan Djilas, the last great dissident from the days of Tito's Partisans. "'What about Yugoslavia?' I asked. He smiled viciously: 'Like Lebanon. Wait and see.'" In late 1989, in what seemed to Kaplan a peaceful easing into democracy, Djilas was still pessimistic, certain that whatever the final outcome "there will be national wars and rebellions. There is such strong hate here." (Kaplan, 1993: 75–76) Djilas's prescience may tempt us into a paralytic despair. The fall of Srebrenica and humiliation of the United Nations in the second week of July 1995 may only confirm the hopelessness.

Misha Glenny, whose reporting has been among the most influential, presents a morality play where the dream of democratization spirals down into a post-apocalyptic nightmare, poised to engulf all Europe, from which he tries to rouse himself, crying "I hate the Balkans. I hate Europe. But we have nowhere else to go." (1993: 234) David Rieff's *Slaughterhouse* is the Sarajevo equivalent of *Belgrade*, though being closer to the action, it offers a richer mingling of blood with plum brandy. Rieff's principal objects of opprobrium are the waffling Clinton administration and what he portrays as the moral duplicity of UNPROFOR, whose tendency "to be *more* sensitive, not less, to the slaughterhouse that our world really is," made all the more shocking by "their insistence that the slaughter had to be allowed to go on." (Rieff, 1995: 170; see also Glenny, 1995a: 63) But this fatalism is subject to the same condemnation West visited upon the politicians of her day. Rieff correctly diagnoses the situation as the product of "moral dereliction," (Rieff, 1995: 193) and if we are not to continue thrashing helplessly about we need to bring together our critical resources to determine what we can do to set right the consequences of this dereliction.

Talk of political morality is likely to sound simpleminded in the face of so much systematically contrived human suffering. Politics, it will be said, is a matter of power and self-interest, and will always resist the constraints of morality. The problem with this popular cynicism is that it is not borne out by the facts. The architects of twentieth-century realism insisted that "an international order cannot be based on power alone, for the simple reason that mankind will in the long run revolt against naked power." (Carr, 1946: 235–236) This is nowhere more clearly borne out than in the study of the laws of war. While the occasional machiavellian will kick dirt on the idea that a sovereign should submit to the rule of law, belligerents have always drawn lines. (cf. Howard, et al., 1994) And even when they lacked either the restraint or resilience to abide by their own moral commitments, most governments have been quick to deny, excuse, or make a show of atoning for their failures. (cf. Walzer, 1992: 323–325. But see also Best, 1994: 410–414) Richard Haass, himself a veteran of the National Security Council, distinguishes four key influences on "what appears in today's newspapers and academic journals:" just war theory; the legal paradigm developed over the last three centuries; theorists of military strategy, from Clausewitz to Liddell Hart; and Cold War analysts such as Kissinger and Schelling, giving primacy of place to the just war tradition, which has "dominated Western thought for centuries and provides a reference point for anyone speaking or writing on this subject." (Haass, 1994: 9) What is this tradition, and what is its place in recent political ethics?

Haass identifies the just war tradition with Christianity, as do Michael Howard and many others. This, however, needs to be qualified in several important ways. Over 30 years ago Paul Ramsey lifted the just war tradition to center stage in the American debate over nuclear deterrence, and through the decade of the sixties he expanded it to cover our involvement in Vietnam, conscientious objection, and a variety of issues in social and political thought. His expressed intention was to address the deficiencies he saw in the Protestant ethics he had learned from the brothers Niebuhr, and to this end he drew unashamedly on the natural law tradition associated with the teachings of the Catholic Church.

Ramsey insisted that "'natural law' judgments do not proceed from autonomous reason alone, but are derivative principles in which *agape* shapes itself for action." (Ramsey, 1961: 33) This foundation in Christian love was important to his theological concern to demonstrate the preferability of Protestant over Roman Catholic moral theology. For Ramsey the natural law tradition associated with Thomas Aquinas could not be understood apart from the Gospel insistence on neighbor love, particularly as interpreted by St. Augustine. If Christian love were at the heart of the just war tradition, and if the shape of that love could be known only through Scripture, as mediated to a community of equals, then the ethics of war would be best explicated in terms of a Protestant Christian community.

Needless to say, this component of Ramsey's analysis did not go without criticism. Natural law thinkers within the Catholic tradition criticized Ramsey's apparent willingness to tolerate injustices in the name of a greater political end. This came out during the mid-1960s in Ramsey's ongoing dispute with a distinguished group of British Catholic thinkers over the justice of deterrence. While Walter Stein, Elizabeth Anscombe, and others maintained an absolute and unequivocal condemnation of nuclear weapons, leaving little alternative to unilateral nuclear disarmament, Ramsey attempted to articulate a theory of deterrence that would retain what he took to be a strategic and moral necessity without offending the canons of justice. (cf. Stein 1961; Ramsey, 1968; and Ramsey, 1988: 183–212) This remained a thorny issue for two decades, receiving its most public airing in the debate over the American bishops' pastoral letter, which some suspected of making too many concessions to the residual realism of Ramsey and his proponents.

From the early 1970s to the present, James Johnson's work has emphasized the multiple intersecting sources that underlie the just war tradition. (cf. Johnson, 1975 and 1987) In 1977 Michael Walzer's *Just and Unjust Wars* appeared, advancing a thoroughly secular approach to justice in war, taking aim in several sections at Ramsey's account of the tradition and its implications. Though Walzer received criticism from all sides, *Just and Unjust Wars*, has been instrumental in fostering a discussion of the just war tradition that goes beyond theological sources to Plato, Aristotle, and other key thinkers in the philosophical tradition. Thinking about justice in war is scarcely a Christian or even a religious matter; it is part and parcel of our best traditions of political reflection in the West.

The flowering of work, historical and philosophical, on the just war tradition has not produced uniformity. Distinctions abound in the foundations and applications of the various versions currently under debate. But whatever their differences on the intellectual underpinnings of the just war tradition, far and away the majority of these thinkers recognize a core to the tradition, made up of a number of criteria that must be met for war to be just. These criteria come in two distinct sorts: those dealing with the justice of going to war—*jus ad bellum*—and those which must be satisfied in the prosecution of war—*jus in bello*. The particulars differ from writer to writer, but the following list is common to all:

Jus ad bellum
1. Proper Authority
2. Just Cause
3. Just Intent
4. Last Resort
5. Reasonable Hope of Success

Jus in bello
1. Discrimination
2. Proportion

Though they can be turned into jargon, the just war criteria are nothing other than the distillate of practical reflection on how reasonable people of goodwill could possibly justify the intentional and protracted use of deadly force against other human beings. Such reflection is unavoidable, regardless of the way the community is constituted. The first criterion for going to war insists that random violence and the indiscriminate injuring of others is always and everywhere an evil. Private individuals may feud, wreak vengence on each other, and undertake vigilantism, but none of these is war, and they are all contrary to justice and the common good. War is an organized, communal action and as such can only be undertaken on the authority of the community. This is as true of a monarchy as a democracy.

To act without just cause manifests indifference to the welfare of friends and enemies alike. Recognizing a just cause rarely requires invoking any arcane theories of justice, any more than recognizing a good play on the baseball diamond requires a theory of baseball. Almost any mature member of the community already possesses the knowledge and experience necessary to determine whether he is behaving properly or doing well. The best evidence of this is our inclination to make excuses, along with our ability to recognize them for what they are. What is surprising is the relatively high standard to which we normally hold ourselves. Most of us, should we find a twenty-dollar bill on the grocery floor, will make some effort to determine its provenance, and the effort we make is likely to increase with the amount. So while I might pocket the twenty, I'd go out of my way to return a thousand dollars, and so would most of us. It's not ours; we're not entitled to keep it. Without seriously extenuating circumstances we would condemn anyone who didn't make a minimal effort to do the right thing.

For most people, twenty dollars would be an annoying loss, but not life-threatening; a thousand dollars might make the difference in a poor family having a place to stay. A prank that might embarrass someone is just childish; one that could maim or kill is unconscionable. To steal is wicked; to rape is worse. To shoot Native Americans attacking your frontier farm is tragic, even in self defense; to appropriate their lands, exclude them from resources, and deploy the army against them is genocidal. No specialized training or expert knowledge is required, though we may sometimes delude ourselves with excuses like "manifest destiny" or protecting the "purity" of the nation.

Just intent is somewhat more complicated, for it plays a dual role in interpreting our actions. On the one hand, it describes the relation of the agent to justice, since the desire to secure and protect the good, with an eye to the general betterment of the community, is something we may reasonably demand of each other. But the agent can be just in his intent without being clear about where justice lies in the prosecution of a war. Thus there is a second sense in which just intent is secured by the commitment to abide by all the just war criteria. To put it another way, we require fairness in resorting to and prosecuting a war, and a failure renders the entire effort defective. If I threaten to gouge out the eyes of a hostage-taker's infant daughter, I have embraced evil, even if he gives in and I do not have to test my resolve. And when I make myself no better than the aggressor, my claim to justice melts away. (cf. Davis, 1992: 103–109)

Last resort and reasonable hope are subordinate to just intent. Should we undertake war as anything other than a last resort, doubt would be cast on our motives. Are we merely looking for an excuse? Do we secretly hope to gain some further advantage? Are we willing to use war, with all its risks and losses, for something less than a just cause? If something less than war will do, then only indifference to the common good would tempt us to resort to arms. At the same time, last resort does not mean trying everything conceivable before going to war. Last resort has been reached as soon as you become certain that nothing less will achieve justice. To take a recent example, the embargo that preceded the Gulf War probably resulted in more noncombatant injury on both sides than a more timely response would have, since it allowed the Iraqi army to consolidate its positions, exploit and destroy Kuwaiti resources, and prepare attacks on Israel, all the while jeopardizing the health and welfare of Iraqi civilians.

In many ways the demand for reasonable hope is the mirror image of last resort. A hopeless war makes no sense. It amounts to throwing away our lives and resources without the prospect of securing the common good. This is contrary to right reason and justice. But to reject hopeless war need not mean meek submission to a murderous power. Accumulating allies and resources may transform a wish into a reasonable hope. Suffering under an oppressive regime may be necessary, but criticism and protest can be surprisingly effective. Flight may be the counsel of prudence, as it was for Jews and others before the murderous fury of Nazi terrorism.

The *in bello* conditions are also clear requirements of justice.

Failure to distinguish those who are subject to attack from those who are not amounts to willingness to kill anyone you want in pursuing your ends, but that is the opposite of justice. A war is a public enterprise, pitting the instruments of one government against another. Only those public forces may legitimately be attacked. Everyone and everything else is immune. This immunity is not a matter of individual conscience. The reluctant draftee may have our sympathy, but on the battlefield he is a just target, while civilians cheering the roundup of Jews and Gypsies must be protected, as despicable as they are. This is not to say that there are no borderline cases; there are. Nonetheless, as John Ford wrote many years ago, the burden of proof falls on "those who want to increase the number of combatants, and include large numbers, even the 'vast majority,' of the civilian population." (Ford 1944: 20) Some occupations, even when they are crucial to an enemy's efforts, may prove immune from just attack. Ford offers a famously prolix list that includes shoemakers, dairymen, telephone girls, reporters, and "all children with the use of reason, i.e., from seven years up . . . all co-operate in some degree in the aggression." (Ford, 1944: 21–22) None of them is a legitimate target, and to attack them is murderous. But soldiering is not on the list. I can directly attack soldiers, but I *must* discriminate between them and civilians.

Even a discriminate attack is not perfect. Bombs do not always fall just where you would like, and children don't always duck and cover. Although tragic, casualties resulting from good faith efforts to avoid noncombatants are not vicious and do not make a war unjust. They may be tolerated, though not welcomed, on the principle of "double effect." Here again, though the term is subject to much abuse, we make judgments based on it every day. If I compete with a friend for a contract or a position, I may know that losing will make him miserable, but that does not mean I shouldn't make my best effort. If I surprise a thief, and in the struggle he cracks his skull, I've done no wrong; he shouldn't have been there in the first place. In the classic example, which gave the principle its name, Thomas Aquinas noted that "the act of self defense may have two effects: one, the saving of one's life; the other, the slaying of the aggressor. Therefore, this act, since one's intention is to save one's own life, is not unlawful." (*ST*: 2a2ae, 64, 7) If my intention is good and my tactics fair and reasonable, we should regret the event, but there is no guilt.

I do, however, have the burden of insuring not only that my actions are necessary to securing justice, but that the good achieved is not outweighed by the unintended loss of life and livelihood that may attend even the best executed actions. There is no simple calculation that can establish by some formula what miseries are acceptable in the pursuit of which goods. Thus determining whether the good to be achieved is proportionately greater than the damage being risked can never be a matter for technicians alone. The just war criteria are intended to clarify conscience when the way is obscure and experience limited, but they cannot eliminate the need to exercise prudence.

War forces my hand; I either submit or act. The criteria offered by the just war tradition help me interpret my actions and test my resolve to do justice. If my attack is out of proportion to the importance of the target, then I do not really care about the lives at risk, and if I do not care, then my willingness to discriminate is superficial. As my commitment to discrimination becomes shaky I may be tempted to pretend that the civilians in my sites are "collateral damages," but this demonstrates a murderous intent, and once I determine to sacrifice noncombatants my cause becomes irrelevant; I am a murderer and my war is unjust.

Haass writes that "the overall effect of this body of thought is to make it more difficult politically to go to war and more difficult militarily to fight one." (1994: 9) This is exactly right and exactly as it should be. War involves great risks and even greater sacrifices for all parties on all sides. The restraints we place on ourselves and our political leaders should discourage self-interest and adventurism not only in others but in ourselves. But this does not mean that war is morally unimaginable. The following essays attempt to bring social and political history together with moral analysis to characterize the ongoing conflict in the successor states to Yugoslavia, a necessary propaedeutic to justifying whatever actions we contemplate or our leaders ask us to endorse.

Michael Sells traces the rhetoric of the contemporary conflict back to a clash of religious communities and the emergent vocabulary of Romantic nationalism. Jean Bethke Elshtain asks us to reflect on the realities of nationalism. Liberals in particular have recently advocated a politics of identity, inviting ethnic and other groups to assert themselves in the face of civil society. Surely this is an important aspect of minority empowerment, but how should we react when "ethnic nationalism," to take a term from Bogdan Denitch, erupts into war and "ethnic cleansing"? If war is intentionally directed against noncombatant civilians, should we tolerate it on the basis of past standards and legal norms? James Turner Johnson investigates this question with reference to the siege of Sarajevo and its crippling effects on the inhabitants of that city. My contribution reflects on the impact that just war thinking might have on American foreign policy, were our leaders to take justice seriously in international affairs. John Kelsay, finally, undertakes to display the impact our actual policies have on the Muslim world, many of whose leading thinkers are already skeptical of the claims of modern, industrial culture to be a vehicle for progress and liberation. Is genocide, some Muslims wonder, anything other than the natural expression of materialist, secularized modernity?

These are not the only questions prompted by the conflict in Bosnia. They are important ones nonetheless. The answers we give will be a direct expression of our ability to make sense out of our own politics, a measure of the health of our own public discourse. "War," wrote Clausewitz, "cannot be divorced from political life; and whenever this occurs in our thinking about war, the many links that connect the two elements are destroyed and we are left with something pointless and devoid of sense." (Clausewitz, 1976: 605)

Religion, History, and Genocide in Bosnia-Herzegovina[1]

Michael Sells

"It's tragic, it's terrible," bemoaned President Clinton, in a June 1995 interview with Larry King. "But their enmities go back five hundred years, some would say almost a thousand years." (*Larry King Live*, June 5, 1995) A month after those words were spoken, the United States government, along with the other governments of the UN Security Council and the North Atlantic Treaty Organization, refused to respond as the Serb army overran the UN-Declared "safe haven" of Srebrenica. The next week, at a meeting in London, the same group of leaders declared that a second "safe haven," Zepa, would not be protected. From six to seven thousand of the approximately fifty thousand inhabitants of Srebenica and Zepa are missing. Amnesty International and the International Red Cross estimate that thousands have been killed. Although leaders of NATO countries expressed surprise at the atrocities, these events surprised no one familiar with the documented behavior of the Serb army and Serb irregular militias in Bosnia.[2]

There is a critical relationship between the facts on the ground in Bosnia (the genocide known as "ethnic cleansing") and the statements of Western leaders such as President Bill Clinton about "age-old antagonisms," "ancient hatreds," and "Balkan ghosts." Such phrases have been used to portray the people of Bosnia as alien, and as historically or even genetically fated to kill one another. The "age-old antagonisms" refrain, as used by UN and NATO officials, served as the primary excuse for the four-year policy that culminated at Srebenica.

In Belgrade, the notion of age-old antagonism is operative in a more primary manner. Serb nationalists used the martyrdom of the Serb prince Lazar at the battle in Kosovo in 1389 as a central component of the ideology of "ethnic cleansing." In the passion play commemorating the battle of 1389, Lazar is portrayed as a Christ figure with disciples (sometimes explicitly twelve), one of whom is a traitor. The Turks are Christ-killers, and the Judas figure, Vuk Brankovic, becomes the ancestral curse of all Slavic Muslims. The ways in which the power of the Kosovo myth and ritual has been harnessed to promote genocide are partially concealed within a symbolic code, but occasionally the ideology is expressed in completely transparent terms. Thus Norris cites the Belgrade academic Miroljub Jevtic:

> Because of this [the battle of Kosovo and the conversion of Bosnians to Islam], the hands of the Muslims who are with us are stained and polluted with the blood of their ancestors from among the inhabitants of Bosnia at that time, namely those who did not embrace Islam. (Norris 1993: 297–98)

This study will show each step in the appropriation and radicalizing of the Kosovo myth to create an ideology of genocide. It should be pointed out at the very beginning that such an analysis is not meant to indict the role of Kosovo in Serb culture as such. Indeed, those who used Kosovo to justify the crimes described below may ultimately be considered by Serbs as betrayers of the values of Kosovo and as having dragged the most cherished themes of Serb culture through internationally recognized crimes against humanity. If that is the case, and Serb tradition is to be retrieved, then difficult theological and cultural issues about the interpretation and place of certain themes from the Kosovo myth will need to be seriously addressed. Yet the same tradition may offer resources for such a retrieval; as the Kosovo legend was taken over by ethno-nationalist militants, the deeper, more human aspects of the Kosovo tradition were submerged, namely those works that managed, through the Kosovo theme, to present the sorrow and loss of the figures portrayed not as the property of Serb militancy, but as Serbia's distinctive contribution to a shared human understanding.[3]

What is "Ethnic Cleansing"?

To understand the nature and goals of the "ethnic cleansing," it helps to begin with the burning of the National Library, a collection of 1.2 million volumes, and Sarajevo's major example of Austrian neo-Moorish architecture, and the events that preceded it. The army of General Mladic systematically targeted the major libraries, manuscript collections, museums, and other cultural institutions in Sarajevo, Mostar, and other besieged cities. Eastern Mostar, with its priceless heritage of ancient Bosnian culture, was leveled by Serb artillery. What the Serb artillery missed, the Croat Defense Force (HVO) hit. The HVO has shelled cultural institutions in Mostar and other cities under siege.

On May 17, 1992, General Mladic targeted the Oriental Institute in Sarajevo, the largest collection of Islamic and Jewish manuscripts in South Eastern Europe. Over five thousand priceless manuscripts, in South Slav Aljamiado, Hebrew, Persian, Arabic, and Turkish, went up in flames. Mladic's forces then targeted the National Museum for destruction. It burned in August.[4]

Behind Serb and HVO lines, the destruction was even more systematic. HVO forces expelled Serbs and Muslims, and dynamited Orthodox churches and Muslim mosques throughout the region, including the centuries-old mosques in Stolac and Pocitelj, two of the more ancient and beautiful towns in Herzegovina. Most Catholic churches and all mosques (over six hundred) have been methodically dynamited or vandalized by Serb militias, including masterworks of South Slavic culture such as the sixteenth-century Ferhadija Mosque in Banja Luka and the "Colored Mosque" in Foca, built in 1551. Graveyards, birth records, work records, and every other trace of the people "cleansed" have been destroyed. (cf. Riedlmayer 1994a, 1994b; Detling 1993; Bollage 1995)

What General Mladic and his Croat extremist imitators destroyed was the graphic and palpable evidence of over 500 years of interreligiously shared life in Bosnia. And despite conflicts in the past, this methodical destruction is new. The art, manuscripts, and artistic monuments being burned and dynamited have existed for centuries, and in cities such as Mostar and Sarajevo, the religious monuments are built next to one another. After all the mosques in the formerly Muslim-majority city of Zvornik were systematically destroyed, the warlord Branko Grujic declared, "There never were any mosques in Zvornik." Once destroyed, the banalities about "age-old antagonism" become irrefutable. History is recreated in the image of the destroyer. What was destroyed was the evidence not only of the five-hundred-year-old Bosnian Muslim civilization of Zvornik, but also of five hundred years of shared living between the two major populations groups in Zvornik, Muslim and Serb. In addition, the names used for such acts can and have been manipulated and abused. Indeed, a premise of this study is that it was the original manipulation of such names in the decade of the 1980s that led to the ideology that fostered the most extreme Serb-nationalist violence in Bosnia in 1992. How are we to name the various components of the "ethnic cleansing" strategy of Serb regular and irregular militias in the spring and summer of 1992? And how are we to properly name what has been called "ethnic cleansing" despite the fact that the alleged "ethnicity" is based merely and solely upon one's religious identification? This latter question can only be answered properly once the individual components of the "ethnic cleansing" program have been properly described.[5]

In each area occupied by the Serb military, killing camps and killing centers were established, and individual massacres were carried out. Such centers included the Drina River Bridge at Visegrad, the Drina Bridge at Foca, the stadium at Bratunac, and schools, mosques, stadiums, and roadsides throughout Serb-army occupied Bosnia-Herzegovina. In such places the killing went on for weeks. Thus the famous Visegrad Drina Bridge, built by the Ottomans in the sixteenth century, was used for nightly killing "sport festivals" by Serb soldiers who would torture their victims, throw them off the bridge, and try to see if they could shoot them as they tumbled down into the Drina River.

After the Serb army had consolidated the seventy percent of Bosnian territory it controlled, the killing switched to controlled intimidation, with a pattern of localized killings and rapes in cities such as Banja Luka and Bijeljina, where significant non-Serb population remained. Various camps, off-limits to all International Red Cross inspection, continued to operate to the time of this writing. Especially notorious is the Lopare camp near Brcko.

The International Red Cross made an extraordinary appeal to the NATO nations to stop the "ethnic cleansings" in Banja Luka and Bijeljina. The appeal was ignored. The first victims were intellectual and cultural leaders: teachers, lawyers, doctors, businesspeople, religious leaders, artists, poets, and musicians. The object of such "eliticide" was to destroy the cultural memory. Gradually, the killing slipped over into something more random as the acts of cruelty and massacre took on an interior momentum and logic of their own.

Those who survived the killings were subjected to a final ritual: the stripping of all property and possession. Buses of refugees were continually stopped by militias and army units. Everything of possible value was taken: not only hard currency, but even shoes and jewelry of little financial value. The stealing of wedding rings (with threats to cut off the finger of anyone whose ring did not come off easily) was a special part of the ritual. From the pervasive nature of this ritual, an interpretation can be made. The stolen wedding rings—of a trivial value in relation to the enormous booty taken by the Serb army and militias—represent the last symbol of a cultural group identity, as well as a symbol of a future procreative possibility. The strange fixation with which militia members persisted in stealing weddings rings, and often in presenting them to their own girlfriends, can only be explained through such deeper symbolism.

The term "genocide" was coined by Rafael Lemkin as part of an effort to learn from the experience of the Holocaust and to develop an international legal consensus about certain kinds of systematic atrocities. The "Convention on the Prevention and Punishment of the Crime of Genocide" adopted by Resolution 260 (III) A of the General Assembly of the United Nations, December 9, 1948, makes the following key provisions:

> **Article I:** The Contracting Parties confirm that genocide, whether committed in time of peace or in time of war, is a crime under international law which they undertake to prevent and to punish.
>
> **Article II:** In the present Convention, genocide means any of the following acts committed to destroy, in whole or in part, a national, ethnic, racial or religious group, as such: (a) Killing members of the group; (b) Causing serious bodily or mental harm to members of the group; (c) Deliberately inflicting on the group conditions of life calculated to bring about its physical destruction in whole or in part; (d) Imposing measures intended to prevent births within the group; (e) Forcibly transferring children of the group to another group.

There can be little doubt that the "ethnic cleansing" practiced by the regular and irregular Serb militias in Bosnia-Herzegovina from 1992 to 1995 constitutes genocide. These practices were a systematic effort to destroy Bosnian multireligious culture and Bosnian Muslim culture, and to destroy the Bosnian and Bosnian Muslim peoples *as a people*.[6]

Christoslavism: Slavic Muslims as Christ-Killers

The antagonism between nationalist Serbs and Bosnian Muslims is, as they say, "old." But it is also recent. While historians dispute the significance of the Kosovo battle of 1389, in which both the Serbian Prince Lazar and the Ottoman Sultan Murat were killed, in Serbian mythology the battle entailed the loss of Serb independence, a loss that was represented in cosmic terms. Yet despite the cliché about "age-old antagonisms," the marshaling of the Lazar legend to place an unbridgeable gap between Slavic Muslim and Serb was achieved only in the nationalistic literature of the nineteenth century. It is in the literature of the nineteenth century that the Lazar Christ-character takes on explicit form. Lazar is now a Christ figure, with knight disciples, who is slain, and with him dies the Serb nation, to rise again only with the resurrection of Lazar. (cf. Emmert 1990; Vucinich 1991) Turks are thus equated with Christ-killers and Vuk Brankovic, the "Turk within," becomes a symbol, and the ancestral curse, of all Slavic Muslims.[7]

The classic illustration of this is *The Mountain Wreath*, written by Prince-Bishop Petar II (known by the pen name of Njegos), which portrays the eighteenth-century Montenegrin extermination of slavic Muslims, the *Istraga Poturica*. The drama opens with Bishop Danilo, the play's protagonist, brooding on the evil of Islam, the tragedy of Kosovo, and the treason of Vuk Brankovic. Danilo's warriors suggest celebrating the holy day (Pentecost) by "cleansing" (*cistimo*) the land of non-Christians. The chorus chants: "The high mountains reek with the stench of non-Christians." One of Danilo's men proclaims that struggle will not come to an end until "we or the Turks are exterminated." The reference to the Slavic Muslims as "Turks" crystallizes the view that by converting to Islam the Muslims have changed their racial identity and have become the Turks who killed the Christ-Prince Lazar.

The conflict is explicitly placed *outside* the category of the blood-feud, common to the Balkans. In tribal Montenegro and Serbia a blood-feud, however ruthless and fatal, could be reconciled; it was not interminable. (Boehm 1984) The godfather (*Kum*) ceremony was used to reconcile clans who had fallen into blood-feud. In *The Mountain Wreath*, when the Muslims suggest a *Kuma* reconciliation,

Danilo's men object that the *Kum* ceremony requires baptism. The Muslims offer an ecumenical analogy, suggesting that the Muslim hair-cutting ceremony is a parallel in their tradition to baptism. Danilo's men respond with a stream of scatological insults against Islam, its prophet, and Muslims. With each set of insults, the chorus chants "Tako, Vec nikako" (this way; there is no other) to indicate the "act" that must be taken. The play ends with the triumphant Christmas Eve extermination of Slavic Muslims as a formal initiation of Serb nationhood.

By moving the conflict from the realm of blood-feud into a cosmic duality of good and evil, Njegos placed Slavic Muslims in a permanent state of otherness. The sympathetic qualities of the Muslims are the last temptation of Danilo. However sympathetic in person, Muslims are Christ-killers, "blasphemers," "spitters on the cross." After slaughtering the Muslims—man, woman, and child—the Serb warriors take communion without the confession that was mandatory after blood-vengeance.[8]

The explicitly Christological patterning of Njegos's portrayal of the Kosovo myth was echoed in other art and literature produced or collected during the Romantic period, in particular a fragment of poetry, known as the "Last Supper," which depicts Lazar's banquet on the eve of the battle. Lazar knows that he will be betrayed, and he suspects Milos, his most faithful knight, who had been slandered earlier. The prince proposes a toast to Milos in which he accuses him. Extremely hurt, Milos promises to prove his loyalty by killing the sultan before the battle. He then points the finger to the real traitor, Vuk Brankovic. (Vucinich 1991: 113) Lazar's last supper is represented in Adam Stefanovic's lithograph "The Feast of the Prince (Lazar)" with Lazar in the center of the banquet table, surrounded by knights in the pose of a thousand depictions of Christ's disciples, with light suffusing the countenance of the prince, and traitor Vuk brooding silently in the background. (Vucinich 1991: 287, Fig. 21)

As part of the preparations for the six-hundredth anniversary of Kosovo, there was a revival of interest in Njegos. The importance of Njegos, the fact that his verses are memorized by a great many Serbs, and the notion that Njegos, himself the poet of Serb crucifixion and future resurrection, was being resurrected, were all part of the Kosovo memorials of 1989. "Throughout Serbia, Vojvodina and Montenegro, people at gatherings carried Njegos's picture and posters with his verses," wrote Pavle Zoric, going on to intone that "this was an unforgettable sight. Is there anything more beautiful, more sincere and more profound. . . . Njegos was resurrected in the memory of people." (Vukadinovic, 1989: 79)

"Race-betrayal" is a major theme of *The Mountain Wreath* and the strand of Serbian literature it represents. By converting to Islam, Njegos insisted, slavic Muslims became "Turks." Ivo Andric, Yugoslavia's Nobel laureate in literature, writes that:

> Njegos, who can always be counted on for the truest expression of the people's mode of thinking and apprehending, portrays in his terse and plastic manner the process of conversion thus: "The lions [those who remained Christian] turned into tillers of the soil, / the cowardly and covetous turned into Turks." (Andric 1990: 20)

If this is the message of "the people," Bosnian Muslims are by definition not part of the people, even though they are regarded as descendants from common ancestors of Serbs and Croats. For Andric, the ancient Bosnian church, persecuted as heretic by both Catholic and Orthodox forces, was a sign of a "young Slavic race" still torn between "heathen concepts with dualistic coloring and unclear Christian dogmas." (Andric 1990: 12) Most Bosnians believe that the members of the Bosnian Church, called Bogomils or Patarins, were the ancestors of the Bosnian Muslims. Andric portrays Bosnian Muslims not only as cowardly and covetous and the "heathen element of a young race," but finally as the corrupted "Orient" that cut off the Slavic race from the "civilizing currents" of the West. (1990: 16ff)

Andric's most famous novel centers on the bridge on the Drina River commissioned by Mehmed Pasha Sokolovic, a Serb who had been taken to Istanbul and become a pasha.[9] To appease fairies, *vile*, holding up the bridge's construction, the builders must wall up two Christian infants within it. Two holes that appear in the bridge are interpreted as the place where the infants' mothers would come to suckle their babies.

The story crystallizes the view that an essentially Christic race of Slavs is walled up within the encrustation of an alien religion. It also represents an obsession with the Ottoman practice of selecting Serb boys to be sent to Istanbul and brought up Muslim; such people, however successful, remain perpetual exiles to themselves, cut off from the Christian essence of their Slavic souls. The key event in *Bridge on the Drina* is the impaling of a Serb dissident by the Turks and their helpers, Bosnian Muslims and Gypsies. The scene contains a long, anatomically detailed portrayal of the death of the heroic Serb, with powerful evocations of the crucifixion.

Andric is a hero to both Serb and Croat nationalists who have been "cleansing" Muslims from Bosnia.[9] On June 28, 1989, approximately one million pilgrims streamed into Kosovo for the Passion Play commemoration of the six-hundredth anniversary of the battle of Kosovo. (Malcolm 1994: 213ff) On this occasion, Serb President Slobodan Milosevic consolidated three years of effort in both fomenting and appropriating radical nationalist sentiment. Within three years, those who directed the passion play, acted in it, and sat in the first rows in 1989, were among the organizers and executors of the most unspeakable depravities against Bosnian civilians. (Glenny 1993: 39)

The Kosovo "Genocide"

You silence the number of atrocities per capita in Kosovo which is unprecedented in the twentieth century. It is forever recorded, but not only on paper. The judiciary groans under the weight of unsolved disputes. And every dispute is a drama. Serbian houses, blinded and empty, sink into the ground together with tombs, so that the houses and tombs will soon vanish. (Vukadinovic 1989: 69)

The above global denunciation of Albanians is from a speech given by Milan Komnenic at the meeting "Serbians and Albanians in Yugoslavia Today," on April 26, 1988. It was then incorporated into one of the memorial volumes on the six-hundredth anniversary of the battle of Kosovo, as a special issue of the *Serbian Literary Quarterly*.

Kosovo has been called by some the "Serb Jerusalem." Not only is Kosovo the place of the archetypal founding event in Serb romantic mythology, it is also the center of many of Serbia's greatest works of religious architecture and the ancient seat of the Serb Orthodox leadership. The Serb Patriarchate was established at Pec in Kosovo in 1346. The Patriarchate was re-established in 1557 by Mehmed Pasha Sokolovic, in the reign of Suleyman the Magnificent, and the first Serb occupant of the chair is believed to have been a brother of Mehmet Pasha. The Patriarchate lasted until 1765 when, during the period of increasing Serb resistance to Ottoman rule, it was abolished.

The notion of purging the majority population of Albanians from

Kosovo had reappeared at periods of crisis during modern Serbian history. In the period between the two World Wars, Albanians in Kosovo were repressed and Serb colonization was encouraged. In 1966 Tito acceded partially to Albanian demands for more autonomy. In 1974 Kosovo was given a special status as an autonomous region, within the Republic of Serbia but with its own vote in the Yugoslav presidency.

In 1986 radical nationalists, Serb clerics, and a branch of the Yugoslav Communist Party began a major campaign orchestrating the dramatic charge that Albanians were engaged in "genocide" against Serbs. The charge of genocide was combined with lurid tales of rape, the beating of nuns, and other alleged atrocities. The high Albanian birth rate, it was now alleged, was part of this genocide. In January two hundred Belgrade intellectuals signed a petition to the Yugoslav and Serbian national assemblies known as the "Memorandum." The memorandum demanded a restructuring of the relationship of the autonomous province of Kosovo to Serbia. It indicted the autonomy and majority rule in Kosovo, established in the Yugoslav constitutional reform of 1974, as a "national treason" and part of an anti-Serb plot. It made references to the "genocide" in Kosovo.

What was the truth of these grave charges, the repetition of which helped galvanize radical Serb nationalism within Yugoslavia? According to police records, the incidence of rape in Albania was at a rate *below* that of Serbia proper. According to the same records there was exactly one recorded instance of the rape of a Serb by an Albanian. When Mihajlo Markovic and two other proponents of the Kosovo genocide charge were confronted with these facts, they had no answer. Instead, they continued to pose unfounded allegations as fact, referring to the Albanian leadership's aspiration to an "ethnically clean" Kosovo. (Magas 1993: 57–58)

Despite protestations by Serb nationalists that Albanians were being given especially lenient treatment, the opposite was the case. Amnesty International reported that Albanians, who were eight percent of the population of Yugoslavia, accounted for seventy-five percent of its prisoners of conscience (Helsinki Watch 1986, 1989, 1990). The claims of genocide, widespread ethnically-caused rape, and systematic annihilation of cultural heritage were in fact not only incorrect and filled with interior contradictions, but they were ultimately insidious. As officials of the United Nations High Commission for Refugees (UNHCR) in Eastern Bosnia reported, the claim by

Serb nationalists of "genocide," "ethnic cleansing," "mass rape," and "cultural annihilation" against Serbs in a particular region was a code for Serbian militias, from within Bosnia and from Serbia proper, to begin the "ethnic cleansing" of a region, practicing in fact all the atrocities that they claimed (falsely) were being practiced against Serbs.

A clear example of the escalation of rhetoric and charges of genocide can be found in the language of Serb Orthodox leaders. In 1969, the Holy Council of Bishops wrote to Yugoslav President Tito to express their concern about vandalism of Serb property and intimidation of Serbs in Kosovo. The language is specific and the concerns are grounded in factual incidents that are described without ethnic or religious vilification or generic blame against all Albanians. (G. Filipovic 1989: 354–55) In 1982, in a Good Friday appeal by Serb priests and monks, the language had changed. With constant allusions to the theme of the crucifixion of the Serb nation, the battle of 1389, the alleged centuries-long plot by Albanians to exterminate Serb culture, the alleged depravity of the Ottoman Turks, the appeal tied all of this history to the charge of genocide:

> It is no exaggeration to say that planned GENOCIDE [emphasis in original] is being perpetrated against the Serbian people in Kosovo! What otherwise would be the meaning of "ethnically pure Kosovo" which is being relentlessly put into effect through ceaseless and never-ending migrations? (G. Filipovic 1989: 355–60)

In 1987, 60,000 Serbs signed a petition protesting the "fascist genocide" in Kosovo. (G. Filipovic 1989: 360–63) In none of these articles, petitions, and appeals was any evidence whatsoever offered of an Albanian program to create an "ethnically pure" state in Kosovo, nor was the allegation that over 250,000 Albanians had emigrated to Kosovo from Albania proper ever demonstrated or even argued.

What started out as a convenient language of "genocide" against Serbs with which to rally Serb nationalists was transmuted by 1992 into a code for genocide by Serb nationalists. The code is apparent in the anti-Albanian hate literature of the period. Thus, Milan Komnenic makes the Serb-nationalist allegation that 300,000 Albanians are refugees from Albania proper and should be returned. Komnenic goes on to cite Njegos himself:

> We do not seek mercy from you, don't you seek it from us. You have
> never given it to us, and we no longer have the right to give it to you.
> Yes, we are, according to the words of Dostojevski, an evangelical
> people, but we are faithful to the mountain gospel of Njegos. . . . Do
> not pretend that you love us, because we do not love you. We have
> long ago eaten up the moldy pretzel of internationalism that falsely
> joins us in brotherhood and falsely unites us. (Vukadinovic 1989: 70)

Such open contempt for the notion of "brotherhood and unity" that
was the widely acknowledged *sine qua non* for holding together the
delicate ethno-religious fabric of Yugoslavia, published in a prestigious
Serbian literary journal, was nothing less than an open declaration of
war.

Such was the contextual backdrop for the six-hundredth anniversary of the Battle of Kosovo. Although the hatred was directed at
Albanians in Kosovo, the literature and archetypes made Slavic
Muslims particularly vulnerable. By the time of the anniversary, the
construction of a language of "genocide" against Serbs in Kosovo was
conflated with the original martyrdom of Prince Lazar. From such a
perspective, there could be no safety. Even the peaceful smile might be
the smile of the traitor, Vuk Brankovic, the Serbian Judas.

The Return of the *Ustashe*

Parallel to the construction of an alleged genocide in Kosovo, Serb
nationalists began alleging the return of the *Ustashe*. Just as Kosovo
Albanians were, as a group, held responsible for German collabora-
tors in the Second World War, all Croats came under suspicion for
Ustashe activities. The Bosnian Muslims were also targeted by the
generic blame. During the Second World War, Bosnian Muslims were
caught on all sides of the battle lines; some fought with the *Ustashe*,
many with the Partisans, and many others were massacred by both
Ustashe and *Chetnik* groups.

As polarization grew, the Serb clergy and Serb nationalists began a
program of disinterring the bones of Serb victims of the *Ustashe* in the
Second World War. The disinterment of the victims of *Ustashe* genocide took place simultaneously with the procession of the bones of
Prince Lazar. In this way the pain and anger of living memory (and
most Serbs had family perish in the Second World War) was combined
with the pain and anger of mythic time—a potent interconnection that
collapses the Second World War and 1389.

Six-Hundredth Anniversary: A Tradition Betrayed

By June 28, 1989, the Kosovo myth and history had been completely nationalized and appropriated. At this epochal moment in Serbian history, Slobodan Milosevic stood upon a podium with an enormous, theatrical backdrop. Directly behind Milosevic was a huge depiction of peonies, increasingly evoked as symbols of the blood of the martyrs killed at Kosovo. Above them was a massive Serbian nationalist insignia: an Orthodox Cross surrounded by the four Cyrillic Ss, standing for "Only Unity/Harmony Saves the Serb" (*samo sloga srbina spasava*). The full symbolic power of the Kosovo theme, the anger and fear generated by the genocide charge against Kosovo Albanians and the resurrection of the Ustashe atrocities, and the fundamental iconography of Kosovo were skillfully combined with the familiar cult of personality from the era of Tito. Pictures of Prince Lazar and pictures of Slobodan Milosevic were seen side by side in Serb homes and at Kosovo celebrations.

What happened in Yugoslavia is not the result of unique Balkan antagonisms; such antagonisms exist in every society. The media campaign took the charges against Kosovo Albanians, the alleged *Ustashe* nature of all Croats, and the alleged betrayal of Slavic Muslims, to a new pitch of repetitive intensity. (Gagnon 1995: 191–92) One barometer of the Serb nationalist media was the work of the cartoonist Milenko Mihajlovic. In May 1989, at the height of the Kosovo dispute and Serb anger over the Albanian birthrate, Mihajlovic published a cartoon showing hordes of baby Albanians, with demented, leering grins, swarming out from a queen-bee-like figure of Marshall Tito. In September 1989, he depicted *Ustashe* members fishing Serb babies with barbed fishing lines. As the Serb media heightened the pitch on its accusations that all Croats were fundamentally genocidal, Mihajlovic published a cartoon in January 1990 showing a Roman Catholic prelate with a rosary made out of the eyeballs of Serb children, with the Serb infants, their eye sockets empty, surrounding the prelate. Mihajlovic's cartoon of September 1990 showed a Roman Catholic prelate and fez-topped Muslim leader arguing over a Serb baby. The prelate wanted baptism, the Muslim wanted circumcision. The second frame shows the prelate gouging out the baby's eyes, while the Muslim, with a demented grin, stretches out the foreskin under a large knife. The cartoons of Mihajlovic were not published in an obscure, fringe journal, but in the *Literary Gazette* of Belgrade, the official organ of the Association of Serbian Writers. (Banac 1994: 36–43)

At the same time, the Yugoslav National Army, the last force of federal cohesion after the dissolution of the Yugoslav Communist Party and federal government, was transformed into a Serb-nationalist controlled implement of the struggle for a Greater Serbia. (Gagnon 1995: 195–96) Major purges of non-Serbs and Serbs who were not sufficiently nationalist began in the early 1990s and continued up until the period of this writing. By 1992, the Yugoslav army had been transformed into an instrument of Serb nationalism and had been hardened by the carnage of the Serb-Croat war and the annihilation of the city of Vukovar.

Finally, the extreme fringe of Serb politics, represented by ethno-fascist leader Vojislav Seselj and militia leaders such as Arkan, Mirko Jovic, and Dragoslav Bokan, was given access by Milosevic to media, political leverage, and military and security protection and patronage. It was these groups—numbered at over forty by the Serb democratic opposition journal, *Vreme*—that worked carefully with the regular Serb forces in early 1992 to spread terror throughout Eastern and Northern Bosnia.[10] Vojislav Seselj's militias committed the most heinous atrocities. (Woodward 1995a: 356) When Seselj challenged Milosevic, Milosevic turned his patronage to another genocide-squad leader, Arkan.

With such a strategy in place, the Kosovo myth was ready for appropriation. Just as Good Friday remembrances of the passion of Christ were used by anti-Semites to instigate attacks on Jews, so the Kosovo Passion Play became the occasion for persecution. When the international "contact group" suggested a peace plan that would give the thirty-two percent of Serbs in Bosnia forty-nine percent of the land, including the areas on which they carried out the most systematic "ethnic cleansing," the Serbian Church vehemently opposed the peace plan as unfair to Serbs and attacked the Serbian government of Slobodan Milosevic for supporting the plan. (cf. Cigar 1995)

As early as 1989, the Kosovo mythology had become a symbolic complex, made up of the Christ-killer theme, the fear of the traitor, the Kosovo "genocide," and the resurrection of the *Ustashe*. Through sheer repetition, the allegations took on a life of their own. They then took the turn into the realm of horror. Reporters and UN officials who witnessed atrocities by Serb forces in Bosnia in 1992 began to notice a pattern. A massacre would take place in a village immediately after the local news began announcing that the Croat and Muslim population was planning to exterminate the Serbs. Indeed, it was by tracing such a pattern that some reporters were able to follow the chain of massacres and killing centers. (cf. Gutman 1993) A vivid example of this process at work was offered by the UNHCR's Jose Maria Mendiluce:

> I knew how the system of ethnic cleansing functioned and in Zvornik I had the opportunity to witness it. For days, the Belgrade media had been writing about how there was a plot to kill all Serbs in Zvornik. The authorities in Zvornik realized that the point in question was a typical maneuver by Seselj's Radicals-volunteers. This maneuver always precedes the killing of Muslims, as had already happened in Bijeljina and many places along the left bank of the Drina River. There were many soldiers, tanks and much shooting in the city. I guess they were so preoccupied with shooting and killing that they did not see me. There were many corpses strewn about and I saw them kill some elderly people who were unable to escape. (*Vreme*, 12/26/94)

Even eyewitness accounts did not shake the ideological structure underlying ethnic cleansing. In justifying the atrocities in Bosnia, Serb nationalists would point to atrocities by Croats. When it was pointed out that the Muslim population had nothing to do with the Croat army and, indeed, had been attacked by the Croat army in 1993, the Serb nationalists shifted to generic blame of all Muslims for the acts of those who fought with the *Ustashe*. When it was pointed out that many of the families who suffered had fought against the *Ustashe*, the Serb nationalists would shift to claims of Ottoman depravity and treat the Muslims as Turks. When it was pointed out that the Slavic Muslims are just as indigenous to the region as Orthodox Christians or Catholics, the discussion would then shift to allegations that the Bosnian Muslims were fundamentalists and that Serbia was defending the West against the fundamentalist threat of radical Islam. When it was pointed out that, in fact, most Bosnian Muslims were anti-fundamentalist by tradition and character, the Serb nationalists would insist that this was a civil war, in which all sides were guilty, there were no angels, and the world should allow the people involved to solve their own problems. These last two positions, although part of the interior Serb nationalist symbol-complex, are also woven into an international discourse of Balkanism and Orientalism. To examine them we must move back from the field of Kosovo to a wider frame of reference.

Between Orientalism and Balkanism

In 1980 Alija Izetbegovic was tried and imprisoned for writing the *Islamic Declaration*. A few years later, he wrote a more extensive work, *Islam between East and West*, that suggested two models—Islam and European liberal democracy—as antidotes to the problems besetting Europe at the time. When Izetbegovic became president of Bosnia in 1989, the vast majority of Bosnians had never read *The Islamic Declaration*.

But Serb ultranationalists not only had read it, they had republished it, and were using it as the key element in their charge that they were defending the Western world from radical Islamic fundamentalists in Bosnia. Although Izetbegovic pleaded with Europe not to recognize Croatia until the issue of Serb minorities in Croatia and Bosnia was settled, Serb nationalists accused him of abandoning Yugoslavia with the purpose of establishing an Islamic state. (Woodward, 1995: 226) Other indications of this alleged militant Islamic plot to establish a fundamentalist state in Bosnia were the fact that Haris Silajdzic (now Prime Minister of Bosnia) stayed in Libya and the fact that some Bosnian Muslims had had special relations with Libya during the period that Libya and Yugoslavia considered themselves allies in the Nonaligned Movement. Ironically, the government of Libya has been one of Slobodan Milosevic's most faithful supporters.

The charges of fundamentalism were placed—without any apparent understanding of the contradiction—with the charge that Bosnian Muslims were plotting to recreate the Ottoman rule over Bosnia. It is not hard to detect in this language traces of "Orientalism," the view that "Orientals"—which invariably means Muslims, of whatever geographical origin—are by nature voluptuaries, aesthetes, authoritarians and, ultimately, perverts. (cf. Said 1976) It was necessary to kill Muslims because the Bosnian Muslims wanted to "Steal Serb women for their harems." Penetrating the "harem" is a standard feature of Orientalizing discourse. Reflecting European racism of the nineteenth century, Orientalism serves as a handy excuse for dismissing the claims of non-Europeans to legitimate moral and political authority.

The term "harem" is the Islamic term for the sacred, and refers particularly to times, spaces, and objects to which access is ritually controlled. The *Ka'ba* in Mecca is the primary Islamic *haram*. The *mihrab*, the prayer niche in each mosque that orients the worshipper toward Mecca, is a sign of sacrality. And the deliberate violation of

Muslim women is then at one with such desecration of other "harems." Despite the fact that Serb soldiers are well aware that polygamy is not practiced by Bosnian Muslims, the notion that Bosnians want to "steal Serb women for their harems" is used by the military as a mode of indoctrination.

The tendency to use "Muslim" in an "Orientalist" manner made it possible to convey, if not a threat, at least a reason for doubting the integrity of the community. Particularly galling to many Bosnians has been the constant reference by NATO power diplomats and by the members of the news media to the "Muslim-dominated government of Bosnia-Herzegovina." Bosnians ask why there are not also, then, references to the Protestant-dominated government of the United States or the Anglican-dominated government of Britain.

Behind the Orientalist propaganda were the Serb-nationalist academics. Miroljub Jevtic, Professor of Political Science at the University of Belgrade, describes the imminent threat to Europe by Muslims, and the Bosnian Muslims as having the "blood" of the martyrs of Kosovo on their hands. Alexandar Popovic, a Serb academic turned nationalist, writes on Islam as a fundamentally "totalitarian" religion because it embraces all aspects of life. (Popovic 1990: 1–10) Use of the term "totalitarianism" equates Islam with Stalinist and Nazi regimes, the wounds of which are still fresh in the former Yugoslavia, and shifts the pain of those wounds in a generic way onto an entire people, identified as Muslim. The diplomats of NATO nations have been careful in public not to reveal anti-Islamic prejudice, but their refusal to allow the Bosnians arms with which to defend themselves, excused on the grounds that such arms would only add "fuel" to the fire or create an "equal killing field," were based solidly on fear of Islam (Malcolm 1994: 1; O'Ballance 1995: 249). Yet by continually urging ethnic partition, they have contributed to the possibility that what remains of Bosnia might indeed become an Islamic state.[11] Ironically, while Bosnian Muslims were prevented by European powers from gaining arms to defend themselves with, out of fear of their possible fundamentalism, support in the Islamic world was slow in coming, partially because some Muslim leaders viewed Bosnians as less than assiduous in their practice of Islam.

Bosnian Muslims are doubly damned in another way. Not only are they prey to dehumanizing Orientalist discourse about Muslims, but they are also the object of an equally dehumanizing discourse about Balkan peoples in general. The Belgrade and Pale regimes, backed continually by voices in the NATO powers, found it convenient to dehumanize all sides in the Balkan tragedy. This is a "civil war," they maintained, and this is the way people in the Balkans have always behaved. The dehumanization of Bosnians as "Balkan" tribal haters, outside the realm of reason and civilization, was promoted by a wide variety of Western diplomats as the major reason for the refusal to stop the genocide when it became known in the early summer of 1992.

The notion that the Balkans are particularly unsuited for civilization goes all the way back to Toynbee. The Balkans are too close, historically and graphically, to the Orient (read Islam) to be truly a part of Europe, the assumption goes. This construction of Balkan peoples and cultures as unamenable to civilized standards of behavior and locked in unchanging, perpetual tribal hatreds, was repopularized in Robert Kaplan's *Balkan Ghosts*, which dwelled on the Balkan border with Turkey as Europe's "rear door." (Kaplan 1992: 283)

A key aspect of the Balkanist stereotype is the mythic history of the superhuman Serb warrior. Serbs, we are told, tied down many Nazi divisions. No effort is made to distinguish between the Partisans of the Second World War, a multiethnic group, many of whose descendants were being annihilated in the Serb army genocide of 1992, from the ethno-nationalist militias of fifty years later. The invincible Serb paradigm served as a "green light" for the conquest and ethnic cleansing by the Serb army of Ratko Mladic. When the Croatian army saw that the NATO powers not only would not intervene to stop the "ethnic cleansing," but were prepared to cede the territories "cleansed" to the cleansers, they began their own "ethnic cleansing" campaign against Bosnian Muslims in the winter of 1992. For over three years, the NATO alliance, the largest military alliance in the history of humankind, maintained that any rolling back of Serb "cleansed" areas would require hundreds of thousands of NATO ground troops and massive casualities.

The policy of containment was the policy of the Bush, Mitterrand, and Major administrations, allowing the Bosnians to be given over, piece by piece, to ethno-nationalist conquest. Candidate Clinton's position, which recognized the genocide for what it was, began to shift as soon as President Clinton entered office, and as it shifted, Balkanist language made a steady entry. On February 10, 1993, Clinton was still acknowledging the massive human rights violations, but speaking now of "containing it." By March 26, 1993, Clinton was talking of a "full court press" to secure "agreement of the Serbs," and, on April 25 of the same year, he reminded us that "Hitler sent tens of thousands of soldiers to that area and was never successful in subduing it." Balkanism was immediately combined with the notion, advanced both by Serb President Slobodan Milosevic, Bosnian Serb President Radovan Karadzic, and the British government, that what was occurring was a "civil war." By February 10, 1994, the dehumanization of the Bosnians had resulted in Clinton blaming the victims: "Until these folks get tired of killing each other . . . bad things will continue to happen." (Sullivan 1995: 14)

The notion that the peoples of the Balkans are somehow genetically or historically fated to kill one another has been a key rationale for UN and NATO refusal to protect Bosnians from the genocide. "Age-old antagonisms," "ancient tribal hatreds," "blood-feuds"—the vocabulary is seldom related to any careful consideration of the history of the region. Just as the genocide against Serbs in Kosovo took on a "reality" of its own through the manipulation of constant assertions, so the construction of the ancient Balkan tribal hatreds—unamenable to the efforts of civilized nations to change—took on its own reality. For the thousands of Bosnian Muslims, Serbs, Croats, Gypsies, Jews, and others, who died trying to save their heritage, the libraries and monuments, the evidence of five hundred years of shared inheritance and civilization, these repeated assertions of an ancient, unchangeable, Balkan, tribal mentality of ethnic hatred and mass murder have been particularly ironic.[12]

At the heart of the Balkanist strategy is a moral equalizing. "There are no angels in this conflict," is one refrain, as if genocide should only be a matter of concern if the victims are angels, rather than human beings. While no side in any war has ever been free of blame, to equalize such disparate programs is to engage in a fundamental act of falsehood.

Moral equalizing was paralleled by political equalizing. While solemnly announcing at the London conference of 1992 that the territorial integrity of Bosnia was to be protected and that no military conquests would be recognized as the basis for peace agreements, the NATO powers immediately developed a competing language in which the Bosnian government was only one of three "warring factions." The political equalization allowed an abandonment of the recognition of Bosnia's sovereignty and culminated in the Stoltenberg-Owen Plan of June 1993, where Bosnia was to be divided up according to a secret

agreement between Serbian President Slobodan Milosevic and Croatian President Franjo Tudjman. (Woodward 1995: 216) The principle, in Lord Owen's phrase, was "reality on the ground." The result
was a peace plan that would have done exactly what the London
Conference, which created Owen's and Stoltenberg's positions as
peace mediators, promised would never be done. Territorial conquest
would be recognized. Serb nationalists would receive most of Bosnia-
Herzegovina, Croat nationalists most of the rest, and Muslims and
any others who wished to remain in Bosnia proper would be relegated
to a discontinuous set of enclaves or ghettoes, with little military,
economic, or political chance of survival.

Perhaps the clearest example of moral and political equalization
occurs in the work of Susan Woodward, a senior fellow in the Foreign
Policy Studies program at the Brookings Institute. In Woodward's
view, the problems in Bosnia are not the result of age-old tribal
hatreds, but the consequences of organizational breakdown following
the Cold War. In such an approach, there seems to be no real crime
and no one really responsible for a crime. Thus "methods of populations transfers varied," "Muslim elites were murdered or brutally
expelled," and "local rivalries were encouraged to play out." (Woodward 1995a: 243) Note how the continual use of passives or intransi-
tive verbs systematically strips the discourse of an agent. There is no
named party carrying out the activities. They just happen in certain
ways. Woodward then goes on to claim that "the victimization of
Muslims through ethnic cleansing was also a result of the political
contest behind the wars, not ethnic or religious hatreds." Throughout,
the killing centers and rape camps, the methodical and consistent
practice of massacre, the systematic annihilation of every trace of the
people targeted are not mentioned. Only the use of siege warfare
(shelling, enforced starvation, and disease) is mentioned specifically,
with the statement that the object of such warfare was "to persuade
civilians of a different ethnicity to leave without putting up a fight."
(1995a: 244) What such language hides is the reality that people who
had already given up all efforts to fight, and would have gladly left
with their lives, were killed in huge numbers. The sanitized language
of procedures and organizations allows the reader no real sense of
either the immensity of the human suffering or the enormity of the
crimes committed. It is not surprising that Woodward finds little
moral or political distinction among the parties in the Bosnian conflict
and treats with undisguised disdain the efforts to establish a War

Crimes Tribunal to reestablish Geneva principles forbidding genocide. (1995a: 323)

Conclusions, Questions

The crimes against Bosnians, and particularly against Bosnian Muslims, have a pervasive religious component. Religious symbols, rituals, and institutions were used by members of the Serb Church, as well as by secular nationalists, in ways that promote an ideology of genocide. The most virulent form of hatred, the cosmic dualism between Slavic Muslim and Slavic Christian, was constructed by Romantic nationalists in the nineteenth century and revived (or, as the Serb nationalist said, "resurrected") at the end of the Cold War. This ideology itself is indeed potent. It was made more potent when rituals were combined: the ritualized charges of genocide against Serbs in Kosovo; the translation of Lazar's bones; the disinterment of the Serb victims of the Second World War; and the passion play observances of 1989. This complex of symbols, by itself, was not capable of causing genocide. Still needed was concerted action by the media, politicians, secret police, militias, and army officers to move from symbolic potency to active aggression. Also needed was the arms embargo on the victims of the aggression, a policy rooted in Balkanist and Orientalist stereotypes. The manipulation of religion and history by Serb nationalists was in this sense supported by the manipulation of Balkan history by Western leaders.

The genocide in Bosnia raises more general questions as well. Will Europe be able to tolerate a flourishing non-Christian cultural entity? If not, are we not drifting toward a new and more dangerous cold war, pitting the Orthodox Slavs, now being inflamed by Russian nationalists, against the NATO alliance, with the world of Islam still in a state of shock and disbelief at what has been done to Bosnians? The outcome of such a conflict can hardly be predicted, but that is no ground for optimism.

Nationalism and Self-Determination: The Bosnian Tragedy

Jean Bethke Elshtain

The headlines scream: "Greatest Tragedy for Western Diplomacy Since the 1930s." Or: "The Worst Humanitarian Disaster Since World War II." The references are to the full unfolding of the tragedy in Bosnia. It is midsummer 1995 as I write. The news is worse and worse. Just yesterday the town of Srebrenica was overrun by Bosnian Serb forces, sending thousands of "stunned Muslim refugees" streaming into "Northern Bosnia today, telling of bodies left hanging from trees and littering the street following the Bosnian Serb conquest of the ostensibly safe haven of Srebrenica." (Kinzer, 1995: 1) The outline of the story is by now an all-too-familiar-one. Women, children, the elderly, and the infirm are forced out of homes and villages, some of the women having been raped; the fate of Bosnian Muslim men who are separated from their families is, as of this writing, unknown. What is particularly disconcerting is the fact that Srebrenica was in 1993 declared to be one of the six enclaves designated as a safe area or "haven" free from armed attack or hostility.

The unfolding of the full extent of the disaster, of course, will take years to assess, but there is no doubt that (a) we have witnessed the worst instances of, and the greatest victories for, genocidal initiatives since the conclusion of the Second World War; (b) the UN has proved to be almost entirely ineffective in dealing with a determined and powerful group intent upon extending its sway through territorial aggression; and (c) the Western Alliance is shaky, and United States leadership is in doubt. It is unlikely that, whatever the final outcome in Bosnia, this can be reversed. The credibility of the United Nations, and of the United States as the leader of the Western alliance, has sustained a series of hammer blows from which it will take years to recover, if indeed recovery is possible. Why this gloomy assessment? What else might we have done and with what justification? Finally, what is to be the scope of the new world order that we see emerging in the name of nationalism and self-determination?

The initial assault on Bosnia took place in April 1992 and was recognized as a case of territorial aggression. But this version of territorial aggression was nothing nearly so clear-cut as, for example, the Iraqi incursion into Kuwait on August 2, 1990, which helped to trigger the Persian Gulf War. That war began on January 16, 1991, with the announcement that "the liberation of Kuwait has begun." Why, then, was the territory controlled by Bosnian Muslims a less exigent case, and *causus belli*, under international law than the Iraqi invasion of Kuwait? The answer is that Bosnia lacked the internationally recognized and sanctioned status of sovereignty. The United Nations Charter makes provision for response to violation of the territory of a sovereign state. But what happens when sovereign states—for example, Yugoslavia—break up, and in the wake of this event a number of what have been called variously microstates or parastates emerge? As Misha Glenny has pointed out, "Until January, 1992, international legal precedent determined that recognition would be granted to states only if they had a 'defined territory.'" (Glenny, 1995b: 46) Generally, this was understood as control over the land in question.

But the territorial muddiness of the face of the new Europe came into view in the Balkans when the European Union recognized first Croatia and then Slovenia. At that point, the president of Bosnia sought recognition for his piece of former Yugoslavian territory, and, when that happened, the situation, for this and a variety of other reasons, began to break down. What emerged were three small entities—the Republic of Bosnia and Herzegovina (predominantly Muslim), the Serb Republic, and the Croat Republic. Although the Bosnian people enjoy a measure of international recognition, that recognition lacked the full-blown status of membership in the comity of nation-states, namely, sovereignty. Thus, the unwillingness of the international community to do anything meaningful to protect and defend the Muslim population of Bosnia indicates just how overriding sovereignty remains as the way in which a polity, defined in part by control over territory, remains the key principle in international affairs.

In effect, what the Western alliance said to Bosnia in 1992 was: "If you lose over seventy percent of your territory, we have no stake in doing much of anything to help you." It's that simple, that abrupt, and that brutal. Having received at least partial recognition, the Bosnian government, vulnerable from the start, began a frantic quest for peace-keeping assistance from the UN, for the lifting of an arms embargo, internationally imposed in 1991 with an eye to stemming the tide of further aggression; and for brokerage of the dispute with some teeth in the settlement—none of which was forthcoming. The Serb rebellion that began in 1992 was, at least until the late summer of 1995, wildly successful. To all intents and purposes, we held the Bosnian Muslims hostage for three years, so to speak, with a series of half-hearted promises about assistance, air strikes, and even, under Clinton's watch, the promise (or threat) of commitment of U.S. troops.

Although many American commentators, beginning with the United States State Department, "deplore" what has happened, few have come up with a rationale for how things might have happened differently. Editorials in *Newsweek*, the *New Yorker*, the *Christian Science Monitor*, and elsewhere speak of the abdication of the major powers and of U.S. dissimulation. Indeed, one editorial writer for *Newsweek* has gone so far as to argue flatly that the president of the United States lied when it came to Bosnia. (Eliot, 1995: 27) The columnist George Will approvingly quotes Senator Daniel Patrick Moynihan's insistence that "everything is at stake here. If principle is everything." If we are willing to stand by in the face of ethnic cleansing, "what have we gone through the twentieth century for?" Will concludes that "the Serbs fighting in Bosnia are bullies led by war criminals collaborating with a dictator. If we don't have an interest in this fight, what are we?" (Will, 1995: 72) The *Christian Science Monitor*, in an editorial entitled "End the Bosnia Posturing," writes that in an electronic age "the genocide in Bosnia can't be contained. We all see it. We learn from it. Will we learn to fight, or watch?" (6/9/95: 20)

What might have been done with what justification? First, it is important to remind ourselves that foreign policy actors and analysts tend to argue with something called *national security interests*, first and foremost, in mind. They generally hold a number of objectives constant in defining these national security interests. These include protecting the U.S. from direct military attack; protecting U.S. citizens and property abroad; preventing adverse shifts in the balance of power; and, finally, deterring aggression and promoting peace in specific geographic regions. Working within these parameters, if an issue is to cross our radar screen, it has to pose a direct military threat to us, or we have to decide if we have an *interest* in deterring this aggression.

Needless to say, this opens the door to almost endless disputation. In setting forth criteria for whether the United States does or does not have a stake in a regional conflict, the overall view is that it is not desirable for the United States to engage in every regional conflict. "It is to be hoped," write two thinkers on strategic policy, "that Washington will choose to exercise leadership primarily in those situations in which U.S. interests and principles are at stake rather than where *only* its principles are tested." (my emphasis) In their view it is imperative that the United States maintain its "traditional commitments," and that policy-makers take prudent steps in the present to avoid worse situations in the future, "particularly in the case of rogue states that refuse to fit peacefully into the world system and are acquiring weapons of mass destruction." When it comes to protecting our "vital interests and principles," they conclude, "the United States must be prepared to use decisive force and must also be prepared to act alone, although acting as part of a coalition is preferable, as long as the United States leads that coalition." (Binnendijk and Claussen, 1995: 120)

Analyses of this kind can be gathered together under the rubric of the so-called *realist* or *realpolitik* position in international relations. This position prides itself on being hardheaded and tough-minded. It sees the world as a configuration of power relations and balance of forces. Those who embrace realism argue that, as tempting as intervention may be in certain situations in which "humanitarian disasters are unfolding," if the makers of U.S. foreign policy cannot discern that an abiding interest is at stake, then the warrant for intervention is simply missing. Thus, the sharp and severe determination in the Bosnian case by former Secretary of State James Baker: "We don't have a dog in that fight." (cf. Will, 1995: 72) This particular assessment is one that, if anything, was extended and deepened in the first years of the Clinton administration, but with far less precision than evinced by Baker.

There are those who argue that United States interests *are* at stake in the Balkans tragedy and, further, that if we do not stem the tide of aggression here, we will face it elsewhere. The favorite analogy for those who make this argument is, of course, with Munich and the policy of appeasement. But the response within the *realist* framework is likely to be that the Bosnian Serbs are not Hitler. They have not the means, the territory, the will, or the power to commit aggression beyond the boundaries of the Balkan peninsula itself. Moreover, it is very unlikely that this regional conflict will spill over and involve Europe in an extension or widening of the war. Thus, realism finds little grounds to engage.

Similarly, those embracing a *pacifist* perspective would urge that the United States and the Western alliance stay out of the situation. For, by definition, pacifism is a doctrine that involves a refusal to fight. Pacifists might, however, call for a widening of the humanitarian effort. The irony for the pacifist is that humanitarian intervention in such a situation can take place only under the covering umbrella of armed force, or with the specific provisos of the aggressors.

One can, however, find grounds for intervention in a just war perspective. Although this essay is not about just war, the just war perspective would ask us to take a look at the clear-cut, unfolding case of genocide under the rubric of "ethnic cleansing," and would find in this possible grounds for intervention. Protecting the innocent "from certain harm" has been for centuries an overriding *causus belli* for the just war thinker. This by no means settles the matter. But the just war thinker would argue that one has to bring *both* principles and interests into play in assessing whether intervention in a given situation is or is not warranted. If our policy makers had been guided by just war principles, my hunch is that we would have intervened earlier with the justification that, under the Nuremberg precedent, genocidal political aggression cannot be permitted to stand.

But the claims of justice have received little hearing, in part because this war has been defined as an *ethnic conflict* fueled and made more hideous by the infusion of narrow, aggressive, and brutal nationalism. Nationalism is the great political passion of our time. That this is so is surprising and, for many, disturbing. Political scientists and analysis over the years predicted confidently that nationalism would cease to be a powerful force as the world moved toward ever-expanding rationalism, Enlightenment, and universalism. Perhaps this helps to account for the shock waves ricocheting through the academic world since 1989. With this "new nationalism" in mind, I want to explore, briefly, the interwoven themes of self-determination and nationalism in the realm in which each takes shape: the world of states, would-be states, political rule, and civic life.

There are some things we ought by now to have learned. One is that the imperial suppression of particular national identities is costly indeed, for these identities, once permitted expression, often take shape in militant, even ferocious forms. As Sir Isaiah Berlin points out, "People tire of being spat upon, ordered about by a superior nation, a superior class, or a superior anyone. Sooner or later, they ask the nationalist questions: 'Why do we have to obey them?' 'What right have they?' 'What about us?' 'What can't we ... ?'" (Berlin, 1991: 20) In her book on nationalism, Liah Greenfield argues: "National identity is, fundamentally, a matter of dignity. It gives people reasons to be proud." Peoples historically—including our own foremothers and forefathers—fought "over respect due to them, rather than anything else." (Greenfield, 1992: 487–488) Václav Havel speaks of the "desire to renew and emphasize one's identity" as a force that lies behind "the emergence of many new countries. Nations that never had states of their own feel an understandable need to experience independence." (Havel, 1993: 8)

Although the nation-state model emerged historically as a Western invention with the Treaty of Westphalia in 1648, this form has been embraced or imposed worldwide. Thus, at present, aggrieved peoples want, not an end to the nation-state, or to sovereignty or national autonomy, but an end to Western colonial, or Soviet, or other "external" dominance of their particular histories, languages, cultures, and wounded sense of identity. Western religious thought has long recognized the validity and importance of self-determination, tying this concept to the need to work to achieve a common good and to a vision of human dignity tied "unquestionably," according to Pope John XXIII in *Pacem in Terris*, to the "right to take an active part in government." (John XXIII: 347) John XXIII, in that great document, reminds us that no human being is "by nature superior to his fellows, since all men are equally noble in natural dignity. And consequently there are no differences at all between political communities from the point of view of natural dignity." (John XXIII: 350) Yet is this not what nationalism always violates by insisting that some states or peoples are in fact not only different from others, given their history and culture, but superior too? Is not equal dignity of all peoples necessarily violated by nationalism?

George Orwell, for one, thought so. Orwell, in "Notes on Nationalism," traces the drastic simplifications and overwrought evocation of competitive prestige in which the nationalist, one who uses all "his mental energy either in boosting or in denigrating," indulges. Orwell calls nationalist thought obsessive and indifferent to reality—persisting on a plane far removed from the concrete truths of everyday social life. The nationalist (by contrast to the civic patriot, of whom I will say more below) classifies people like insects and assumes that "whole blocks of millions or tens of millions of people can be confidently labelled 'good' or 'bad'." (Orwell, 1968: 362–363) The nationalist insists, as well, that no other duty must be allowed to override or even challenge that to the nation-state. He evokes power as force—we need more of it, we can never have enough of it, somebody else is creeping up on us and may soon have more than we do—and he sinks his own individuality into an overarching identification with the collective.

Orwell endorsed a robust version of patriotic or civic identity, a form of identification always wary and cautious of nationalistic excess because the temptation of national identity is to push in a triumphalist direction. How do we sort this out? How do we chart a moderate but firm course between the Scylla of sovereign absolutism, or an absolutizing of particular national identities, on the one hand; and the Charybdis of an arrogant universalism, or imperialism running roughshod over self-determination and diversity, on the other? Let us examine this possibility further.

Identity with a nation goes deep. In *The Political Life of Children*, Robert Coles found attachment to a homeland, or an imagined homeland, in the symbolism and imagery deployed by children. "Nationalism works its way into just about every corner of the mind's life," Coles writes. Children have ready access to a nation's "name, its flag, its music, its currency, its slogans, its history, its political life," and this personalized yet political identity shapes their outlooks and actions. Entrenched notions of a homeland are double-edged, at once inward looking, a place where one "gets one's bearings," and outward projecting, distinguishing and perhaps protecting "us" from "them," from foreigners who, all too easily, may become enemies. Both aspects of homeland and nationalist imagery turn up "in the developing conscience of young people" everywhere. (Coles, 1986: 60–63)

John Keane, a British theorist of civil society, that realm of associations and solidaristic possibilities greater than the individual but "beneath" the state, writes that "the birth of democracy required among its citizens a shared sense of nationhood." This shared sense becomes a "collective identity of people who share a language or a dialect of a common language, inhabit or are closely familiar with a defined territory, experience its ecosystem with some affection, and share a variety of customs." Most importantly, this identity includes "a measure of memories of the historical past." When these memories are called into play, the past is "experienced in the present tense as pride in the nation's achievements and, where necessary, an obligation to feel ashamed of the nation's failings." (Keane, 1992: 10) All of this sounds quite unexceptionable. But we all know the troubles that national identity trails in its wake and why there is so much cause for concern.

Bosnia focuses our attention on the negative features of national identity. What are these? They include: ruthless granulation of political entities in the name of a principle of the unimpeachable singularity of national, linguistic, cultural, even racial identities, coupled with the dangers of "mixing" any group with any other. Let me suggest that we not rush to judge the Balkans, to dismiss this region and its people as primitives and fanatics, but rather that we permit these terrible events to instruct us on the *always* present dangers in nationalism and national self-identity. We can and must be thus instructed without abandoning altogether the inherent integrity implicit in the *ideal* of self-determination, an ideal tied to self-respect and to the possibility that men and women, acting together, may know a good in common they cannot know alone.

What we see unfolding in the Balkans is a very old phenomenon, one from which our own society is by no means exempt. In harsher forms of multiculturalism, for example, do we not see an assertion of the absolutism of particular identity? Going beyond rightful claims to self-respect and civic equality, multicultural absolutists insist that identities must not be mixed; that, quite literally, whites and blacks, or men and women, or homosexuals and heterosexuals, inhabit incommensurable epistemological universes.

This is a view the civic pluralist cannot accept. For the civic pluralist embraces universalist aspirations and possibilities, affirming the idea that we can and must reach out in gestures of solidarity, friendship, and citizenship to those different from ourselves. As G. M. Támas puts it, the "ethnocultural" version of identity and nationalism is that "others ought to be elsewhere; there is no universalistic, overriding, trans-contextual principle 'legitimising' mixture, assimilation or diversity within the same politico-symbolic 'space.'" (Támas, 1993: 120) Those who break bodies politic "into warring ethnocultural enclaves" disdain nineteenth-century liberal and civic republican ideas of citizenship, which accepted the possibility of, and in some instances the necessity for, a form of national identity not reducible to ethnicity or culture as that which is simply given. The "new" ethno-cultural nationalism, "particularly in the extreme shape it had taken in Eastern Europe, cannot and does not want to answer political questions. It is mostly a repetitive reaffirmation of identity." (Támas, 1993: 121) The only precept proffered by the ethno-culturalist is "Be what you are," as an essentialist prescription. This, then, is by contrast to an alternative *civic* ideal, one chastened by recognition that "others are before and among me," that I am not hunkered down, alone, with others exactly like myself.

Christians, too, are *obliged* in this matter. Christianity is not primarily a civic religion. It arose in opposition to Empire and has from its inception engaged in a struggle with political authority over what rightly belongs to *regnum* and to *sacerdotium*. At the same time, the Christian insists that human beings are always in "the Empire," in a political formation of some sort or another. But the claims of a body politic, including the vast pretensions embodied in the classical notion of sovereignty, must always be checked and balanced against other claims. Identity with and obligation to a nation-state are never absolute. We rightly fear forms of nationalism that feed on hatred of other ways of life. But much of the new nationalism, the remarkable outbursts of civic energy from suppressed peoples, speaks in and through a rhetoric that taps universal claims and concerns.

The independence movements in the Baltic states—Solidarity, Civic Forum, and others—protested their control by the Soviet Empire, first, because it violated principles of self-determination imbedded in international law and shared understandings and, second, because it trampled on basic human rights, including the right to participate in, and help to choose, a way of life. Such appeals are at once universal *and* particular, tapping old identities but energizing new political recognitions. One must hope that peoples who proclaim their devotion to human rights as a universal principle can be held accountable in ways rapacious, nationalistic destroyers, who scoff at such niceties, cannot. Though one must, of course, *attempt* to hold those who would murder, rape and plunder accountable. This "middle way"—once again as an alternative to warring racial and ethnic groupings or the homogenized stability of efficiently managed imperialism—seems to me the only possible course that respects claims to self-determination yet holds forth the prospect of a painfully attained and perhaps, for that reason, even more deeply cherished civic order based on universal principles of recognition.

Perhaps a concrete example of this delicate balancing act is necessary. I rely here on press reports of Pope John Paul II's visit to the Baltic states in September 1993. Anatol Lieven, in *The Tablet*, writes that the situation in Lithuania was particularly delicate for John Paul because "Polish nationalists for their part have tried to exploit the alleged mistreatment of the 300,000 strong Polish minority in Lithuania." It is worth reminding the reader that much of current Lithuania was once part of Poland. The Lithuanian capital, Vilnius, is Poland's "Wilno," dear to the hearts of Poles everywhere, in part because it is the home of Adam Mickiewicz, the greatest Polish poet. Thus, "the Pope had to be very careful not to offend Lithuanian sensibilities," he being not only the Pope but a Pole associated with Polish aspirations to self-determination.

And so John Paul, while acknowledging the love Poles have for that particular place, used the Lithuanian name "Vilnius" and not the Polish "Wilno" throughout his pastoral visit, including the one time he spoke Polish—when he delivered mass in the main Polish-language church in Vilnius. For the rest of his visit, "the Pope spoke Lithuanian which he had learnt for the occasion" and "this made a tremendously positive impression on the Lithuanians." The Poles, reports Lieven,

> were not so pleased, but coming from the Pope they had to accept it. The Pope exhorted the Poles to identify fully with Lithuania, and not to dwell on the past—by which he meant not to endlessly recall the time when Vilnius was part of Poland. (Lieven, 1993: 1208–1209)

This subtle account shows the ways in which ethical space can be created or expanded for a form of civic identification *sans* irredentist or chauvinistic aspirations. One might say that eternal vigilance is the price of civic moderation.

Take a powerful example from the new South Africa as reported by the theologian John W. deGruchy, a longtime foe of the apartheid system. In a piece called "Waving the Flag," deGruchy begins by telling us that he "never thought I would be seduced by civil religion. After all, part of the struggle against apartheid was against the civil religion of the Afrikaner nationalism that gave it birth." He then asks us to imagine his feelings of "confusion" as he "unashamedly" applauds "the civil religion of the new South Africa and experience deep feelings of patriotism welling up in my soul." Now, deGruchy continues, he has a "flag on my desk, a flag in the kitchen, a flag pinned to my pocket."

But deGruchy knows there are limits: the fear of idolatry, warnings against making gods "in our own national image." For that reason, the flag of the new South Africa will not go into the sanctuary. "It is painful to do this—we would so much like to bring it in. But we need to do this to keep ourselves in check. The temptation of conflating civil religion with revelation has to be resisted." (deGruchy, 1994: 597–598) This is an example—a powerful example—of how Christians are (rightly) drawn toward the civic goods embodied in a particular order, or the promise of one, but must at the same time refuse any moves, however tempting and apparently innocent, to forge too tight an identity between their religion and their national loyalty.

Post-Nuremberg claims of sovereignty and self-determination cannot trump all other claims in any instance of conflict. The issue of crimes against humanity and human rights has been a shaping force in the world arena and will continue to be such. Human rights may be a weak reed against deadly force, but this is often the only weapon beleaguered peoples have, and it offers a lever others can use to enforce the notion that geopolitical and cultural definitions of nationhood must, at this time in history, be open to chastening by universal principles. Of course, the Church has always advocated such chastening. But as we enter the twenty-first century, a bevy of international associations promulgates and nurtures this conviction as well.

At the same time, the plurality of cultures is irreducible. A world of many nations, each with its own particular marks of self-identity, reminds us that we are not alone and that we cannot and ought not make the world "one" by cruelly obliterating diverse ways of life. Indeed, one of the most insidious aspects of Communist "universalism" was precisely its need to crush difference, "to make everything," in the words of Vaclav Havel, "the same." Havel goes on to recall that "the greatest enemy of communism was always individuality, variety, difference—in a word, freedom." Orwell's Big Brother needed to preside over every aspect of life:

From Berlin to Vladivostok, the streets and buildings were decorated with the same red stars. Everywhere the same kind of celebratory parades were staged. Analogical state administrations were set up, along with the whole system of central direction for social and economic life. This vast shroud of uniformity, stifling all national, intellectual, spiritual, social, cultural, and religious variety, covered over any differences and created the monstrous illusion that we were all the same. (Havel, 1993: 8)

No, we are not the "same." But we do *share* a capacity for identification with the idea of a plural political body; we all require self-dignity; we all yearn for a decent life for our children.

This latter universalism is as different from the false universalism Havel scores as the night is to the day. In the words of John Paul, speaking of the Soviet Empire, "a falsely united multinational society must not be succeeded by one falsely diversified." What makes these unities and diversities false, the Pope continues, are the "racist pretensions and evil forms of nationalism." (John Paul II, 1993: 1599) A universalism that sustains respect for difference is a universalism aware of our human need for concrete reference groups in order to attain and to sustain individuality and identity. As a version of national identity, the form of membership I wish here to commend softens but does not negate altogether the idea of sovereignty. The alternative to strong theories of sovereignty that place duty and loyalty to the nation-state above all other duties and loyalties is "sovereignty . . . in the service of the people," in the words of the U.S. Bishops. (NCCB, 1993: 453)

Havel writes of politics—a politics of civic self-determination—as a form of "practical morality . . . humanly measured care for our fellow human beings." Scoring the "arrogant anthropocentrism of modern man," an arrogance that has its political culmination in triumphalist accounts of sovereignty and nationalism, Havel opts for limited ideals of identity and responsibility. Politics, on this account, has to do with having a home, with being at home, with tending to one's particular home and its place in the wider world in which one gets one's bearings.[2]

John Paul II has also elaborated an alternative to statist versions of sovereignty. Early in his papacy, in a homily at Jasna Gora in 1983, he argued that "the state is firmly sovereign when it governs society and also serves the common good of society and allows the nation to realize its own subjectivity, its own identity." (cf. Ash, 1989: 43) Insofar as I grasp the version here advanced, sovereignty is located neither "in" the state per se, nor in an unmediated construction of the "sovereign will" of the people, but rather in the multiple associations of civil society in dialogue with one another as "subjects." This dialogue creates, or concatenates into, a political body whose legitimate purpose is to see that rules for civil contestation are followed and that the various loci of human social existence, necessary to human dignity and freedom, are protected and served. The coexistence of overlapping, porous entities is assumed. This is a dialogical by contrast to a monological political ideal.

With Isaiah Berlin, I "do not wish to abandon the idea of a world which is a reasonably peaceful coat of many colors, each portion of which develops its own distinct cultural identity and is tolerant of others." (Berlin, 1991: 21) Indeed, this ideal offers the strongest alternative to the cruelty and torment of a rapacious and narrow nationalism, on the one hand, or a watery universalism or impositional empire that either cannot inspire or cruelly commands people's loyalties, on the other. We live in a dangerous time, shaped by powerful forces most of us had no direct hand in shaping.

A powerful book on the "new nationalism," Michael Ignatieff's *Blood and Belonging: Journeys into the New Nationalism*, reminds us that the new nationalism takes many forms.[3] It can look as menacing and behave as horribly as the term "ethnic cleansing" suggests, a new name for a very old and, alas, pervasive phenomenon. It can also creep up on cat's paws in the form of sad little tales of past injustice coupled with a no doubt unrealistic but very human desire for reparation, for putting things right somehow. We know, or are coming to know, the big stories of shelling of cities, massacres, detention camps, the breaking up of old multiethnic enclaves and ways of life. Writing of the "ethnically lÿeansed microstates that have taken the place of Yugoslavia," Ignatieff, in this wonderfully crafted and sobering journey of discovery, laments that "ethnic apartheid may be an abomination, but for the more than two million refugees who have fled or been driven from their homes, apartheid is the only guarantee of safety they are prepared to trust." This holds for aggressors and victims alike— and bear in mind that who is the tormentor and who the one being tormented shifts from week to week. Although the Serbs bear the major responsibility for the disaster in the Balkans, they are not solely responsible. Indeed, the West must take its fair share of the blame for what has happened there. "For the West," Ignatieff notes, "failed to save Sarajevo, where Muslim, Croat, and Serb lived together in peace for centuries." In light of this, "it is asking the impossible to believe that ordinary people will trickle back to the multi-ethnic villages they have left behind, simply in order to vindicate our liberal principles." (Ignatieff, 1993: 37)

What Ignatieff tries to get the reader to grasp, perhaps dipping into this volume in the comfort of an office or a soft reading chair in a den, is *fear*—the fear everywhere at work in struggles over the new nationalism, whether in the Balkans, Germany, Ukraine, Quebec, Kurdistan, or Northern Ireland, the sites that form the basis of his political ethnography. "There is one type of fear," he writes, "more devastating in its impact than any other: The systematic fear that arises when a state begins to collapse. Ethnic hatred is the result of the terror that arises when legitimate authority disintegrates." (Ignatieff, 1993: 24) That all-pervasive fear is unknown to us in contemporary Western democracies in its most primordial, most overwhelming form. But it is no stranger to many of our fellow human beings.

Mind you, Ignatieff is not out to demonize nationalism. He recognizes, as all serious scholars of the subject must, the historically close connection between nationalism and democracy. "Nationalism, after all, is the doctrine that a people have a right to rule themselves, and that sovereignty reposes in them alone," he writes. The "tragedy for the Balkans," then, was that when democracy at last became possible, "the only language that existed to mobilize people into a shared social project was the rhetoric of ethnic difference. Any possibility of a civic, as opposed to ethnic, democracy had been strangled at birth by the Communist regime." (Ignatieff, 1993: 25) For in Tito's Yugoslavia there were no competing political parties, no independent loci of social and political life—the divisions were based on ethnicity alone, with the *apparat* perched on top holding everything in dictatorial order. People had no experience of democratic contestation in and through the category of civic citizenship. What existed in the old Yugoslavia was "manipulated plebiscitary democracy that ratifies one-man rule." (Ignatieff, 1993: 54)

Ignatieff wants to disabuse us of a certain sort of liberal prejudice: the notion that what we see in the Balkans, or Northern Ireland, or elsewhere is an outburst of atavistic irrationalism. Rather, he carefully situates us in complex political and social contexts, helping us to understand how and why and when people are driven to extremes of ethnic identification and contestation, even as he is horrified at the result. He reminds us of just how important "national belonging" really is, and how it has come about that nation-states remain the dominant form of constituting and maintaining political bodies, for better or for worse. He suggests it is a good bit of both. "It is only too apparent that cosmopolitanism is the privilege of those who can take a secure nation-state for granted," he notes provocatively. For cosmopolitanism, a blithe "post-nationalist spirit" depends, in ways its advocates and practitioners often resolutely refuse to recognize, "on the capacity of nation-states to provide security and civility for their citizens." (Ignatieff, 1993: 13)

Ignatieff's is a vivid and sad journey. He takes us into the heart of fraught and fractured situations. He never adopts a stance of superior Western smugness toward those he interviews, encounters, sups and drinks with. We hear voices and see faces. For example, we hear a "skinhead" in the old East Germany.[4] Ignatieff's interview with "Leo," who embodies contemporary "skin culture," is filled up by Leo's talk, at once enraged and riddled with pathos. "If you see the world from his point of view," Ignatieff writes, "he comes from the only country in Europe that isn't allowed to feel good about itself." Germany is still required to atone for its sins. But young men like Leo were born well after the Third Reich and they are tired, apparently, of bearing the stigma of "Germanness." Perhaps Leo, then, is an example of what happens when a country "loses peaceful ways of being proud about itself, when the language of national pride is forced underground, when patriotism is hijacked by criminals." (Ignatieff, 1993: 83) For Leo, "This isn't home, this is just misery." (Ignatieff, 1993: 84) And from the darkness of that misery he lashes out.

Ukraine, Quebec, Kurdistan—we follow Ignatieff on his mordant quest. The fears of his respondents come alive for us. The great tragedy, he concludes, is that ethnic nationalism, as a quest for sure and certain identity, must fail because it does not allow people to be truly themselves. They must lose their individuality in that of the group. It becomes an ethnic crime to fall in love and to marry outside the group. It becomes an ethnic crime to think in and through categories other than ethnicity. Nationalism, Ignatieff hastens to asure us, is not what is wrong with the world: "Every people must have a home, every such hunger must be assuaged." What is wrong is the "kind of nation, the kind of homeland that nationalists want to create and the means they use to seek their ends." (Ignatieff, 1993: 249) If hatred of others is necessary in order to achieve your own group solidarity, you are on the road to bitter disappointment and in thrall to a likely cycle of recrimination and revenge.

"I began the journey as a liberal, and I end as one," says Ignatieff, as he brings his story to a close:

> But I cannot help thinking that liberal civilization—the rule of laws, not men, of argument in place of force, of compromise in place of violence—runs deeply against the human grain and is achieved and sustained only by the most unremitting struggle against human nature. The liberal virtues—tolerance, compromise, reason—remain as valuable as ever, but they cannot be preached to those who are mad with fear or mad with vengeance. (Ignatieff, 1993: 248)

That is his sober lesson for us, here in the waning years of the twentieth century. To those who preach wholly abstract sermons about peace and harmony and goodwill, Ignatieff would probably say, "Grow up." What we must come to realize is that nationalism is the chief political passion and force as we enter the twenty-first century. How will we, in the stable and privileged West, respond? With moral superiority and more preachments or with a tough-minded preparedness to engage in order, just perhaps, to help those who seek and need our help to arrive at least at those conditions of some safety from depredation that alone might help them to learn or re-learn the lessons of tolerance and moderation?

Sometimes, as I suggested above, the "new nationalism" is a story in miniature. A recent story from the *Wall Street Journal* invites us to consider the fate of Karlovy Vary, also known as Karlsbad, the *belle epoque* spa famous in literature, frequented by the likes of Nietzsche, Freud, and, in an earlier generation, Goethe and other luminaries. Karlovy Vary is in the Sudetenland, "a region once home to 65,000 Jews, 800,000 Czechs, and three million Germans." When the Germans annexed the Sudetenland, they sent the Jewish population packing. Next the "Czechs eliminated the Germans. Eduard Benes, the pre-Communist post-war president, decreed their expulsion in 1945. At Potsdam, the Allies approved. As Germans fled toward Bavaria, Czechs took revenge: They murdered 40,000 Germans; many died at the end of a rope."

This episode was long buried in the Communist deep freeze. But since 1989, "the expulsion has become a national nettle. . . . Czechs know that every Sudeten German wasn't guilty of Hitler's crimes."[5] Although President Václav Havel has condemned the Sudeten expulsion, the current regime wants to keep the episode closed. In the meantime, children of Jewish and German victims of expulsion and murder are seeking, one by one, the return of their family houses. These are people with real names, and faces, and quite specific and—

in the grand scale of things—small stories and claims. Each is heart-breaking, of course. The current policy permits Jewish families with claims to regain their houses; but German families cannot. The German descendants do not understand why their troubles count for nothing. One says, "My only crime was that for 800 years my ancestors lived in that place." They want repeal of the 1945 expulsion decree. They want a chance to get their property back. They want to return to their "homeland," not just homes in Karlovy Vary but villages long emptied—ethnically cleansed—of their kind. (*WSJ*, 7/15/94: 1–8)

But it won't happen. Not every wrong can be righted. Not every injustice can be reversed. Perhaps, at this juncture, Hannah Arendt's insistence that "forgiveness" is the greatest contribution of Jesus of Nazareth to politics should be noted. Perhaps there is nothing left for the expelled and expropriated people of German descent to do but to forgive. This gesture is made possible, in part, by President Havel's recognition of the past injustice they suffered. But forgiveness from the side of the aggrieved itself helps to make possible forms of soul-searching and recognition from the "other side." Forgiveness is the hardest thing of all to do, of course, but it may be the only way to forestall quaffing the bitter brew of injustice suffered and recompense sought even unto future generations.

The injunction to forgiveness is vital and important, but it must go hand in hand with the claims of justice. Where justice is not served, indeed not even honored, forgiveness is more difficult, and rage collects like the incessant drip of a leaky faucet. It is the view of a number of important commentators in central Eastern Europe—a view that I share—that the new Europe will be haunted well into the next century by the failure of the West to stem the tide of ethnic cleansing in the Balkans, knowing as they do that there was and is no easy course of action. The ghosts of the Second World War continue to haunt Europe, and to these specters has been added the face of ethnic cleansing in the Balkans at century's end.

War for Cities and Noncombatant Immunity in the Bosnian Conflict

3

James Turner Johnson

A. The Stakes

The armed conflicts that have erupted as part of the breakup of the former Yugoslavia have weighed especially heavily on noncombatants. Media accounts of harm to noncombatants of all sorts and in various circumstances have dominated the coverage of both the war in Croatia and that in Bosnia-Herzegovina; yet the extent of this harm and the fact that often it has been intentional are not inventions of the media but simply an integral element of these wars. Alongside battles between fighting forces of the belligerents—the sort of combat by which war is ideally conceived—these conflicts have employed various tactics whose intended and immediate target has been not fighters but noncombatants. Such tactics include the driving out of refugees in the name of ethnic cleansing; the splitting of families, with all but the very youngest and oldest males taken prisoner and often mistreated; rape and other sexual mistreatment of women and girls that, even if reports are magnified, spread terror; siege warfare in which not the defending forces but the inhabitants of the populated areas themselves are the targets; and the targeting of United Nations peacekeepers and taking of hostages from their ranks.[1]

Commenting on this character of the warfare in Bosnia, with specific reference to the siege of Sarajevo, the *New York Times* notes that some military analysts have begun to call such war "postmodern" or "future" war. Such conflicts, according to the *Times* account, are defined by three main features. First, states and disciplined military forces are often replaced by tribal groupings and informal groups of fighters or militias not answering to higher command. Second, the conflicts are intractable, being rooted in deep cultural differences that do not lend themselves to negotiated settlements or compromise. Third, the conduct of such wars, the *Times* notes, quoting military historian Martin van Creveld, tends "to be very bloody, because there is no distinction between armies and peoples, so everybody in the way gets killed." (*NYT*, 5/21/95)

This is not so much a new form of warfare, though, as one unexpected for this age and place. Such conflicts have long existed, as well as names for them. Holy wars and ideological wars involve distinct cultural communities at odds with each other over deeply rooted and often nonnegotiable differences. Civil wars, rebellions, and revolutions involve belligerent parties at least one of which, by definition, may not be recognized as a state, and whose exercise of authority may be fragmented by factional differences or difficulties in communication between the political leadership and the military forces. Partisan and guerilla warfare involve armed groups of fighters whose main loyalty may be to themselves or to the particular subcommunity out of which they have come, so that not only is the direction of these groups by central command and discipline difficult, but also the means they employ may be especially bloody and they may target noncombatants and combatants alike. Indeed, there are many past wars that include all the characteristics of the ostensibly "postmodern" or "future" wars named above.

Moreover, the whole history of Western moral and legal tradition on limiting war has sought to impose restraint by removing these very characteristics, defining the form of warfare that is acceptable as justifiable only for specified reasons, which are in principle open to negotiated settlement; involving political communities with a strong enough central authority to exercise effective government, including military command and control; and military forces answering to such command, wearing distinctive emblems or uniforms, and conducting their operations according to the laws and customs of war. These concerns are not a minor and somehow dispensable part of the moral and legal tradition on warfare; they are at its very heart. Giving up on them means giving up on the main line of the effort to restrain war in Western cultural tradition and modern international law, and this would be a massive loss.

The point is that whatever the descriptive value of identifying how such wars differ from the norm of wars between states fought with regular military forces observing the international law of war, it should not be allowed to become a prescriptive acceptance of their character as a new form of war for the future. "Postmodern" wars are not new at all, either in the West or elsewhere. The alternative to simply accepting the nature and means of such warfare as normative for the future is to recognize that these are precisely what is rejected in the major normative traditions on war, and to challenge the allegedly "postmodern" or "future" war accordingly. While the concept of "civilized" or "humanized" war is, for many persons, an oxymoron, these concepts do make sense; the principles of civilization and of humanity are at the basis of the international law of war. (cf. Schwarzenberger, 1962: I; McDougal and Feliciano, 1961: 521ff) More than just a reference to the cultural history and moral tradition that undergird the rules for the conduct of war, these terms point to what is lost if the rules are flouted: civilization itself, accepting a shared humanity with the enemy even in the midst of conflict.

The focus of the present essay is not all contemporary wars that flout the normative tradition on civilized or humanized war, but the present war in Bosnia and Herzegovina; not the character of the entities who are the belligerents in this conflict or their justifications for fighting, but the conduct of the war. More specifically, this essay focuses on one particular aspect of the Bosnian conflict, the practice of siege warfare by the Bosnian Serbs against the Bosnian government/Muslim-held cities, and the implications this form of warfare has for noncombatant immunity. Clearly there have been other deeply problematical issues in the conduct of this war: the shelling and taking hostage of United Nations peacekeepers, for example. The Serbs are not the only ones who have overstepped the bounds of morality and the laws and customs of war, but the conduct of the Bosnian Serbs has been especially reprehensible and directly harmful to noncombatants. Their practice of siege warfare poses the question of right and wrong treatment of noncombatants in a way deeply characteristic of this conflict. The siege as a form of war has, moreover, been neglected both by moral analysts and by modern military thinkers, and its importance in the Bosnian conflict provides the occasion to right the balance in some small way.

B. Setting Limits on the Conduct of War

All wars, of course, produce noncombatant casualties. Except in a few kinds of cases—naval battles on the high seas, land battles in unpopulated areas such as deserts, air combat—it is practically impossible to avoid injury to noncombatants. Real wars, as opposed to particular elements of such wars or idealized scenarios of "surgical" warfare, take place in territory inhabited by noncombatant populations. Consequently the destructiveness of war as a matter of course extends over these populations, sometimes as a blanket in which whole areas are damaged or destroyed and the human suffering is general, and sometimes as essentially random harm in which one person may be killed or wounded but many others left unscathed.

But incidental harm to noncombatants from military acts directed at an enemy's armed forces is not the same, morally or legally, as harm done by acts whose direct and intentional target is noncombatants. There is, moreover, a limit beyond which even unintentional collateral harm to noncombatants should not go. The former distinction follows from the concept of noncombatant immunity itself, often stated in recent moral discourse as the principle of discrimination; the latter follows from the idea that acts of war should not cause disproportionate damage as compared to the ends which justify them. Together these two concerns define the *jus in bello*, the doctrine on what conduct in war is justifiable, for the just war tradition. They are also implicit in the requirements of positive and customary international law on war. It will be useful to take stock of where contemporary moral argument has staked its position regarding the requirements of noncombatant immunity and proportionality in the conduct of war.

The major thrust of recent moral argument is that noncombatant immunity, understood through the principle of discrimination, is an exceptionless moral rule. This conception is found in both religious and philosophical ethical analysis. The Catholic Church's *Pastoral Constitution on the Church in the Modern World* puts this understanding of the requirements of discrimination explicitly in terms of means of war aimed at cities and populated areas:

> Any act of war aimed indiscriminately at the destruction of entire cities or of extensive areas along with their population is a crime against God and man himself. It merits unequivocal and unhesitating condemnation. (Abbott, 1966: *Pastoral Constitution*, #80)

Commenting on this, the American Catholic bishops' 1983 pastoral letter, *The Challenge of Peace*, rendered the requirement as follows: The lives of innocent persons may never be taken directly, regardless of the purpose in doing so." (NCCB, 1983: #104)

The fullest and in many respects the definitive statement of such an understanding of the principle of discrimination remains that of Paul Ramsey.[2] For Ramsey's analysis, based principally on a reading of the fourth- and fifth-century Christian fathers Ambrose and Augustine, the key element is a core norm "from the interior" of Christian ethics, Christian love of neighbor or charity. Charity is known directly by Christians and indirectly, as a requirement of natural justice, by non-Christians. This love simultaneously justifies Christian participation in just warfare and limits what may rightly be done in such war. "The justification of participation in conflict," writes Ramsey, "at the same time severely limited war's conduct. What justified also limited! Since it was for the sake of the innocent and helpless of the earth that the Christian first thought himself obligated to make war against an enemy whose objective deeds had to be stopped." At the same time, "he could never proceed to kill equally innocent people as a means of getting at the enemy's forces. Thus was twin-born the justification of war and the limitation which surrounded noncombatants with moral immunity against attack." (Ramsey, 1968: 143–44)

This limitation, Ramsey continues, defines the distinction between legitimate and illegitimate military objectives; direct, intentional attack on noncombatants can never be legitimate. The immunity of noncombatants from such attack, because of its source and nature, can never be given up. The only harm to noncombatants that does not violate this immunity is that which is indirect and unintended, as when noncombatants are harmed by acts of war aimed at legitimate targets. Ramsey allows this latter sort of harm by reasoning from the rule of double effect. "The death of an innocent man," he writes, "might be brought about, without guilt to the agent, as the unavoidable yet indirect effect of an action whose primary intention and physically independent effect was to secure some good." (Ramsey, 1961: 47) Elsewhere Ramsey explains further what this implies:

> The principle of discrimination is shorthand for "the moral immunity of noncombatants from direct attack." This does not require that civilians never be knowingly killed. It means rather that military action should, in its primary (objective) thrust as well as its subjective purpose, discriminate between directly attacking combatants or military objectives and

directly attacking noncombatants or destroying the structures of civil
society as a means of victory. (Ramsey, 1968: 428–29)

The gist of Ramsey's understanding of noncombatant immunity is
thus threefold: (1) its source is the Christian ethical requirement of
love of neighbor, which is known both directly by Christians and indirectly as a requirement of justice by non-Christians; (2) what such
love requires is that noncombatants may never be the object of direct,
intended attacks in war—their moral immunity from such attack is
absolute; (3) at the same time, acts of war against legitimate (combatant) targets do not violate this immunity even if they harm noncombatants, provided such harm is genuinely collateral—that is, indirect
and unintended. Only in connection with this last consideration does
the principle of proportionality enter in. As a concept requiring calculation and judgment of harms and benefits, costs and effects, it is not a
factor in moral judgment of acts that are wrong in themselves, as
direct, intended attacks on noncombatants are.

The approach to the *jus in bello* limitation of war just described
depends fundamentally on a theological analysis of a religious norm,
though the norm in question, Christian love of neighbor, is also understood as being present through conceptions of natural justice accessible to all humankind, regardless of religion. This provision, though,
demands demonstration. On its face, it says more about the nature of
the theological analysis than about perceptions of natural justice by
all humankind. Thus while it opens the door to dialogue with a more
general human community, it is not a realistic basis from which to
argue that the conception of *jus in bello* in question is able to be
perceived even by all Christians, let alone non-Christians.

Nonetheless, a similarly restrictive argument as to noncombatant
immunity can be made on the basis of human rights. "The rules of
'fighting well'," writes Michael Walzer, "are simply a series of recognitions of men and women who have a moral standing independent
of and resistant to the exigencies of war. A legitimate act of war is
one that does not violate the rights of the people against whom it is
directed." (Walzer, 1992: 135) This applies even when the people in
question are citizens of a state that has gone to war wrongly, for
these people "do not forfeit their rights when their states wrongly go
to war," and soldiers fighting against their state "cannot violate the
life and liberty of enemy civilians." (Walzer, 1992: 137) The immunity of noncombatants is thus, for Walzer, vested in their own moral

standing vis-à-vis the war, and unless they change that standing by virtue of their own acts (not merely sympathies), they retain their moral immunity.

Walzer's subsequent analysis of the implications of this conception is shaped by reflection on a number of historical cases intended to show the meaning of this restriction and its limits. Noting that "military necessity" is often invoked to justify direct attacks on noncombatants, Walzer rejects this argument. "'Reason of war'," he insists, "can only justify the killing of people we already think are liable to be killed." (Walzer, 1992: 144) At the same time, the rule of double effect means that the rights of noncombatants do not prevent military activities aimed at legitimate targets but which endanger the noncombatants by reason of their "proximity." In such cases what is required is "that some degree of care be taken not to harm civilians." (Walzer, 1992: 152) What Walzer has in mind mixes considerations of proportionality in with noncombatant immunity. He argues for a modification of the rule of double effect so that it includes a "double intention": "first, that the 'good' be achieved; second, that the foreseeable evil be reduced as far as possible." He explains, "Simply not to intend the death of civilians is too easy. . . . What we look for in such cases is some sign of a positive commitment to save civilian lives." (Walzer, 1992: 155–56)

Walzer's rights-based argument for a strong, restrictive concept of noncombatant immunity thus parallels Ramsey's love-based argument. In both cases, considerations of *in bello* proportionality regarding noncombatants come into play only as a consequence of the implications of the rule of double effect. Yet even here Walzer seems to hold to the more fundamental moral argument from the rights of noncombatants, calling for a "positive commitment" to save their lives.

The principle of proportionality also limits the harm that may rightly be done to combatants; on this both Walzer and Ramsey agree. Walzer, though, goes a bit further, arguing that in one sort of case, that in which an individual enemy soldier is exposed to fire by another individual, there is some reason not to kill him though doing so is not against the rules of war. Sketching several cases in which this opportunity presented itself and the decision was taken not to fire, Walzer suggests that in such cases the "naked soldier" in question presents himself as another man, not an enemy, and thus partakes in the immunity that noncombatants bear by right. He further notes one circumstance in which the rules of war historically tried to protect one kind of "naked soldier": the requirement in the United States Army's *General Orders No. 100* of 1863 that "outposts, sentinels, pickets are not to be fired upon, except to drive them in." (Walzer, 1992: 143)

In general, though, Walzer and Ramsey agree in assigning the priority of protection of noncombatants from harm in war to the highly restrictive and noncontextual principle of noncombatant immunity: an implication of Christian love and natural justice for Ramsey, a right possessed by all noncombatants for Walzer. Limitation of harm by proportionality becomes a factor only in cases in which noncombatants are endangered as a result of attacks intentionally directed at legitimate targets. But proportionality also protects those legitimate targets, including enemy combatants. It is a consequence of these authors' focus on noncombatants that the limitation of harm to combatant targets by the principle of proportionality is not examined in any detail. The practical result is that in their analyses proportionality is clearly secondary to discrimination or noncombatant immunity as a moral restraint on the conduct of war.

It should be noted that the historical development of Western moral tradition on war reveals, overall, a less theoretical conception of the *jus in bello* restraints, one in which the immunity of noncombatants has been approached through lists of classes of people who, as a result of social function or ability to bear arms, normally take no part in war and thus should not have war made against them. In historical perspective the concept of proportionality in the conduct of war has had concrete expression through efforts to limit particular weapons thought to have disproportionate effects. These ways of approaching the problem of restraining the conduct of war have carried over to the development of positive international law on war, including the protections placed on certain classes of people by the various Geneva conventions and protocols beginning in 1863, the restrictions on weapons adopted by the Hague conferences of 1899 and 1907, and other agreements such as the 1925 Geneva Protocol on gas and germ warfare. (cf. Roberts and Guelff, 1989)

In terms of the moral argument, the difference between the historical tradition of defining noncombatant immunity through lists of classes of noncombatants and the approach through the principle of discrimination employed in recent moral analysis is not important for the context of this essay; yet the difference between this recent analysis and the protection to noncombatants offered in positive international law is a somewhat different matter. The law deals with discrete possibilities within the conduct of war, and determines that some are to be prohibited. What is not prohibited is, by the structure of the law, allowed. As we shall see below, for the case of siege warfare, this divergence of approach between the law of war and moral reasoning leads to significant differences between the two on elements of the protection of noncombatants under conditions of siege.

While such differences are regrettable, the dynamic of positive international law has been to establish agreement to its content regardless of whatever cultural or normative background may be read through it. In this way it provides not an ideal, on which it may be difficult to achieve agreement, but a positively stated floor below which the conduct of war should not fall. Nations which have agreed to be bound by the content of a particular agreement are bound by it. There is, however, no convenient enforcement mechanism for such law, including the provisions of the law of war. During a conflict, one of the surest methods of inducing an enemy to act according to these rules is the threat of reciprocity if the rules are flouted. The threat of war crimes trials, both during and after a war, represents another way to seek to enforce compliance and punish noncompliance. A third means is to exert international pressure on violators, pressure ranging from informal to diplomatic contacts to the use of economic sanctions to the resort to military force. The various options have had various degrees of success under different conditions.

The Bosnian War illustrates the failure of all the means thus far tried. Accepting such failure in the means of securing compliance with the laws of war does not mean giving up on the ideas of restraint contained in these laws or the various ideals that underlie them, but it does mean giving up on the concept that compliance may be enforced, and thus it implies functional ineffectiveness in the law itself. For this reason accepting noncompliance is, in international law terms, a dangerous course that undermines international law as such and makes the world a considerably more dangerous place.

C. Warfare against Centers of Population and the Problem of Noncombatant Protection

How to think ethically about attacks on centers of population is the problem that, more than any other, has been at the center of ethical analysis of war during the nuclear age. Here again Paul Ramsey, in *War and the Christian Conscience*, laid down the baselines for discussion at the beginning of the nuclear period: countercity or counterpopulation warfare is not ethically justifiable, as it is a direct violation of the principle of discrimination/noncombatant immunity; yet a legitimate military target in a population center may still be attacked, although such an attack will also, indirectly and unintentionally, kill or otherwise harm the noncombatants who live and work around it. (Ramsey, 1961: Chs. 3, 8, 12; cf. Ramsey, 1968: Chs. 6, 7, 11) What allows the latter sort of attack is reasoning from the rule of double effect. If harm to the noncombatants is not direct or with purpose, it is not forbidden by the principle of discrimination, even when it is reasonably expected or foreknown; it may still, however, be ruled out by considerations of proportionality.

The same sort of reasoning, utilizing the rule of double effect, runs throughout Michael Walzer's treatment of "The War Convention," his term for the rules of war, *jus in bello*. It also figures prominently elsewhere, as in William V. O'Brien's *The Conduct of Just and Limited War*, where the central concern is relating the requirements of just war tradition to the actual conduct of limited war in the contemporary era and recent history. Even "just war pacifist" and "nuclear pacifist" authors have employed a related form of reasoning, though they inverted it to argue that under the conditions of modern war the conditions set by the just war theorists could never be met, and therefore, lacking the possibility of satisfying the *jus in bello* requirements, there can never be a *jus ad bellum*. (cf. Ramsey, 1968: 271–78)

The line of argument laid down by Ramsey and employed by Walzer and others does not, of course, apply only to the use of nuclear weapons. The immediate precedent for Ramsey's development of the argument was Catholic theologian John C. Ford's use of it to critique so-called obliteration bombing in the Second World War. (cf. Ford, 1944) During the Vietnam War Ramsey applied it to the context of insurgency-counterinsurgency warfare (Ramsey, 1968: Ch. 18); Walzer employs it in a variety of contexts in Part Three of *Just and Unjust Wars*; O'Brien has applied it to ethical analysis of the Israeli-PLO conflict. (O'Brien, 1991) It is, moreover, a line of argument reaching back at least to Thomas Aquinas.

Direct application of this rule for moral reasoning to war dates to the work of a self-conscious Thomist, the sixteenth-century Spanish theologian, Francisco de Vitoria, whose *De Jure Belli* includes a discussion whose particulars anticipate the analyses of Ford, Ramsey, Walzer, O'Brien, and other contemporary theorists. Vitoria's discussion, moreover, more directly engages the kind of warfare characteristic of the conflict in Bosnia: not war involving nuclear weapons or even strategic conventional air warfare, but attacks on cities in which noncombatants are to be found alongside combatants. It is useful to gauge the flavor of his argument.

If a war is just (in the *jus ad bellum* sense), Vitoria asks, is it lawful therefore to kill the innocent? His answer is straightforward: "The deliberate slaughter of the innocent is never lawful in itself." This prohibition holds even "in war with the Turks," that is, even in war with an enemy who does not share the same religion or culture. (Vitoria, *De Jure Belli*, #35–36; 1991: 314–15)[3] In this context he goes on to list as not to be harmed directly and intentionally all those classes of persons named in the canon law as formulated by the thirteenth century: women, children, "harmless agricultural folk," as well as "the rest of the peaceable civilian population."

Yet sometimes the innocent (noncombatants) cannot be separated from the guilty (combatants), as is the case during sieges and during attacks on fortresses and cities. Vitoria argues as follows:

> Sometimes it is right, in virtue of collateral circumstances, to slay the innocent even knowingly, as when a fortress or city is stormed in a just war, although it is known that there are a number of innocent people in it and although cannon and other engines of war cannot be discharged or fire applied to buildings without destroying innocent together with guilty. The proof is that war could not otherwise be waged against even the guilty and the justice of belligerents would be balked. In the same way . . . if a town is wrongfully besieged and rightfully defended, it is lawful to fire cannon-shot and other missiles on the besiegers and into the hostile camp, even though we assume that there are some children and innocent people there. (*De Jure Belli*, #37; 1991: 315)

He follows this by adding that, even in just uses of force of this nature, the principle of proportionality must be applied, for "it is never right to slay the guiltless, even as an indirect and unintended result, except when there is no other means of carrying on the operations of a just war." (*De Jure Belli*, #37; 1991: 316).

Vitoria's findings here depend on participation in a *just* war; if one's cause is *unjust*, fighting is not allowable in the first place. When neither side has justice on its side, the war itself, by definition, is not justified. In practice, though, as Vitoria recognized, one or both sides in a conflict may, through ignorance, wrongly believe themselves to be fighting justifiedly. In such cases the requirements of the *jus in bello* restraints are to be observed by both. (*De Jure Belli*, #32; 1991: 313)[4] This concept is the operative base of the international law tradition growing out of Vitoria and other sixteenth- and seventeenth-century just war theorists.

As the modern understanding of international law developed, first sovereigns and then states were placed on a formally equal footing and given *compétence de guerre*, the right to determine whether they had justification for taking up arms in a dispute. At the same time, greater attention was given to restraining the conduct of war. In positive international law these restraints began to appear as early as the 1860s, as noted above. By contrast, the first substantive effort in positive international law to define justified and unjustified resort to force was the Pact of Paris of 1928, which anticipated the United Nations Charter by defining this difference in terms of aggressive versus defensive use of force (for further discussion see Johnson, 1973; 1975: 266–72). In practical terms, efforts to ensure compliance with the law of war still go on, regardless of judgments as to the justice of one or another belligerent's cause.

The implication of Vitoria's reasoning, ratified by the subsequent development of international law, is thus to hold all sides in a war to observing the *jus in bello* limits, even when conflicts take place across major cultural divides. Vitoria did not go so far as to argue that failure to observe these limits renders the war itself unjust. The structure of his argument requires that the question of overall justice, whether there is a *jus ad bellum*, must be settled merely to the satisfaction of the sovereign power under whose authority the war is fought; the persons who then fight the war may take this as a settled matter. Their moral problem is how they fight, and this is the subject of the *jus in bello*.

Returning to attacks on cities and fortresses, though Vitoria lays out the exception allowed through the rule of double effect to the general prohibition against harm to noncombatants, it is important to note that he structures the case, as do later theorists who have employed this line of argument, in terms of an attack directed at a legitimate target. Indeed Vitoria goes beyond what most of his successors have explicitly said by stipulating that, apart from such an attack, "there is no other means of carrying on the operations of a just war." He meant this, I think, as an observation about what is possible given the nature of war as he knew it. Yet this observation also implies a moral imperative to change the means available so as to serve discrimination and proportionality better, an implication in line with Walzer's desire, noted above, for "a positive commitment to save civilian lives" when attacking targets containing a mix of combatants and noncombatants.

Vitoria's structuring of the overall argument by the rule of double effect, however, leaves several important questions unaddressed. First, in saying that there can never be any justification for deliberately attacking noncombatants, he does not anticipate the kind of question raised by Walzer in his discussion of the "supreme emergency" argument for the British bombing of German cities in the Second World War. (1992: Ch. 16) Second, he does not take into account the fact that the distinction he makes between deliberately and collaterally harming noncombatants puts no restrictions on the choice by belligerents, for reasons of expected effectiveness, to attack mixed combatant-noncombatant targets as opposed to targets containing combatants alone. And third, Vitoria's argument from the rule of double effect does not take notice of the fact that in siege warfare the very nature of the operation targets noncombatants first. All have direct bearing on the case of the Bosnian conflict.

First, what of the "supreme emergency" argument? Is this a case in which extenuating circumstances trump the general prohibition against direct, intentional attacks on noncombatants? If so, what are the characteristics of such circumstances? I have elsewhere argued (Johnson, 1981: 20–30) that, as Walzer develops his analysis of the "supreme emergency" argument, the implication is that the general prohibition of deliberate harm to noncombatants may be overridden when the value system from which this prohibition derives is itself threatened. On this reasoning, the British would have had to believe that the Nazi threat was not only to their government but to the underlying values of Western culture, that the defeat of Britain would have led to the loss of those values, and that without counter-city bombing Britain would be defeated. There is evidence in the material Walzer cites that the parties responsible for the decision to bomb German cities held all three beliefs, and that in the circumstances they were reasonably held.

Such belief points to a deeper question than the factual one of whether there would still be other nations (such as those in the Western hemisphere) left to uphold the normative values of Western culture if Britain had fallen to the Nazis. Rather, the concern is more subtle and perhaps more realistic as a reading of history as well. Had the Nazis defeated Britain, as they had already defeated and subjugated virtually all the rest of Western and Central Europe, the values which the Nazis embodied would themselves have been in a position of relative triumph, and in the subsequent struggle Nazi values would have had an enormous, perhaps insurmountable advantage. The "supreme emergency" argument, then, is that, faced with a threat of this dimension, the British had an obligation to preserve the values it professed by overriding them, not in their general conduct of the war, but in a calculated and deliberate way. Only in such extreme circumstances is it ever allowable to violate noncombatant immunity directly and intentionally.

Since the reasoning from moral duty and/or rights that establishes an absolute form of noncombatant immunity must always presuppose the existence of a value system that establishes those duties and/or rights, this line of argument has considerable force. Turning it around, it means that, in any conflict where the protections due noncombatants by these terms are systematically disregarded, there is a moral obligation on the part of other nations who themselves hold to the value of these protections to seek to end the violations in order not only to save the people threatened but also to maintain the principle of such protection and the value system underlying it. How far they should go in this is a matter for *jus ad bellum* analysis, but to my mind the systematic violation of such protection qualifies as a wrong that may be righted even by resort to force, a case of "vindicative justice" in the sense of the widely used medieval just war proof-text, Romans 13:4: "For [the Prince] does not bear the sword in vain. He is the minister of God to execute his wrath on the evildoer."

At the same time, the "supreme emergency" argument as I have interpreted it may be construed as opening the door to all-out warfare over major differences in values, ideologies, or cultures. Vitoria may be anticipating such an argument for the case of war for religion, in noting pointedly that the prohibition of deliberate harm to the innocent applies even in war against the Turks. In other words, one may not do wrong even if the heavens are in danger of falling. But the "supreme emergency" argument provides its own corrective, for it is an argument about the conditions for an exception to the rule, not an overthrow of the general rule itself. It is thus substantially the same as the argument that allows reprisals in kind in order to stop an enemy's violation of the rules of war. Thus it establishes the outer limit of the moral in the rules for determining the exception to the rules.

The second problem Vitoria and his twentieth-century successors do not take into account is that under the conditions of war, belligerents may choose mixed combatant-noncombatant targets deliberately, rather than targets containing combatants alone, under cover of the collateral harm to noncombatants allowable by the rule of double effect. While the distinction this rule makes possible is of great utility for individual moral reflection about one's own intention, it is of only limited use for external judgment of a particular action. Given a mixed target, there is no way of objectively distinguishing between an attack against a legitimate military target that collaterally harms noncombatants and an attack on a mixed target deliberately chosen for its broadened shock effect. Ramsey acknowledges the potential attractiveness of mixed targets as the targets of choice, and argues on moral terms against such choice, specifically in the case of nuclear weapons with "overkill" capacity and conscious strategic decisions to "widen the target." (Ramsey, 1961: Chs. 11, 12) While I agree with the thrust of his argument, which is toward defining what he called "rational, politically beneficial armament"—weapons genuinely capable of being used in a counterforces manner—my point here about the double effect argument is somewhat different. Given even the most accurate and proportionately sized weapons, it is still possible to choose to employ them in relatively discriminate and proportionate ways or to indiscriminate and disproportionately harmful effect. This is the hole in the effort to restrain the conduct of war that is opened up by the argument from double effect.

In the case of the Bosnian conflict, the nature of the problem is immediately apparent. Leaving aside the fate of rural villages engulfed by the tide of a war over control of territory, how should we understand the status of the urban Muslim enclaves surrounded by Serb-held territory and, at least nominally, under United Nations protection? Are they legitimate military targets because they serve as bases from which Bosnian Muslim forces operate against the Serbs, because they represent a threat to the Serb forces' rear from the perspective of the front lines of the conflict running down the middle of the country? Or are they properly described as the United Nations describes them: population centers that should be "safe havens," within which noncombatants may be sheltered from the potential for harm that is all around them?

The answer is: both of these and neither. They are of a mixed character, still having Bosnian Muslim fighters in them, still serving as a base for some of the activities of those fighters, yet being also centers where the noncombatant populace of surrounding areas have been gathered as refugees from the fighting, swelling the numbers of noncombatants already living in what were before the war significant regional centers of population, trade, and culture. In my own judgment, the preponderance of the noncombatant portion of the mixed character of these urban areas, and the fact that they have been designated "safe havens" by the international peacekeeping forces present, together with the comparatively minimal military danger they represent, should for practical purposes remove them from the list of potential targets. The military presence, however, makes them legitimate targets for attack, and allows invoking the rule of double effect to legitimize also the harm to noncombatants sheltered in those cities.

My concern is that in such cases this sort of reasoning wrongly skews the argument at the expense of the noncombatants. What is needed additionally is something like the domestic legal standard of the "reasonable person" to judge whether the means of attack (and the means of defense as well) can reasonably be described as meeting the requirements of discrimination and proportionality. In the Bosnian Serb attack on Srebrenica, for example, there seemed to be a conscious policy to use military force to sow panic in the noncombatant population, to drive them out toward the next safe haven so as to create panic and confusion there as well, and, in short, to aim at the Bosnian Muslim military through the noncombatants. (*NYT* 7/14/95, 7/15/95) Similarly, the shelling of other Muslim-held cities, including Sarajevo, as well as the Croatian capital city of Zagreb after the Croatian takeover of Okucani in May 1995) have consistently had this character. (cf. *NYT* 5/29/95, 6/1/95, 6/30/95, 7/23/95a, and 5/3/95) Because of the military presence in each of these cities and, in the case of Sarajevo, also its character as the seat of government, these are mixed combatant-noncombatant targets, and damage to noncombatants may be argued legitimate by the rule of double effect. Yet reasonable judgment would require that the means used be genuinely employed against combatant targets, and the aim seems to have been just the opposite.

A further complication is that under certain circumstances the law of war, while forbidding direct attacks on noncombatants or on undefended cities, nonetheless allows a belligerent to make use of the enemy's noncombatant population to disadvantage the enemy's military. This is in particular the case with sieges. Thus we now move to the third kind of problem with double-effect reasoning as applied to the protection of noncombatants, the problem posed by siege warfare.

D. Siege Warfare and the Protection of Noncombatants

Siege warfare raises particular moral problems, but despite this it is largely ignored in contemporary ethical writing on war. Of the major contributors to ethical discussion and analysis of war over the last half-century, only Walzer has directly addressed the subject of sieges. (1992: Ch. 10) Indeed, I am unaware of any other writer on ethics and war during this period who has even in passing treated this subject. This lack of attention reaches back much earlier. The sieges of Leningrad and Stalingrad during the Second World War have not occasioned the same ethical critique as has been directed to strategic bombing, though the approximately three million civilians trapped in Leningrad at the beginning of the German siege is of similar order to the numbers of noncombatants put at risk by the strategic bombing campaign against Germany. Civilian casualties at Leningrad by the time the siege ended totaled over a million, of which it is safe to say the majority were genuinely noncombatants. (cf. Walzer, 1992: 165–66; Salisbury, 1969) Nor did the prolonged and deadly siege of Richmond during the American Civil War, despite the privation and suffering of the noncombatants in the city, occasion the attention of ethical analysis such as was focused on the problem of partisans and treatment of civilians in occupied territories. (cf. Halleck, 1863; Lieber, 1862)

Indeed, there are fashions in the ethical analysis of war, and, apart from Walzer's probing examination, the Western ethical tradition on siege is substantially where Vitoria left it, with its restricted focus on the specific consequences of military weapons targeted on the besieged place and the treatment of noncombatants when such a place is taken by storm. There are also, as we shall see, other pressing ethical issues in siege warfare against places containing a mix of combatants and noncombatants. These issues often press against or exceed the boundaries of existing discussions of discrimination and proportionality in the conduct of war, so that the siege needs to be examined in ethical terms much more closely as a form of war different in significant moral respects from those that are the focus of existing ethical analysis and judgment.

Ethics is not the only field in which siege warfare has been ignored or given short shrift. Modern military theory and the law of war also reveal a pattern of neglect of the siege and forms of conduct in war associated with it. The last serious engagement of siege warfare by military theorists was in the 1830s, when both the major military theorists of the time, Jomini and Clausewitz, gave it limited treatment in the context of the style of warfare of the Napoleonic period. (Jomini, 1862: 102, 133–40, 344–48; Clausewitz, 1976: 393–415, 551–55) International law has sought to prevent bombardment of undefended places, at the Hague in 1907 and again in 1923, adding damage to cultural property as a crime in 1954, (Roberts and Guelff, 1989: Documents 5, 10, 13, and 22) but the focus of development of positive international law on war has largely been elsewhere, and the provisions found in those places do not address the full range of problems raised by siege warfare.

Different forms of war have different purposes. Siege warfare is a form of war aimed at control of territory. Indeed, control of territory was once the dominant conception of the purpose of all warfare in both military theory and the practice of war. Beginning with Clausewitz, however, the main line of strategic thought has conceived the paramount aim of conventional warfare differently, as the destruction of the enemy army's ability to fight. This way of thinking about the overall purpose of war is reflected in two major innovations in twentieth-century warfare. First, strategic bombing reaches behind the enemy's strength and over his territory with the goal of destroying support of his armed forces by attacking his general populace. In the Cold War era, the role of strategic bombing was redefined in the form of strategic nuclear targeting for deterrence, but its goal remained essentially the same. Second, the increased emphasis on mechanized forces and air support able to bypass enemy strong points to attack relatively weakly defended but significant targets embodies a conception of war in which particular places, whether defended or not, are of relatively low importance.

The air-land strategy of NATO forces at the end of the Cold War period illustrates this concept of war of maneuver, highly refined to take account of new mobility and high technology applied to warfare. The strategy and tactics of allied forces against Iraq in the Gulf War provide a textbook example of the effectiveness of means of war based on maneuver and deep air strikes against the enemy, though the limited aims of this war did not extend to the Clausewitzian goal of compelling the enemy by force to do one's will.

The war in Bosnia is, however, different in important respects from the Gulf War and from the sort of conflict envisioned between NATO and Warsaw Pact forces in Cold War era planning. First, the overall goal is different. Both the Bosnian Muslims and the Bosnian Serbs aim at establishing a secure state in the area of the conflict. Their conflict is over the political government of these states, the territory each will cover, and the character of their populations. Neither side has the military power to destroy the opponent's armed forces, and doing so in any case is for both sides distinctly subordinate to the goal of establishing control over territory, an aim that includes having a population in place that supports the political aims of the side in question. While the parties to the conflict may be forced ultimately to accept a limited outcome to the fighting, their fundamental war goals are totalistic rather than limited.

Second, the terrain is different. Bosnia is a land of mountains and valleys, with limited routes of maneuver for large land armies and limited lines of attack for supporting air forces. Here, control of territory is of paramount importance, for it determines military advantage. Cities are important strategically not as centers of culture or population centers but as junctions of lines of communication and supply. The heights around the cities are important because of the superiority they give to whoever controls them, either to attack or to defend the cities below. These factors dictate a war with two main components: limited maneuvering (and fighting while maneuvering) to seize and control the heights and lines of communication, together with siege warfare against the cities because of their importance as communication centers.

Third, the means available to fight the war are different. The Bosnian conflict is not a high-technology war fought with large, well-trained armies, but a war of conventional (and somewhat dated) technology fought by poorly trained forces of modest sizes, whose units often do not work well together nor observe discipline and the chain of command. Neither side is oriented toward seeking a pitched battle with the main force of the enemy nor well enough organized to do so; the need to occupy and defend territory in any case places strains on the resources of both sides. Both, however, have the capability to do a great deal of harm to noncombatant and mixed targets.

The Serbs, with their superiority in tanks and artillery and control of the high ground around the eastern cities and Sarajevo, have the ability to wage a kind of strategic war by bombardment of the Muslim-held areas, particularly the cities. Yet this is not strategic warfare properly. The aim of strategic bombardment is to turn the sentiments of the general population away from support for their armed forces and their government, and thus undermine the will of the side under bombardment to continue the war. In the case of the Serb bombardment of government-held cities, this is one aim. But more dominant is the purpose of bombardment as an element in siege warfare, which is different: to kill or drive out the inhabitants and the defending forces so as to make it possible to take over the city. Within the context of the overall war aims, this is a purpose to which the Serb guns and mortars are well suited, and even the tanks, which in less mountainous territory would be weapons of maneuver warfare, in this conflict function mostly as movable gun platforms.

Fourth, the conception of the enemy is different. This is a total war not only in the sense of the overall war goals, but in the sense of who the enemy is. That definition is religious and cultural, based on identities shaped by deep historical experience. While Serb practice acknowledges a distinction between combatants and noncombatants, the former category, according to media reports, has repeatedly been broadened in practice to include all males judged able to bear arms, including those aged from approximately puberty to the sixties. (NYT, 7/17/95, 7/23/95b) Acknowledging the latter has not included protection against direct targeting with the aim of undermining morale and driving out refugees, as in the shelling of the eastern Bosnian "safe havens," (NYT, 7/15/95, 7/20/95, 7/23/95a) or even as retaliation for military attacks launched elsewhere, as in the shelling of Sarajevo as response to the Bosnian offensive against the Serb position north of that city. (NYT, 6/28/95, 6/30/95)

Siege warfare as practiced in this conflict embodies the results of all these differences. "Siege," Walzer comments, "is the oldest form of total war." Such war, he notes, exposes noncombatants inside the circle of siege to the same risks as combatants, "or perhaps not equally so: in this kind of war, once combat begins, noncombatants are more likely to be killed. The soldiers fight from protected positions, and the civilians, who don't fight at all, are quickly made over ... into 'useless mouths'." The fate of noncombatants is worse than that of soldiers. "Fed last, and only with the army's surplus, they die first." (Walzer, 1992: 160)

If this were the entire picture, it would be bad enough, but relatively easy to apportion the blame for the noncombatant deaths: it would belong with the noncombatants themselves, if they decided to stay, or with the defenders, who have intentionally situated themselves in the midst of a populated urban center, perhaps with the aim of using the populace as a shield, and who may be guilty of depriving the noncombatant population so as to feed the army, as Walzer suggests. On this construction, the analysis used by Vitoria and others in his tradition, on up through Ramsey and beyond, fits adequately well. The harm done to noncombatants by the besiegers' actions—cutting off supplies, bombardment, attacks aimed at taking the place by storm—can be described as a secondary, unintended effect of these actions, so that blame for such harm does not rest with the besiegers but with the besieged. This was, Walzer observes, the attitude of the Roman general Titus during the siege of Jerusalem in 72 A.D.: he lamented the deaths of the inhabitants of the city, but called God to witness "that it was not his doing." (Walzer, 1992: 162)

But sieges are not the kind of occurrences to which the rule of double effect in war seems designed to apply: essentially random events in which those persons collaterally hurt are simply going about their normal business when an otherwise legitimate act of war impinges on them. Several factors often present in siege warfare work to define an importantly different context. If the entire besieged area is the target, and not simply the military defenders, then it is hard to see how the besiegers may be properly described as aiming only at the defenders within it. Yet it is clear that the besieged area, rather than the defenders alone, is the target; otherwise how to explain that tradition in siege warfare by which the defending forces are allowed to surrender the place while being given their own freedom, often with their arms intact? Further, there is a question as to why the noncombatants are present at all: they may be there under coercion from the besiegers, who have driven them in or forcibly prevented them from leaving, or under coercion from the defenders, who want them for the services they provide or for the measure of protection their presence can give, or because they are actually not true noncombatants but involved in the city's defense, or there because they judge that conditions would be proportionately no better elsewhere, a possibility that turns out to collapse into the first. Finally, there will be some persons present in a besieged place who are genuinely noncombatants seeking, as best as possible, to go on about their lives in peace, waiting for the storm of war to pass.

Such considerations as these are no doubt part of the reason why there developed historically a conception of siege warfare in which, according to the Talmudic maxim, the besieged place is to be surrounded only on three sides, not four, allowing an escape route for noncombatants and combatants alike. (Walzer, 1992: 168) Such a conception of proper warfare against places was counseled by the great strategist of the Napoleonic period, Jomini, and practiced during the American Civil War at the Union siege of Corinth, Mississippi, in May 1862 (though not in later sieges, where the aim was not simply territorial but destruction of the enemy's forces). Such an escape route was also available at the siege of Leningrad, though it was a difficult one, across Lake Lagoda. This particular opening was not intentional on the part of the besieging Germans, who simply had no way of extending their lines around the lake. Their aim, as will be discussed below, was to seal the noncombatants inside with the defenders, not to allow them a route by which to escape the city.

In any case, there is a difference between sieges in which only the noncombatants are allowed to leave and those in which combatants are allowed an escape route as well. For our purposes, the more directly important case is letting noncombatants depart while defenders remain. An argument can be made that in such cases, those who choose to remain, if they have done so voluntarily, have forfeited any claim to immunity from harm by the besiegers, that they have taken onto themselves responsibility for that harm. In terms of subjective responsibility, there is merit to this argument; a person who chooses to live or work in an area he or she knows to be dangerous bears responsibility for this choice. Firefighters, deep-sea divers, and a number of other civilian occupations come to mind.

But when the danger is caused by the acts of another, as in the case of war, then this case defaults to the kind of situation to which the rule of double effect has traditionally been applied. In such cases the person who is the source of the danger also has a responsibility, namely to use means of harm not indiscriminate or disproportionate. Direct targeting of the noncombatants who remain is still wrong, though they have chosen to be there. Indirect and unintentional harm to them is not wrong, according to the rule of double effect. But if the besiegers employ means of attack that are by nature indiscriminate or disproportionate in their effects, then I am less willing to grant the double effect excuse, and if these means are chosen so as to increase the burden of possible harm on the noncombatants present and may be judged so because they are likely to have their primary effect against these and not the combatant defenders, then double effect reasoning emphatically does not apply.

Let us consider a case from the siege of Sarajevo. Here, from time to time, the besiegers have cut off the power supply, which has in turn shut down the supply of water to portions of the city, or have directly attacked pumping stations to the same effect. In such cases the besieged inhabitants are forced to get water from a small number of exposed sites: public taps, even above-ground water mains. When they do this, the besiegers fire upon them. (cf. *NYT*, 6/28/95) How should this be analyzed ethically?

The first thing to say is that cutting off power supplies and water during sieges is as old as sieges themselves; this is part of what a siege is. Such acts aim properly at the defenders, even though all persons inside the circle of siege are equally endangered. If the defenders take more than their share of the reduced supply, this is a moral burden on them, not on the besiegers. If besiegers fire on the noncombatants seeking water, not to kill them but to drive them back away from the supply, this too is allowed by the military tradition regarding sieges, though it is morally questionable, as I will argue below. But the Serb tactics against Sarajevo appear to have the noncombatants as their particular target. They appear to use the seeking of water as an opportunity to target the noncombatants. This is wrong in itself, and calls into question the whole tactic of cutting off the power and water supplies, for these now seem but a step toward inducing the noncombatants to expose themselves so they can be shot. Whose moral responsibility are these wounds and deaths? The answer is that even if the noncombatants are in the besieged place and expose themselves to fire voluntarily, the entire responsibility is that of the besiegers, who have directly and intentionally targeted the noncombatants and coerced them to expose themselves so that they can be targets.

The same is true if the noncombatants in the city are present not from their own free choice, but as a result of coercion by the besiegers. It should be noted that here ethical analysis and the practices accepted by the law of war and military history part company. As Walzer notes, it was judged no violation of the laws and customs of war when the German forces besieging Leningrad in 1942 fired upon Russian noncombatant civilians seeking to escape the city. The critical reasoning focuses on the burden noncombatants place on the defending forces and the corresponding benefit their remaining in the place under siege confers on the besiegers. In such cases "it is lawful, though an extreme measure, to drive them back so as to hasten the surrender." (Walzer, 1992: 166) But it is clear that the noncombatants fired upon are being directly targeted, and it is not *morally* important whether the besiegers are firing for hits or near misses. In either case, if any one of the noncombatants is hit, it is the result of a direct and intentional act by the besiegers.

Now let us consider the state of those noncombatants who manage to return to the besieged city or, knowing they would be fired upon if they tried to escape, have chosen to stay. They are present in the place under siege involuntarily, as a result of coercion by the besieging forces. In such cases I am unwilling to grant that the harm done to them is properly described by reference to the rule of double effect. Rather, I would argue, the decision to keep them in place makes them part of the target. Their presence is integral to the war against the city, and harm to them is intended as harm to the defending forces, on whom it imposes a burden. Indeed, the type of relationship assumed in the argument from double effect is inverted in such cases, as the combatants become the indirect (but emphatically not unintended) targets of acts of war aimed directly and intentionally against the noncombatants in the besieged place.

Though allowed by the laws and customs of war, this is a violation of the moral concept of noncombatant immunity. It exemplifies a deep moral problem not only with war by siege, but with other kinds of "strategic" warfare against enemy cities in which the target is intentionally enlarged by the attackers. At the same time, it suggests one reason why strategic nuclear targeting of a potential enemy's cities has not been banned outright in the law of war: it is similar to what is allowed—that is, not prohibited—in the laws and customs of war for counter-city warfare in the case of sieges.

Bosnian Serb siege tactics have repeatedly enlarged the target to include noncombatants as a primary target. The case described above is one example, and many others are found in the news accounts. The problem here is not only with the Serb forces; it is with the state of the law of war. Indeed, the problem has two dimensions: first, the lack of recognition of the direct nature of the targeting of noncombatants in such cases, and second, the lack of prohibitions or limits on the connected series of activities that subject noncombatants in such cases to direct and intentional endangerment by a besieging force.

E. Implications for Other Contemporary Forms of War

These two problems reach beyond the case of siege warfare to include other contemporary forms of war as well. In particular, I think, there are implications for ethical discussion of strategic targeting and bombardment (whether conventional or nuclear) and blockades. The former, of course, has drawn the attention of much recent ethical analysis. The latter, by contrast, has received only sporadic attention.

In the case of strategic targeting and bombardment, the rule of double effect has played a central role in ethical analysis directed at this subject for the last thirty-odd years. While the circumstances of siege warfare are not identical with those of strategic bombardment, there is an area of overlap, and I suggest that the concerns raised above regarding the application of double-effect reasoning to sieges must also be raised for strategic attacks. Double-effect reasoning depends on drawing a distinction between combatants, who may morally be targeted, and noncombatants, who may not be directly and intentionally targeted but may receive collateral harm. This is a useful moral distinction, but at the practical level certain problems arise.

First, the populated area itself, and not simply the combatant elements within it, may in fact be the target. In the case of sieges, this is intentionally so; in the case of strategic bombardment, the use of weapons disproportionately large and/or not capable of discrimination in targeting makes it so in practice, whatever the stated intention. Indeed, the history of argument for strategic bombardment suggests that it is intentionally so for populated areas targeted for such bombardment, since the stated purpose is to undermine civilian support for the war effort. But even without such stated purpose, the weapons employed do make a difference. To reduce an entire city by fire, high explosive, or nuclear attack calls into question the plausibility of arguing that combatants in the place were the actual target and noncombatant deaths were only collateral. This is a problem in terms of both the principle of proportionality and also that of discrimination.

A second issue, discussed above for the case of siege warfare, is why the noncombatants are present in the target area. As noted, there may be various reasons, some of them involving voluntary choice but others involving one or another kind of coercion. For practical purposes the citizens of a city targeted for strategic bombardment, like those of a city about to be placed under siege, may have nowhere else to go, or they may be impeded in various ways from going. Merely including them in the target places a burden on the military units in the target area and suggests that it is in the attacker's interest to keep them there. This might include, for example, preventing noncombatants from leaving by destroying or threatening lines of transportation away from the target area—acts which, in themselves, might satisfy double-effect reasoning but in the larger context would be aimed at coercion of noncombatants. Conversely, it is possible that military installations have intentionally been placed in areas of noncombatant population as an effort to protect these installations, on the reasoning that a potential attacker will be deterred by the deaths of so many noncombatants if he strikes the military targets. There are strong similarities to the decision by the combatant defenders or political authorities in a place under siege to keep noncombatants present as a form of screen to protect the place from at least some forms of attack.

Moving beyond the question of coercion, whether the responsibility of the attackers or the defenders, to that of the means employed, I would argue that certain kinds of means inherently have their major impact on noncombatants and thus are properly described as indiscriminate, whether or not they are also disproportionate. Siege warfare in general, as Walzer notes (1992: 166), impacts disproportionately on noncombatants in the besieged place, and the same has often been said about nuclear attack on a populated area in which there is a mix of combatants and noncombatants. But there is a difference between using means that may be directed at the combatants present and means that must be directed at the entire area; this is what I mean by means capable of discrimination. In the case of sieges, cutting off food, water, and power is indiscriminate, though in some respects not disproportionate (compared, for example, with an extended and thorough bombardment). It is implausible to argue that such cutoffs are not aimed at noncombatants, maybe even more at the noncombatants and combatants alike; indeed, in the case of siege warfare, no denial is attempted, for this is how sieges are conducted according to the laws and customs of war. Perhaps the analogy with siege warfare can make moral analysis of the case of strategic targeting both more realistic and more honest: the aim is not simply the combatants but the noncombatants as well, when a means is used that has effect over the entire area.

The moral problem inherent in the use of such means is also the main moral problem with warfare by strategic blockade. In this case an entire nation is in effect put under siege, and all its inhabitants are affected by the privations imposed by the blockade. But, in Walzer's phrase, "perhaps not equally so": the noncombatants are hurt more and have fewer resources to fend off and repair the damage. Of course, the political and military authorities of the country under blockade may be assigned the blame if they divert a disproportionate share of what is available to themselves and away from the noncombatant population.

The blockaders may, with the Roman general Titus before Jerusalem, call on God to witness that the harm to noncombatants from the blockade is not their fault. Yet three concerns here, as in the case of sieges, argue that the blockaders do in fact bear some measure of the responsibility for the harm done to the noncombatant population. The blockaders know, for practical purposes, that the main force of the blockade will fall on the noncombatants. The aim of a general blockade, as opposed to one limited to specific items of potential military use, is in fact to exert pressure on the population at large and through them on the political and military authorities. And the choice of a general blockade is the choice of a means that has its principal effect not on combatants but on noncombatants. The general blockade thus violates the principle of discrimination in its effect, though in some respects it may be argued to be a more proportionate means of war than other possible choices. In the case of the Gulf War, for example, a considerable lobby supported a general blockade rather than the military action taken because of a conviction that military action is always worse in itself than a blockade (Johnson and Weigel, 1991: 119, 137, 147–48). I would argue just the opposite: because of its direct and intentional effect on noncombatants, a general blockade, whether of a country or of a city under siege, is always wrong, while other means may or may not be wrong depending on their nature.

The thrust of these last comments on strategic targeting and bombardment and on blockades has taken us away from the Bosnian conflict as such, but they show how this particular conflict carries in it lessons for thinking about other forms of war in other places and times. Indeed, the Bosnian conflict—a relatively limited, relatively low-technology war with more likeness to conflicts of the past than to the warfare imagined for the nuclear age—serves to open again lines of moral analysis long forgotten or deemed irrelevant to the modern age. In this respect, the considerable role played by siege warfare in this conflict is important both because it calls on moral analysis to pick up threads almost lost in the history of the modern era, and because it sheds new and distinct light on other problems of modern warfare: war against whole peoples, war by strategic targeting, war by general blockades of entire societies. These are all factors in contemporary war, and all exemplify a totalistic conception of war in one or another way. Siege warfare is, in Walzer's memorable phrase, "the oldest form of total war." (Walzer, 1992: 160) Thus its prominence in the Bosnian conflict, a war conceived totalistically by many measures, should not have been unexpected. At the same time, the presence in the Bosnian conflict of this form of war, which is generally ignored in ethical analysis, brings to the surface some important issues integral to the conduct of war in general. In particular, moral analysis of the problems of restraining harm to noncombatants in siege warfare provides a new perspective on limiting harm to noncombatants in other forms of contemporary war. More generally, if the siege is the oldest form of total war, perhaps it is possible to learn from moral examination of siege warfare in the Bosnian conflict what issues need to be addressed in order to make the conduct of future wars less totalistic.

Bosnia, the United States, and the Just War Tradition

4

G. Scott Davis

There is an inherent asymmetry between the moral status of nations at war and their nonbelligerent neighbors. Warring states can neither avoid conflict nor worry about taking sides, while third parties typically do both. If the conflict is sufficiently contained and far away, it may be relatively easy to let loose a spate of hand-wringing and disapprobation, and be done with it. To many, both at home and abroad, United States policy on the Yugoslav wars has appeared to be just this. For not a few in this country that is just what it should be. In conversation and in the press it has been common, these last three years, to hear warnings against foreign quagmires, reminders of Vietnam, and general puzzlement as to why the United States should have any interest in risking American lives and resources on a small country in a contentious part of the world that lacks even the redeming political benefit of oil.

The downside, of course, is that the petty invasion or murky civil war that we ignore today may become tomorrow's sinkhole, opening wide to receive our blood and resources. Vietnam comes rather obviously to mind. Even when a third party can successfully avoid entanglement in its neighbors' conflicts there may be compelling reasons to intervene, be they geopolitical, humanitarian, or both. Bangladesh, Biafra, Cambodia, Somalia: here the list is too depressing to dwell on. In any event, the justification for intervention or indifference says much about the self-image of a state and the moral identity of its citizens. This essay reflects on two approaches to U.S. foreign policy, with an eye to a critical analysis of American options for action in the conflict over Bosnia.

In recent decades, justifications for American action have relied heavily on one or another brand of "realism." In most of its forms, realism sees states as essentially hostile, driven to cooperate solely by the desire for security, and willing to use whatever forms of power are at their disposal to maintain the balance of power or, if possible, tip it just a bit in their own favor. Realists are not, or at least need not be, amoral monsters in the service of ruthless strategies of domination. Whether their origins be theological, like Reinhold Niebuhr's, or grounded in political history, like E. H. Carr's, most realists are moralists at odds with one or another form of optimism that they fear blinds its adherents to the real evils being perpetrated right and left. Thus Niebuhr excoriates the pacifists for committing themselves to "the perverse judgment that Hitlerism is really preferable to British imperialism because it is 'more honest', or because bombing cities is morally preferable to a blockade." (1957: 270) Carr, also writing on the brink of war, insists that we "can discard as purely utopian and muddle-headed plans for a procedure of peaceful change dictated by a world legislature or a world court," concluding that, if peace and justice are what we want, "we shall do our best to make ourselves as powerful as we can." (1946: 222) For the realist it is the idealist, of whatever stripe, who is the threat to promoting legitimate values.

The classical paradigm of political realism is the debate over the fate of Mytilene, which revolted against Athens in the fourth year of the Peloponnesian Wars. Having suppressed the revolt, the Athenians "decided to put to death not only those now in their hands but also the entire adult male population of Mytilene, and to make slaves of the women and children." (Thucydides, *HPW*: III, 36) The next day, as Thucydides tells the story, some repent of their zeal, provoking a heated debate. Like a good realist Cleon advocates swift and ruthless measures in showing what happens to those who would resist Athenian power. Diodotus speaks for the opposition, but he is quick to insist that he is advocating neither compassion nor a misplaced sense of justice. "This is not a law-court," he reminds the assembly, "where we have to consider what is fit and just; it is a political assembly, and the question is how Mytilene can be most useful to Athens." (III, 44)

Diodotus proves an even better realist than Cleon by arguing that to destroy an entire city is counterproductive. If the Athenians exterminate a disobedient ally, they will create a disincentive to future alliances. Not only this, but there is no appreciable deterrent effect since rebels, like thieves and murderers, typically act on the assumption that they will not get caught. Finally, destroying the whole of Mytilene will inspire those rebels who do get caught to fight all the harder since they will believe they have nothing to gain by capitulating. After reflection, the assembly rescinds its death sentence.

Here is the essence of realism. We believe, Diodotus acknowledges, that right is on our side. But we also need to secure our prospects for the future. Giving in to indignation is no more prudent than the idealism that would spare Mytilene out of misplaced mercy. Like any wisely governed state, Athens should act with measured restraint to secure the optimal outcome. In recent American politics realism characterized the Cold War policies of "containment" and "constructive engagement," as well as the debate over nuclear deterrence. While almost everyone agrees that nuclear war would be unimaginably horrid, and that threatening to bomb large civilian populations is monstrous, realists insist that unilateral disarmament would tempt our enemies to strike first. Putting ourselves at risk in this fashion, they maintain, would be politically irresponsible and would threaten the extinction of an entire civilization. Despite vigorous criticism from peace groups of all sorts, the realists dominated the strategic policy of the Cold War period. (cf. Freedman, 1986)

Much of the credibility of this realism came from its emphasis on strategy firmly grounded in scientific analysis. Typical of the emphasis on hard science and technical analysis were Herman Kahn and Thomas Schelling. Kahn's realist credentials were impeccable. His massive *On Thermonuclear War*, with its account of doomsday machines and advocacy of strategic planning, is said to have inspired Stanley Kubrick's *Dr. Strangelove*. (cf. Kahn, 1960: 144–153) Schelling's *Strategy of Conflict* hoped to provide "the retarded science of international strategy" with scientific foundations by deploying the recently formulated theory of games. (cf. Schelling, 1960: 7–16; but see Brams, 1975: 46) The place of game theory in realist analysis is worth a look.

Game theory, since its birth in the mid-1940s, has produced some remarkably powerful analyses in economics, collective bargaining, and, most to the point here, military and political strategy. By assigning values to outcomes, it is possible to make fairly specific claims about which is the most reasonable strategy. The example traditionally used to illustrate the game theoretic method is the Prisoner's Dilemma. Imagine that you and your partner have been arrested for securities fraud. Yes, you did it, but if you both keep quiet you will get just a five-year sentence for tampering. If either of you cop to it, saving the state a trial, you can bargain for ten. Here it would seem obvious that the thing to do is clam up; why choose ten years in jail if you can get away with five?

The problem is that the DA knows this too, so she offers probation on both counts to the first person who turns state's evidence, with the other taking the full twenty-five years. How much do you trust your partner? When it was in both of your best interests to keep quiet, perhaps you could trust him a lot, but now you could be in for twenty-five years and he could be on the way to Vegas with the proceeds of a previous job. The only stable strategy is to rat each other out, with both of you taking ten rather than risking twenty-five years, even though keeping quiet still buys you only five. Solidarity between you and your partner would produce the better result, but Prisoner's Dilemma and related games seem to show that the only stable point is where both sides give up solidarity for self-interest.[1]

Steven Brams and Marc Kilgour, applying game theory to superpower quests for security, argue, however, that it is possible to achieve some cooperative goods while retaining stability. Consider their account of the problem of nuclear weapons. If we value justice over security, then unilateral disarmament is the way to go, but this seems to the realist too much like Russian roulette. It is possible, however, to envision a gradual build-down. After all, if I have a dozen rifles trained on your baby's crib, I can send one or two out for cleaning without your thinking it is safe to make a break for it. Couching the risks in probabilistic terms, Brams and Kilgour argue that de-escalation is stable in game theoretic terms, if coupled with the deterrent threat of robust retaliation. (Brams & Kilgour, 1988: 51–53) We can, theoretically, reverse the arms race, albeit this requires, for stability, that the retaliation for cheating become increasingly certain and severe. (1988: 71) This is a promising finding for the realist, who would like to reduce nuclear arms in general, but is not willing to run the risk of going it alone.

There are, however, two problems. The first is related to Alasdair MacIntyre's critique of the role of social scientific experts in policy deliberations. The most sophisticated tools of the social sciences, MacIntyre argues, are crippled by three factors: the ability of the players to render themselves inscrutable by acting unpredictably; the limits of knowledge obtaining in almost all real-world situations; and the fact that no game modeled on real world conflicts can accurately represent that situation. If, for example, I have a reputation for conservative card-playing, this makes my occasional bluff all the more effective. If I vary the pattern of my play, sometimes playing boldly and at others reverting to form, I can keep you guessing and provide myself an advantage.

In cards, of course, my strategy is a limited variable within a fixed game. We all know the cards in our own hand and some, depending on the game, of the cards held by our opponents. With a little practice we can compute our odds fairly precisely. That's why casinos play with multiple decks. The level of predictability goes down as the amount of relevant knowledge goes up, particularly if what we need to know depends on the changing strategies of our opponents. Since strategies alter with changes in resources and technology, which the other side is making valiant efforts to conceal, our ability to get the knowledge is strained, the higher the stakes. This is why we have spies and counterspies, in industry as well as politics.

This might be enough to make us suspect the experts, but the third factor clinches it. MacIntyre invites us to consider a board game of the Battle of Gettysburg, "which reproduces with great accuracy the terrain, the chronology and the units involved in that battle. It had this peculiarity, that a moderately good player taking the Confederate side can win." (MacIntyre, 1984: 98) This is noteworthy for the obvious fact that Lee lost, and lost *because* he did not have the very knowledge essential to the game player. The contemporary player can win because he knows what the possible outcomes are. He knows the relative troop strengths, their abilities, and how long the battle will last. He can, in short, ask himself "What would have happened if, at Gettysburg, Lee had played it differently?" But this makes the game invalid as a method of predicting. For, as MacIntyre puts it, "Lee did not and could not know that it was the *Battle of Gettysburg*—an episode on which a determinate shape was conferred only retrospectively by its outcome—which was about to be fought." (MacIntyre, 1984: 99) The *prospectively* indeterminate nature of historical events stands in the way of identifying them with those past. Attempting to do so is little more than creative, sometimes brilliant, guesswork. The would-be scientific theories that underlie the games suffer from being unrepeatable and untestable, thus undermining the predictive power of even the most sophisticated model. Without strong predictive claims, it is hard to see why the "expert" deserves our deference.

Proponents of game theory have countered that there are reasonable methods of eliminating such problems, (cf. Harsanyi, 1990)[2] but the success of these strategies is suspect. Suppose that it were possible to convince our erstwhile enemies that de-escalation was incomparably better than anything to be gained by cheating or attack. Imagine, that is, that the sentence for securities fraud was instant death, and nobody was making deals. This would transform the noncooperative situation of an arms race into a cooperative game, where you and partner have no disincentives to solidarity. In this sort of situation we would want to be as forthright and careful in de-escalation as we try to be in building nuclear plants for peaceful purposes at home. And this is the problem. Even our best efforts sometimes fail, and if Charles Perrow is correct, the prospects for failure are endemic to complex technologies.

In *Normal Accidents*, Perrow distinguishes between mishaps that are beyond reasonable expectations and those that are normal given the nature of the system. He takes his cue from the nuclear accident at Three Mile Island, but let us begin more simply. There is a current TV car commercial in which a bird picks up a tortoise, but drops it in mid-flight. The falling tortoise dislodges a boulder, the boulder rolls down the road into the path of a four-wheel drive vehicle driven by a couple who are hopelessly lost. At the moment of impact, the commercial breaks away to the reassuring message that this model, fortunately, comes with dual airbags. This is *not* a normal accident, but the stuff that sitcoms are made of. Contrast it with a winter scene on a major New England highway. The traffic circle outside Portsmouth, New Hampshire, has a dusting of snow, but nothing the locals would worry about. Unfortunately, grabbing brakes on a eighteen-wheeler lead to the truck jack-knifing, its rear end whipping around into the path of an oncoming station wagon, killing a family of six. This is a tragedy. It is also a normal accident.

Normal accidents are failures that we should expect, given the complexity of certain kinds of components and their interaction with other components in the system as a whole. Any complex system, to achieve its goals, must direct energy down numerous paths to drive diverse but interlinking subsystems. In theory, the interactions are smoothly coordinated and work with smooth efficiency to achieve our ends. But if the parts are tightly coupled, like cars on a train, the consequences of failure anywhere follow immediately. The highway is designed for travelers, the breaks within certain tolerances, and the tires to provide a reasonable grip on the road. But it should not surprise us that tiny glitches happen, and when they do, the very design of the system facilitates the tragedy.

To avoid catastrophes, we build in safety measures, such as the bindings on ski boots and automatic decouplers, designed to release before the damage is done. But the more complex the system gets, the more difficult it becomes to monitor the stress points, see what is going on, and act before the next problem occurs. This was initially the case at Three Mile Island. Nonetheless, it was a normal accident. Because they are both highly complex *and* tightly coupled, nuclear plants are among the highest risk of all technologies, approached, in Perrow's discussion, only by the likes of nuclear weapons systems, air travel, and chemical plants. (See the graph he calls the "Interaction/Coupling Chart," Perrow, 1984: 327) To call such failures "normal accidents," he notes, "is an expression of an integral characteristic of the system, not a statement of frequency. It is normal for us to die, but we only do it once." (Perrow, 1984: 5) In normal accidents, disaster can occur without any malice aforethought, even if, unlike Three Mile Island, all involved continue to do their best to cooperate. In political affairs the situation is still worse.

Consider the following. Two army pilots take a helicopter on a routine mission to familiarize themselves with a new environment. In the course of their flight, they stray over a border clearly marked from the ground, but difficult to discern from the air. If this were the border between Denmark and Germany the event would be inconsequential, but because this particular border marks an ongoing hot spot, the matter is grave. The chopper goes down and one of the pilots dies, creating the possibility for a major international incident. Perhaps apologies and face-saving are possible all around, but unfortunately the Commander in Chief has been having image problems at home, and the military authorities of the aggrieved nation have themselves been grumbling about the effectiveness of a recently installed leader, particularly when contrasted to his deceased father. What of the remaining serviceman? What about next time?

Perrow shows that even in the most cooperative game, where smooth coordination is in everybody's interest, we should expect accidents neither predictable nor avoidable in game-theoretic terms. Managing high-risk operations places enormous and sometimes conflicting demands on those in charge. In the most general case, crises in tightly coupled, complex systems call for measures whose "demands are inconsistent. Because of the complexity, they are best decentralized; because of the tight coupling, they are best centralized." (Perrow, 1984: 334) I'll call the result the "Strangelove Effect." If deterrence is to work, the adversary has to believe that there is nothing to be gained from striking first. The way to demonstrate this is by building a system so tightly coupled that, once triggered, the consequences cannot be avoided. But the more complex the system becomes, the more likely it is that a short circuit, human or mechanical, will trigger a catastrophe.

Taken together, Perrow and MacIntyre cast considerable doubt on the claim that crises and conflicts can be predicted and managed by the practical social scientist, standing shoulder to shoulder with the hard-nosed engineer. This is something of a blow to the political realist. Game theory looked like a very promising method of policy-making, high in scientific credibility and free from any adventitious idealisms. Implementing it with the high-tech proposals made familiar by the likes of the RAND Corporation seemed to promise a respite from our modern political jitters. Now it seems that, even if the technologies could be made to work, programs like SDI are fool's gold, more glitter than the hard currency needed for peace of mind.

What alternatives might there be to the realism of the Cold Warriors? Perhaps there is another lesson to be learned from the Prisoners' Dilemma. Early on, psychological researchers noticed that "there is initially either a reservoir of good intention or a lack of appreciation of the strategic structure of the game." While the theory dictates that it is safest to confess, this strategy "is not born out on the first play." (Rapoport & Chammah, 1965: 200; also Brams, 1975; 32–34) The cynic may read this as idealism or naïveté, but it points to an important feature of our social and political lives. Our ordinary abilities to negotiate daily life depend on reserving fear and mistrust for abnormal situations. Unless I have very specific intelligence, and the need to gather it, I am not likely to begin the day by checking my car for bombs. If I point out to the young man ringing up my groceries that the machine read something twice, or that it did not register the sale price, I take it for granted that he did not intend to cheat me, that the manager is not going to threaten me with a gun, and that the extra $2.17 will come off my total.

This doesn't mean that I'm oblivious to the waiter's gentle attempts to suggest another bottle of wine, or the fact that some parts of town are more dangerous than others. But our suspicions are reasonable only against the larger background of minimal goodwill and cooperation that makes ordinary life possible. We are normally committed to cooperation at the beginning of any enterprise we choose of our own accord. It is only when we are given reason that we are disposed to heighten our suspicion. Recognizing this marks the difference between the paranoid and the pragmatist. The paranoid is convinced that everyone is dissembling, and by treating all acts as hostile, he heightens the danger for himself and others. The pragmatist acknowledges that there is no way to eliminate risk and uncertainty, but insists that this is no excuse for acting contrary to principle.

Brams and Kilgour register some sense of this in remarking that "when threats themselves become provocative and severely undermine trust, one must ask whether their deterrent value outweighs the cost of creating an inflammatory situation." (1988: 53) How is it possible to make a threat without being inflammatory? Traditionally the answer has been to limit threats to those consistent with justice. A commitment to justice says that, as the temptation to cheat becomes greater, we will exert ourselves all the more to resist it. We will not only exercise restraint at the top, but will decouple our own system in order to avoid the "Strangelove Effect." Of course this leaves us open to the malicious intruder, but then nothing, in ethics or the social sciences, can eliminate malice. The most effective, and to our adversaries most reassuring, guard against it is submitting our policies and acts to the scrutiny of justice.

I want to be clear that I am not offering an argument for justice. To demand a reason to be just is to show that you do not understand what the word means. (cf. Davis, 1992: 6–26) My strategy is, rather, to disarm a certain strand in political rhetoric that urges us to believe that "moral talk [does] not bear" on problems of policy and strategy. (Wasserstrom, 1969: 79) I am certainly not advancing the absurd claim that justice is always in our best interest. Sometimes it isn't. Nor am I making the slightly less implausible claim that justice is its own reward. Maybe it should be, but that is a matter for moral psychology, and the realist will rightly dismiss it. I am making the more complicated claim that in any strategic situation each side hopes to maximize its ability to predict the moves of the other. The more we can trust our opponents, the more predictable they become. If cooperation to a mutually desired conclusion is the goal, then each side should make itself predictable to the other, and this means convincing them of their trustworthiness.

An interesting illustration of the failure to command trust emerges from Lawrence Freedman's account of American nuclear policy in the early 1950s. The policy of "massive retaliation" enunciated by John Foster Dulles, writes Freedman, led interpreters at home and abroad to assume that the United States was willing to resort to nuclear weapons as a means of countering Communist expansion. There is ample evidence that presidents and their advisors had substantial moral, not to mention practical and strategic, reasons for not initiating any nuclear exchange. Nonetheless, Dulles's position seemed so dangerous that it both provoked opponents and alienated allies. Thus, "rather than leading America's allies to support the administration's Indochina policy, their suspicions probably encouraged them to keep their distance." (Freedman, 1986: 742) Mutual mistrust fueled the ongoing arms race, with the result that even the rather perverse stability of mutual assured destruction gave way to the clamor for ABMs, MIRVs, and ultimately Star Wars. (cf. Freedman, 1986: 758–761) For the realist to remark sagely that we avoided nuclear war neglects both logic and the economic impact of the arms race. So while justice may not always be in my best interest, being trusted is. The easiest and most effective way to achieve this is by actually being trustworthy.

But we should be clear about the limits of our efforts at trustworthiness. There are, broadly speaking, three sorts of reason for trusting another person: family ties; shared endeavors; and commitments to principle. Neither of the first two were appropriate to the Cold War, nor are they appropriate to the conflict in Bosnia. The misplaced perception of family ties is clearly an impediment to reasonable policy in the Yugoslav context; it is one of the problems. Virulent forms of this "genetic" fallacy would have us support the most vicious attacks on the innocent merely because we and the attackers come from the same "stock." The appeal to shared endeavors is less offensive but not much more stable. With the end of the Cold War, even the strongest of past alliances are more likely to find themselves competing for key markets and technologies, without the global worries that used to mollify those competitions. Only their commitment to principle makes it possible for one side to trust its rival. It is not surprising that the rhetoric of global threat has shifted to one of political principle, and that we hear more and more about justice and the just war theory.[3]

In fact, it has been a good decade for the just war tradition. The eighties opened with debates over the Catholic bishops' *Challenge of*

Peace, keeping just war thinkers and their critics highly visible in the popular media, before and after the pastoral's publication in May of 1983. This visibility provoked, in its turn, no small amount of collegial rivalry, leading to analogous pastorals by the French, German, Belgian, and Irish Catholics, as well as Lutherans and Methodists, among others, in this country. These official pronouncements were themselves only the tip of a publishing iceberg that spanned the full spectrum of conservative and liberal, evangelical, and secular thinkers.

The hubbub might have abated with the fall of the Berlin Wall had it not been for Saddam Hussein and the invasion of Kuwait. Just war arguments once again flew almost indiscriminately through the press, and the impact of those arguments was, by all the evidence, felt deeply in administrative circles. President Bush's January 16 address from the Oval Office bears detailed consideration. "This military action," said Mr. Bush, "taken in accord with United Nations resolutions and the consent of the United States Congress, follows months of constant and virtually endless diplomatic activity." (Bush, 1991: 311) Not only did the Iraqi invasion of August 1990 not only violate the sovereignty of Kuwait, he continued, but "while the world waited, Saddam Hussein systematically raped, pillaged, and plundered a tiny nation no threat to his own. He subjected the people of Kuwait to unspeakable atrocities ... moved massive forces into Kuwait," and "met every overture of peace with open contempt." (1991: 312) The President insisted that "we have no argument with the people of Iraq. . . . Our goal is not the conquest of Iraq. It is the liberation of Kuwait," (1991: 313) and he expressed his certainty "not only that we will prevail, but that out of the horror of combat will come the recognition that no nation can stand against a world united. No nation will be permitted to brutally assault its neighbor." (1991: 314)

Less than a month later, in his *Washington Post* column of February 14, Charles Krauthammer invoked the just war tradition to defend the bombing of sites in Baghdad, asserting that "by any moral calculus, if our intelligence indicated no more than, say, a one-in-five chance that it made biological weapons, the Allies had not just the right but the duty to destroy it." (1991: 332) He goes on to remind his readers that "one of the criteria for just war is proportionality of means to ends," acknowledging that "civilian pain in war is a horror beyond words. But when the war is just, it must be faced with a kind of nerve." (1991: 333)

Here in narrow compass we have the traditional criteria for initiating and prosecuting a just war. From at least the thirteenth century there has been general agreement that entry into war requires the following: proper authority; just cause; right intent; last resort; and the reasonable hope of success. These are, of course, the conditions Mr. Bush insists have been met, thus justifying American involvement in Kuwait. Krauthammer invokes the criteria for justice in war: discrimination and proportionality, governed by the principle of double effect.

When President Bush announced the liberation of Kuwait on February 27, there were more than a few legitimate grounds for thinking that moral resolve and technological prowess enabled the fighting of a war that satisfied the demands of justice. The international community had responded to manifest aggression with thoughtful, cooperative action to coordinate military resources in order to repel the aggressor and restore the legitimate government of Kuwait. There were skeptics, of course. Many could not quite shake the suspicion that oil played just the tiniest role in shaping our intentions. But this points up the power of the just war tradition to shed light on our actions and intentions. If oil, rather than justice, made the difference, we could hardly be said to be acting morally. If securing our "sphere of influence" were the principal motive, we might as easily have back the aggressors. Had we not done so earlier in the Iran/Iraq War? Mr. Bush himself didn't seem to notice that on just war terms his predecessor's incursion into Grenada, Operation Just Cause in Panama, and American involvement in Nicaragua were all immoral.

And the past matters. In order to praise you for acting well, I have to believe you knew what you were doing. After all, it would just be dumb luck if kids out ringing doorbells happened to save a family from a gas leak. But even when someone knows what he is doing, he has to do it for the right reason. The psycho who rescues his prey in order to subject her to satanic tortures is hardly a humanitarian. So in order to think you are trustworthy, I must believe you are virtuous, that you would habitually do the right thing for the right reasons. (Cf. Aristotle, EN: 1105a–b) And you really are trustworthy only if my beliefs are true. The evidence for those beliefs is your doings up to now, and a tradition of *realpolitik* may make the claims of justice seem too much like grandmother's nightgown: sheer fabrication over a nonexistent concern.

Nonetheless, invoking the just war tradition seemed at least a laudable first step toward shaping policy in the light of justice. That Mr. Bush and his minions found it important to offer a just war account of their actions argues for some awareness of its claims. And though progress in political ethics may only come in fits and starts, cynicism in politics is not likely to help in ameliorating the miseries we find and inflict. "Critics," as Michael Walzer put it, "have to argue for a consistent policy, which is to say that just-war theory, with its definitions of aggression and self-defense and mutual aid, should be applied impartially across the society of states, to the critics' own state as well as to all the others." (1992: xxiii) The way to get better is practice, for states as well as individuals.

But even as the Gulf War wound down, the difficulties of applying just war criteria "across the society of states" were becoming painfully clear. Since the death of Tito, in May of 1980, conflict had been growing among the constituent republics of Yugoslavia. An emergent Serbian nationalism lobbied for control of Kosovo, the legendary locus of hopes for a greater Serbia. The Albanian majority objected to dramatic assaults on their independence, and civil strife erupted in 1988. Mutual suspicions and the decay of the economic order, along with the dramatic transformation of neighboring Communist states, led the republics of Slovenia and Croatia to contemplate secession, a move taken by both on June 25, 1991.

Slobodan Milosevic, who had come to be identified with Serbian nationalism, assumed leadership of Yugoslavia and deployed the Yugoslavian National Army (JNA) first against Slovenia and then Croatia, but was unable to reverse their movement out of Yugoslavia. Both were recognized by the European Community in January of 1992. In February of 1992, the republic of Bosnia and Herzegovina held a referendum on independence, boycotted by the majority of those identifying themselves as Serbs. The European Community and the United States recognized Bosnia and Herzegovina on April 7, 1992.[4]

As moves for secession went forward, violence escalated in Bosnia, predominantly carried out by separatists in the name of Serbian nationalism. The day before recognition, reports came in that paramilitary forces from Serbia, led by the notorious Arkan, had attacked and murdered Muslim worshippers. (Kajan, 1993: 87) Shortly thereafter the American ambassador to Yugoslavia, Warren Zimmermann, confronted Milosevic, who insisted that the fighting was an internal matter, pitting Bosnians against Bosnians. "But," said Zimmermann,

"I saw Arkan on your own Belgrade television boasting about his capture of Bosnian villages." "You shouldn't take it so seriously," Milosevic replied. "Besides, you needn't worry about trouble in Bosnia. Serbs have no serious grievances in Bosnia; they're not being abused there." The chilling irony, Zimmermann concludes, is that under the guise of this reassurance, "Milosevic reduced the Serbian argument for naked aggression to the assumption that Serbs had a right to murder, torture, and expel simply because they did not want to live under an independent multiethnic government that was not abusing them." (Zimmermann, 1995: 19)

Radovan Karadzic, who had emerged as the leader of Serbian separatists within Bosnia, made the point even clearer. "You have to understand Serbs, Mr. Zimmermann," said the erstwhile psychiatrist:

> They have been betrayed for centuries. Today they cannot live with other nations. They must have their own separate existence. They are a warrior race and they can trust only themselves to take by force what is their due. But this doesn't mean that Serbs can hate. Serbs are incapable of hatred. (Zimmermann, 1995: 20)

This hateless attempt to secure "what is their due" resulted in over three years of war, by far the bulk of it directed at noncombatants.

Any moral tradition that did not condemn the atrocities in Bosnia would, by that very failure, demonstrate its own bankruptcy. But acknowledging the inhumanity of war takes little effort. The harder question is what guidance the just war tradition gives in circumstances like these. This in itself divides into two steps. There is, first, the status of the belligerents and the justice of their acts. Here the just war thinker wants to know who initiated hostilities and with what provocation, how the war is being conducted and to what end. Only when answers can be given here are third parties such as the United States in a position to ask what justice demands of them.

Again the Gulf War is instructive. That the Iraqi army had carried war into Kuwait was not in doubt. As a sovereign nation Kuwait was entitled to appeal directly to its friends, allies, and the community of nations for immediate assistance against the invaders. Had Saudi Arabia, the United States, or any coalition of states immediately joined hostilities against Iraq, it would not have been an intervention, because interventions imply a third party's inserting itself, as opposed to allies coming to each other's aid. Debates about oil and our "vital interests" would have been beside the point; the relevant question would have been the mutual obligations created by shared treaties and alliances. The minimal level of trustworthiness to which a country can be held is honoring its commitments.

If we shift our attention from Kuwait to Bosnia, how did things stand on April 1, 1992? Serbian nationalists and some commentators in Europe and America maintained that Bosnia had no independent history. Without historical precedent, went the argument, a community has only accidental status and no independent claim to political recognition. Alex Dragnitch, for instance, writing in May of 1992, systematically minimizes the historical status of Bosnia. When he comes to consider the fates of Yugoslavia's republics, Dragnitch remarks that:

> Plebiscites in Bosnia-Herzegovina and Macedonia indicated a desire for independence, but neither had ever existed as an independent state. The only independent states making up the new Yugoslav state in 1918 were Serbia and Montenegro. In a plebiscite in 1992, Montenegro voted strongly for remaining with Serbia as a part of Yugoslavia. (1992: 191)

The implication seems to be that prior independence is a prerequisite for political standing; that being a republic in 1918 conveys some privileged status; and that the preferences of Serbia and Montenegro have greater weight than those of Croatia and Slovenia. But none of these claims is credible. Political identity is less a metaphysical brand, impressed somewhere on the soul, than a serpent's skin, sloughed off regularly in the course of political change. We either embrace or eschew the identity imagined for us by our predecessors. The spectator, in particular, begins with the present and works back, making what sense he can of historical claims.

Bosnians and those sympathetic to their claims insist that "there had been a Bosnia since the Middle Ages . . . maintained through the Ottoman and the Austro-Hungarian period, and at the end of the Second World War it became part of Tito's Yugoslavia as one of the constituent republics of the federation—the only republic which was multinational by definition." (Rabia & Lifschultz, 1993: xxi) This seems to be confirmed by most recent historians. A printed map from about 1492, to take a date at random, shows Bosnia, with Srebrenica in the east and Bihac in the west, divided from "Zervia" and

"Sclavonia" by the rivers Sava and Drina. (Campbell, 1987: pl. 49) Ivo Banac, in his study of Yugoslav nationalism, notes Bosnia as a minor presence whose "regional consciousness" expanded throughout the thirteenth and fourteenth centuries, to the point where "Tvrtko, the greatest of all Bosnian rulers, assumed the royal title and laid claim to the thrones of Serbia, Dalmatia, and Croatia." (1984: 39) Much the same emerges from Malcolm's and Fine's recent sketches of Bosnian history. That Bosnia fell under Ottoman, then Habsburg, domination scarcely differentiates it from its neighbors. That Bosnians converted to Islam hardly implies that Bosnia ceased to exist.

But none of this matters. History makes a difference in determining who did what to whom, but it is the nature of history that land passes from group to group, person to person. It is sadly rare that land passes justly from one group to another, but responsibility does not pass eternally down the generations. The most we can be asked to do is to insure that the transfers we witness are conducted fairly, and when they are not, to defend the victims.

Suppose, for example, that the heirs of Odysseus were to emerge, fully verified, and claim their rights to Ithaca. Should we cede them the land, along with sovereignty and the right to set policy as to the public good? It is hard to imagine how we should respond, though it might help to consider the plight of the modern Ithacans, established for a mere century or two. Would it be fair to displace them in favor of the Odysseans? Would they be acting unjustly in rising up to defend their farms? The contemporary Ithacans have as good a claim as can be had to their land. They have, in fact, exactly the same claim Odysseus would have had against the heirs of his neolithic precursors: they received it from their fathers, who could not remember a time when it was not theirs.

Invoking memory here is anything but arbitrary. The urgency of claims to redress injuries diminishes over time, and this for two reasons. First, the longer the hiatus the less it can be shown that the original injury has any impact on the heir. The claimant has less reason to believe that he would have been the beneficiary of the victim, and the fact that he is here shows that he has been able to make his own life in the world. Second, as time goes by, those who receive ill-gotten goods have less reason to suppose them ill-gotten. There is a difference, for example, between an injury done to your great-grandfather and one received by yourself. Had he not been swindled out of his land grant in 1883, perhaps all those oil wells lining La Cienega would be yours, along with all that great real estate. But this is a big perhaps, resting on a lot of hypotheticals. It is also possible that the surviving beneficiary, the great-grandson of that particular robber baron, will be appalled by ancestral vice and make you a handsome offer. But it is hard to see that he is obliged to give up what he has received. Nor is there, morally speaking, any reason for the law to prefer you over him, though it should have protected your ancestor from his great-grandfather.

Notice that time and memory are not the only factors. There are different sorts of injury and loss. Suppose, for example, that you have inherited an heirloom baby quilt from a beloved aunt. The baby, one spring morning, happily lets it flap out the car window, without your noticing. Roger, some hours later, comes across it, stuffs it in his backpack for no other reason than it is pretty, cleans it up and drapes it over his antique Shaker rocking chair. Some years later—this is no normal accident—you arrive to pick up your grade-schooler, who is playing with Roger's daughter. Whatever the law, and even if Roger has grown fond of the quilt, he should give it back. Unless he would would suffer substantial injury in restoring the *status quo ante*, then the current holder has no reasonable claim. And this injury must be of a special sort. Substitute for the quilt, a Stradivarius. Roger does not play, nor does his daughter; they kept it because it was pretty. Once it is appraised Roger discovers he has a very valuable instrument, but if the act of having it appraised reveals its provenance, as happened in the recent case in California, Roger should return it. To argue that he might have sold the violin for a million dollars, while true, is irrelevant, for prior to discovering the nature of the violin he had invested nothing of himself in it, and now that he knows its rightful owner, he is not entitled to profit from it. The return should be unconditional and uncontested. Anything else is venal, whatever the law allows.

If memory has been kept painfully alive, as in the case of the occupied territories in Israel, there is absolutely no excuse for conveying or occupying the land. In the eyes of the Palestinians, claims to divine instauration are no more legitimate than those of Odysseus. Nor should they be for third parties, even if they believe in the God of Israel. Thus, in denying the claims of the conquistadors, Vitoria points out that, whatever God's ultimate purposes, empires "have been handed down by inheritance or conquest or some other title until our own times." There is no divinely appointed emperor, and that of Spain "is not entitled on any such grounds to arrogate to himself the dominion of the whole world, nor, as a consequence, of these barbarians." (Vitoria, *de Indis*, #25; 1991, 255) The relevant borders are those obtaining at the time of the conflict, and it is the memory of these that brands the occupied territories for what they are. There is an argument for holding the Golan Heights against attack in an ongoing conflict, but this is rather different from annexing and settling somebody else's land. Past injuries cannot be redressed by new injustices. Whether in Palestine, Bosnia, or the United States, when governments perpetrate injustices, they perpetuate conflicts.

Dragnitch's complaint that the European Community "actively contributed to the destruction of another sovereign European state—Yugoslavia—in contravention of clearly understood principles of international law and the Charter of the United Nations," (1992: 190) if true, is a more powerful argument. The Europeans would then be guilty of fomenting civil war, and this is manifestly unjust. Furthermore, any external intervention would be improper, for in civil war, justice places special conditions on third parties. In a civil war, sovereignty is the issue. What may once have been a single body has degenerated, with the pathology playing itself out in armed conflict. If some minimal apparatus of government exists, then the conflict remains a domestic matter, and entering on either side prejudges the issue. If the situation has degenerated into murderous confusion, it is unclear where justice lies. In either case, third-party action attempts to decide the very question prompting the war, thereby subverting the notion of political independence. Civil war, the tradition argues, should be met with strict neutrality on the part of spectators. (Walzer, 1992: 96–97) If Germany and Austria connived to foment revolution in Croatia and Slovenia, this would indeed have been unjust.

But recognizing the seceding republics is another matter. There was much to be said against the breakup of Yugoslavia. Few thought that the constituent republics would fare well, given their mutual dependence. But, beyond wise counsel and best wishes, there was little that the other countries of Europe, much less the United States, could legitimately do. Whatever the wisdom of the original secession, Croatia and Slovenia made it stick, in the face of a concerted military assault directed from Belgrade. Milosevic's invocation of a Greater Serbia inspired legitimate concern over a revival of *Chetnik* aspirations that, as recently as 1941, called for a state "which is to be ethnically pure and is to include Serbia, Montenegro, Bosnia and Herzegovina, Srijem, the Banat, and Backa." This purity was to be achieved through "the cleansing of the state territory of all national minorities and a-national elements." (Tomasevich, 1975: 170) It was not unreasonable for the Croatians to see the war that broke out in the summer of 1991 as an extension of these *Chetnik* hopes. The brutality directed against Croatian civilians is itself grounds for believing that the government in Belgrade did not act for the common good, thereby forfeiting what claim it might once have had to the allegiance of the other republics. With the moral collapse of the federal government, the only viable candidates for political recognition were the republics that had made up Yugoslavia, with the borders that defined them.

As for Bosnia, once Slovenia and Croatia made good their secession, the old Yugoslavia was over. The conduct of the war in Croatia, and before that Milosevic's repressive measures against the Albanians of Kosovo, could hardly reassure the people of Bosnia and Herzegovina. It is not clear whether the referendum of February 1992, with some sixty percent of the electorate voting for independence, was required by justice, but it lends further legitimacy to the default Bosnian government. It signaled the willingness of the government of the new state of Bosnia and Herzegovina to reaffirm a commitment to the common good. This is what governments are supposed to do.

That the Bosnian Serbs boycotted the referendum is irrelevant. Dragnich, in a letter to the *Times* of June 4, 1995, invokes the Serbian desire for "self-determination," but self-determination does not take place in a vacuum. It happens either within or against the system of prevailing law, and it is reasonable to insist that all groups abide by laws that are justly framed and applied in good faith. Had there been substantial repression it would be one thing, but Milosevic and Karadzic did not claim this. Local disagreements over policy and services do not justify taking arms. Not for the Bosnian Serbs, not for our own militias. Refusal to vote, in any event, hardly licenses revolution. If the aim of political action is justice and the common good, we are required to ask whether the good to be achieved is sufficiently weighty to justify the threat to those with whom we share a common living space.

For the third-party spectator, neither history nor law justifies the mayhem in Bosnia before or after April of 1992. Still less do the claims of Serbian national identity justify rising up against government and neighbors.[5] From the perspective of the just war tradition they are of little substance, for if justice is no respecter of persons it is also no respecter of peoples. The most distressing component of

Karadzic's exchange with Zimmermann is his unproblematic assumption that Serbs are entitled to other people's goods *simply by virtue of being Serbs*. It is as though we came upon a rape in progress and the perpetrator were to defend himself by saying he was a man. So what. He is still not entitled to take from his victim what is not his. Even if he were to reply that men have sexual needs, that frustrating these needs leads to misery and desperation, he would still have no excuse. Personal or collective aspirations do not justify any attack on otherwise innocent persons or groups.

Both before and after the advent of Bosnian independence, Karadzic and his followers were engaged in criminal activities that the government had an obligation to put down. Before April 7, 1992, the failure of Belgrade to secure the peace in Bosnia confirmed the moral failure of the Milosevic government. Once independent, Bosnia and Herzegovina could, as a sovereign community with clearly defined borders, request and receive whatever aid seemed appropriate from the international community. As in the case of Kuwait, this would have required neither appeal to nor act of the United Nations. United States and European failure to go to Bosnia's aid reflects either indifference, confusion, or lack of moral resolve. Perhaps the critics of the Gulf War were not altogether mistaken in their doubts.

But that initial failure was allowed to stand. Karadzic, with the early help of Serbian paramilitary groups and the consent of Bosnia's neighbors, took control of some seventy precent of the republic's territory. In the eyes of the just war tradition this satisfies the "self-help test," with the rebels acquiring "belligerent rights and an equality of status with the government." (Walzer, 1992: 96) On this account, what would have been aiding a recognized member of the international community came to be seen as a potential intervention, and interventions are always suspect. In just war terms they are typically guilty of violating one or more of the criteria for *jus ad bellum*. Consider Operation Urgent Fury, the American incursion into Grenada in October 1983. The expressed purpose of landing some three thousand troops on the small Caribbean island was to rescue several hundred medical students, said to be threatened by a recent coup. Although he considers it a successful intervention, Richard Haass seconds what many thought at the time, that the Reagan administration took advantage of the situation "to replace a government friendly toward Cuba and the Soviet Union with one more pro-Western and democratic ... and to show that the United States could still act effectively." (Haass, 1994: 25) The students were a pretext that allowed the United States to claim an interest in the situation and the authority to act. But if the students were in little danger, and the real intention was changing the political balance, then there was no genuine authority. In lieu of proper authority there was no justification for interfering in the political life of another sovereign country. Without cause the act was illicit.

Two other of Haass's examples, Panama and Somalia, display violations of different just war criteria. As "the largest military engagement of U.S. forces up to that point since Vietnam," (Haass, 1994: 30) Operation Just Cause was out of all proportion to the injury received or the good to be done. This is not to say that Noriega is a good guy; he's a murderous, drug-trafficking, dictatorial criminal. But he is only one criminal, and not particularly worse than our homegrown varieties. In order to arrest him the United States deployed 25,000 troops and air forces, including a stealth bomber. (Haass, 1994: 31) Because of press restrictions, there is very little sense of the casualties and collateral damages, though they are estimated to have been noteworthy. Imagine the outcry had the ATF used this amount of firepower against the Branch Davidians. Overkill in all of its worst senses. Did Mr. Bush escape scrutiny because the civilians killed and rendered homeless were not U.S. civilians, but only Latinos? This does not speak well for the president or the rest of us.

Somalia began as a humanitarian mission, but in the summer of 1993 came to be "nothing less than nation-building." (Haass, 1994: 45) Not only do we lack the authority to build someone else's nation, but any such mission was destined to fail the demand for a reasonable hope of success. Nation-building takes time and enormous reserves of money and resources, none of which Mr. Clinton had a mandate to expend on Somalia, even if the United States had had the authority to do so. To attempt it with inadequate forces, in the face of belligerent factions on the ground, was to embrace failure and gross political embarrassment. Even a well-intentioned operation can become an occasion for regret and recrimination. The strictures on interventions are well observed.

Recently, however, Walzer has argued that "nonintervention is not an absolute moral rule," but one that may, and in the case of Bosnia must, be overridden "to put a stop to actions that, to use an old-fashioned but accurate phrase, 'shock the conscience' of humankind. . . . Active opposition to massacre and massive deportation," he concludes, "is morally necessary." (1995: 36–38) Sovereignty, and with it the principle of nonintervention, are central to a just political order, and thus to the possibility of justice in war. Nonetheless, Walzer seems to argue, there may come a point when conflicts become unintelligible as political actions. This he takes to be the case in Bosnia. The nationalist aspirations of Karadzic and his followers are not creating political problems, they *are* the problem. They license what can only be called bestiality, a condition, Aristotle noted, more horrifying than vice because what once distinguished us from the inhuman has been willfully eradicated. (*EN*: 1150a) The appropriate analogy is with a cancer threatening the viability of the entire body politic. Whatever its origins, we do what we can to kill it off, and the cancer itself has no claim to justice against our assaults. "It isn't enough, to wait until the tyrants, the zealots, and the bigots have done their filthy work and then rush food and medicine to the ragged survivors," insists Walzer. "Whenever the filthy work can be stopped, it should be stopped. And if not by us, the supposedly decent people of this world, then by whom?" (1995: 41) The conflict in Bosnia, he implies, is a cancer that will spread to the conscience of us all.

To deplore the enormity of the evils perpetrated in Bosnia and to wish them stopped is the only human response. Still, worrying about authority and the reasonable hope for success is not, as Walzer suggests, a matter of "reciting high-minded principles." (1995: 41) Reasonable hope of success is not simply a matter of political prudence but a measure of the preference rightly shown by a community for the people who make up its military and the citizens who will be asked to make sacrifices in exchange for deploying forces. As Walzer admits, intervention can quickly become coercion, and the history of such coercions accounts in no small measure for what drives nationalism, be it in Serbia, Kashmir, or Northern Ireland. The chaos of war, which generates new and unpredictable animosities on top of the old, works against our best attempts to imagine an equitable outcome, or to propose plans for securing it. Face-to-face with reports of execution, rape, and the consequences of ethnic cleansing, the pressure becomes enormous to do something, anything, to make it stop. But will the lives lost in intervening seem a noble sacrifice when we watch the spectacle of the saved devouring the children of their oppressors? We should beware of giving in to the Medea syndrome that tempts us to sacrifice innocents in the face of an intolerable evil. Even when scandalized by the enormities perpetrated abroad, the insistence on hope for success remains as a break on intervention.

But in fact, the situation was made more complicated than Walzer's argument accounts for by United Nations Resolution 713, adopted on September 25, 1991, which established an arms embargo on the whole of what was then Yugoslavia. The expressed purpose was to minimize the violence and contain the war in Croatia, and these were laudable objectives. Nonetheless, the justice of the embargo was questionable, even at the time. If the conflict then under-way between Croatia and Serbia was a civil war, then the embargo shifted the balance in favor of Serbia, which had inherited the bulk of the Yugoslavian National Army's munitions and materiel. If Croatia and Serbia were sovereign states, then the embargo begged the question of justice in favor of Serbia by denying Croatia the opportunity to defend itself. This should have been particularly offensive given the conduct of the Serbs, who had already displayed the willingness to attack civilian targets and to condone atrocities. In any event, the embargo violated the just war constraints on intervention. The claim that it stopped, or minimized, the fighting is disingenuous in the extreme. The foreseeable result was a redirection of energies against Bosnia, where the whittling away of people and their homes was hardly less repulsive for being more leisurely.

After April 7, 1992, when the United States and most of Europe recognized Bosnia as a sovereign state, the embargo remained, and this is extremely puzzling. From the perspective of the United States and the European Community, there now existed at least four sover-eign entities: Yugoslavia, consisting of the republics of Serbia and Montenegro; Slovenia; Croatia; and Bosnia and Herzegovina. The entity against which the original embargo was established no longer existed. The successor state, the new Yugoslavia, might have been a legitimate object of embargo insofar as the behavior of the Milosevic government toward Croatia and Bosnia was an affront to interna-tional standards of political justice. But insofar as they were applied to Croatia and Bosnia, the embargoes stood in need of further justifica-tion. For part and parcel of sovereignty is the responsibility for defense, and this responsibility had been acknowledged at least tacitly in the formal act of recognizing the new republics.

It is worth reflecting for a moment on the logic of the situation. Had the international community not acknowledged the new states, then it would have been possible to consider the conflicts in Croatia and

Bosnia as parts of an ongoing Yugoslavian civil war. Under those circumstances, as indicated above, neutrality would be dictated, though it would still have been legitimate to restrain interventions by others, including the United Nations. This is the point being made by those critics calling for a "level playing field." But with recognition, the argument from civil war neutrality can no longer be made. At the beginning of April 1992, the case for civil war in Bosnia was very weak. The conflicts in Slovenia and Croatia had seriously altered the status of the Belgrade government, and though many of the immediate players were native to Bosnia, they had cast their lot, as Karadzic demonstrates, with Serbia. They were the first wave of a foreign attack even more murderous in its hopes than the Iraqis in Kuwait. In light of the Gulf War, Izetbetgovic and the majority of Bosnians voting for independence might have expected a similar outcry from the international community. They could at least have expected an end to the arms embargo, which now constituted an intervention in their sovereign affairs.

The mere declaration of a Bosnian Serb Republic should not have been an impediment to international support for the Bosnian government, for at the beginning of the Bosnian war this was not a matter of taking territory, but laying claim to those parts of Bosnia inhabited by Serbs. The ersatz Serb republics in Bosnia and Croatia were no more legitimate than an Aryan Republic would be in the mountains of Idaho. Would we, after all, tolerate the Canadian government doing nothing to curtail shipments of arms to the Michigan Militia, should it take up arms against the government? Would we accept the Canadian excuse that it didn't want to take sides? This hardly seems credible. Nor do most of the other arguments offered from time to time by the UN, the Europeans, and the United States. For example, to justify their refusal to call in air strikes, UNPROFOR emphasized "the difficulty of hitting Bosnian Serb Army gun emplacements," but David Rieff seems on the mark in pointing out that everyone on the scene in Sarajevo "knew the guns were sitting ducks for air attack . . . the guns stood in plain view, often only a few meters from the road." (Rieff, 1995: 159) There was, throughout, an equally disingenuous ring to professed fears of Russian involvement.

At the onset of the conflict, the proper response would have been lifting the embargo and supplying aid directly to the Bosnian government. Furthermore, it would have been legitimate to restrain the Milosevic government from aiding Karadzic and his followers. Failure here is particularly offensive given the conduct of the war. Claims and counterclaims about who raped whom and whether or not there were death camps could not, at the time, be settled, but there was no doubt that General Mladic's artillery rained shells down on civilian targets. Had there been *no* rapes, *no* ethnic cleansing, the conduct of the military operations alone demonstrated that the Bosnian Serbs were engaged in terrorism and mass murder. The on-again, off-again Clinton strategy of arming Bosnia and striking against the Serbs would, if restricted to Milosevic's aid to the separatists, have been the just strategy. That our European allies refused to acknowledge what their own recognition of the former Yugoslav republics implied was, at the very least, a gross failure of moral analysis. That the United States failed to exercise its considerable powers of persuasion says much about the political immaturity of the Clinton administration, and even more about sacrificing the demands of justice to the so-called realities of power politics.

For in the end, the European Community and the United States both allowed inaction and neglect to do the work of policy. A comparatively porous embargo made it possible for Franjo Tudjman to build the Croatian army into a formidable fighting force, while the economic embargo on Serbia made it more and more difficult for Milosevic to maintain his ascendency at home, much less supplement the resources of the Bosnian Serbs. All the while a steady flow of small arms and Mujahedeen fighters from Afghanistan and elsewhere kept the Bosnian government army on its feet. The remarkably swift and ruthlessly successful Croatian offensive that retook the Krajina in the summer of 1995 may have set in motion the move to negotiation, but it finally took a systematic NATO air offensive to crush the military will of the Bosnian Serbs and pressure them into accepting Milosevic as their negotiator in Dayton.

And what of the so-called Dayton Accord and the prospects for Bosnia? Having earlier chastised the excesses of our political science experts, it would be unwise here to indulge in the parlor game of predictions, and ultimately that is not the focus of this essay. Whatever the outcome of the ongoing conflict between Bosnia and its neighbors—and the conflict, in one form or another, is sure to be ongoing—it should be remembered as one more failure for the politics of power and self-interest. In her contribution to this volume, Professor Elshtain ruefully remarks that, "the credibility of the United Nations, and of the United States as the leader of the Western alliance, has sustained a series of hammer blows from which it will take years to recover."

(above, p. 46) This remains true even with the implementation of the Dayton Accord, for the Bosnians and many of those who looked on will not be able to forget that the major powers tolerated four years of nationalist terrorism without recent precedent; made excuses for their own refusal to act on the obvious implications of their own policy decisions and professed values; and finally acted only under the mounting pressure of public outrage at the bestiality of the Bosnian Serbs. To suggest that Srebrenica was one massacre too many will invariably provoke some cynics to ask "How many massacres aren't too many?" When American diplomats congratulate themselves for turning the Bosnian Serbs' control of seventy percent of the territory into fifty-one percent control for the Bosnian government, the same cynics are likely to wonder why anyone should be congratulated for giving away half of his neighbor's house in the first place. Credibility is sometimes at the mercy of external forces, but in this case the loss of credibility is a direct function of the failure to do justice.

Recovering credibility, in the Balkans and elsewhere, will depend on the willingness of our political leaders to do justice for justice's sake. This will mean bearing with the causalities that are already beginning to mount, from landmines, snipers, and the dangers that attend any military action. It will mean, even more importantly, eschewing excuses and pursuing justice without the arbitrary limit of twelve months or a dozen years. Finally, Serbia, Croatia, and Bosnia should be held to the most rigorous conceivable standard of postwar justice, and this cannot be done unless those who would help them are consistently mindful of what justice demands. The obstacles to recreating the communal life of the Yugoslav republics before the breakup are enormous. Nothing can guarantee success; memory is long in these lands. But however they are reconstituted, the future governments of Bosnia and its neighbors will need to prove *themselves* trustworthy to their own citizens, of whatever religious or ethnic background. Every failure to do justice now makes its future claims that much harder to sustain, but sustain them we must to have any chance of building a trustworthy international system. This is a hard demand. It means putting away those identifications, friendships, and alliances that tempt us to excuse injustice in ourselves and others. And it will mean dramatic change, at home and abroad. For justice may be easy in a foreign desert, but it will insinuate itself at home, in the army, the hospital, the cathedral, anywhere and everywhere that conscience is constrained to act.

Bosnia and the Muslim Critique of Modernity

5

John Kelsay

In contemporary discussions of justice and war, Islam is in the dock. Of this, there can be little doubt. The association of various groups claiming the mantle of Islam with kidnapping, terror bombing, and other violations of just war norms runs deep in the consciousness of Europe and North America. The judgment that follows—that Islamic practice and "just war thinking" are at opposite poles—finds expression at every level of Western discourse.

With respect to popular media, consider the following: Less than twenty-four hours after the Oklahoma City bombing, newspapers throughout the United States ran headlines asserting that the leading suspects in a criminal investigation were "radical" Muslim groups. Grasping for explanations of a seemingly inexplicable act, journalistic accounts gravitated toward an Islamic "other," widely viewed as willing to kill and be killed in ways that defy ordinary standards of justice. When the investigation moved on to persons and groups more typical of the cultural and geographic heartland of the U.S. itself, the sense of shock was palpable: Americans, too, can sometimes do terrible things.

Again, with respect to scholarly opinion, the following is hardly unusual:

> In Islam the struggle of good and evil very soon acquired political and
> even military dimensions. Muhammad, it will be recalled, was not

only a prophet and a teacher, like the founders of other religions; he was also the head of a polity and a community, a ruler and a soldier. Hence his struggle involved a state and its armed forces. If the fighters in the war for Islam, the holy war "in the path of God," are fighting for God, it follows that their opponents are fighting against God. And since God is in principle the sovereign, the supreme head of the Islamic State—and the Prophet and, after the Prophet, the caliphs are his viceregents—then God as sovereign commands the army. The army is God's army and the enemy is God's enemy. The duty of God's soldiers is to dispatch God's enemies as quickly as possible to the place where God will chastise them—that is to say, the afterlife. (Lewis, 1990: 49)

Crafted by no less an authority than Bernard Lewis, this passage serves as background for an explanation of contemporary "Muslim rage." Thus we are given to understand that acts that violate ordinary standards of justice in war flow from the roots of the Islamic tradition itself. Muhammad's war tradition—the Islamic war tradition—operates with a conception of collective religious guilt. One reading this account would hardly know of the efforts of classical jurists, much less of contemporary Muslims, to deal with Muhammad's charge to his troops: "Do not cheat or commit treachery, nor should you mutilate anyone or kill children." (Khadduri, 1966: 75–76) Lewis's reader can only conclude that Islam is a tradition that authorizes violations of just war standards, and that in the name of God.

It is tiresome to multiply examples. Let the reader bear with one more, however. With respect to discussions of policy, one reads with interest a pair of reports developed by staff working for the Republican members of a House of Representatives Task Force on Terrorism and Unconventional Warfare during 1992 and 1993.[1] The first entitled "Iran's European Springboard?" is concerned with a question of indisputable strategic importance. Will Iran, in its quest for leadership among Muslims, seek to exploit the suffering of Bosnian Muslims? According to the authors of the report, the answer is yes. The argument proceeds with a number of interesting observations concerning the possibilities for Iran to use the Bosnian conflict as a way to increase its influence with disaffected Muslim populations in Europe and North America, as well as to discredit other "Muslim" states.

As estimations of actors in the "great game" of international politics is one of the tasks of policy-makers, one can hardly object to the questions raised in a report. It is instructive, however, to read on and consider that, as the authors develop their suggestions about Iranian objectives, they (1) turn the Bosnian Muslims from victims whose tragic fate may be exploited into active representatives of a long-standing drive of Islam to dominate the Western world; and (2) present an understanding of Islamic tradition that makes the efforts of Muslims seeking to participate as citizens of the Western democracies an anomaly. (HRRC, 1992)

At this point, one feels the authors are no longer dealing strictly in matters of policy; they are making normative judgments about Islamic tradition. Thus, one can hardly read "Iran's European Springboard?" without thinking of the argument of Serbian fighters: Islam and Christianity (or more generally, Western culture) cannot share the same geographic and political space. This is so because Islam demands that its adherents strive to build a political entity in which the head of state is a Muslim and Islam the established state religion. Muslims who seek to define themselves as "secular," or as participants in a religious and moral tradition ready, along with other traditions, to offer guidance in accord with the spiritual needs of modern humanity, are not real Muslims. Islam and the West are mutually exclusive realities.

When the same staff followed "Iran's European Springboard?" with a report entitled "The New Islamist Internationale," the further development of their position was clear. Islam is the new enemy of the U.S. and its allies. Policies should be crafted along the lines of an analogy between the new conflict and the great power rivalry of the Cold War period. The new enemy, like the old, seeks to build an international, ideologically founded alliance whose aim is the defeat of the Western democracies. Again, like the old enemy, Islam is ready to attack Western interests by any means available. The Islamist enemy will seek to advance its position through acts of terror aimed not only at power elites, but at the industrial and popular bases of European and North American civilizations. Muslims and others who protest against such depictions of the Islamic tradition are naïve, at best. In the post–Cold War world, Islam is in the dock—ironically, even in the instance of the undisputed and tragic case of anti-Muslim warfare in Bosnia-Herzegovina. (HRRC, 1993)

It is not my purpose to offer an apologia for Islam against such a trend. Muslims do have questions to answer, for themselves and others, about the relationship of practices by certain contemporary groups to the Islamic tradition. I do, however, think that the tendency to view Islam as inherently opposed to the just war tradition has unfortunate consequences. In particular, the current view of Islam prevents those who would think about justice and war from hearing the wisdom of a religious and moral tradition which has, through the long history of its development, fostered a deep and serious set of reflections on the purposes of and rules for war. It is my hope to encourage such hearing, through some reflections on the ways the conflict in Bosnia relates to Islamic writing about religion, society, and justice in war. As I see it, this requires two steps. First, we must come to understand that many Muslims see Bosnia as the latest (and to this time, most profound) example of certain crucial weaknesses in the social-cultural structure of "Western" or, more precisely, European and North American society. To gain perspective on this point, I take the reader through a line of writing in which Muslims over the past century have engaged in a critique of various aspects of that society, generally characterized in terms of "modernity."

The second step flows from the first. Having grasped that many Muslims see Bosnia in the context of the failure of modernity, I turn to some specific applications of the Islamic tradition on justice and war. As I shall argue, Bosnia makes clear the ways that the Islamic tradition pushes us to focus on the ways particular conceptions of the rules of war—in particular, the *jus in bello* criteria of proportionality and discrimination—relate to larger issues of the nature of justice and the form of a good society. I argue that the momentum of Islamic thinking about justice and war leads to an emphasis on such *jus ad bellum* concerns as right authority and just cause, and ultimately to discussion of how conceptions of the nature and destiny of human beings set a framework for discussions of war. In the end, Bosnia suggests that it is not just Islam but European and North American civilization that are in the dock. That, I shall argue, is the implication when we connect Muslim critiques of modernity with the discussion of justice and war.

Modernity and Islam

Let us admit at the outset that both of our terms can bear multiple interpretations. In the case of modernity, I shall be thinking of selected aspects of the type of society associated first with Western Europe and North America since the sixteenth or seventeenth centuries; here, I shall draw on some ideas from Max Weber, Talcott Parsons, and

Richard L. Rubenstein. My selection is dictated, in part, by the arguments developed in a line of Muslim writers that includes (among others) Jamal al-Din al-Afghani, Muhammad Iqbal, the Ayatollah Khomeini, and Alija Ali Izetbegovic, President of the Bosnian Republic.

From Weber's analysis, let us take the notion that one of the central tendencies of modern society lies in the advance of instrumental rationality (*zweckrationalität*).[2] As Weber described it, instrumental rationality involves a particular type of means-end reasoning; in an exemplary study of Weber's analyses, David Little suggests we think in terms of a specifically "this-worldly and relativistic form of consequentialist reasoning." (Little, 1974: 5) Further borrowing from Little, we may distinguish five specific characteristics of instrumental rationality. First, it justifies actions in consequentialist terms. Results make the difference in determining the nature of a rational or justified act.

Second, instrumental rationality refers to formal or procedural norms that are thought to issue in results that can be quantified. To use an economic example, we might consider the way that participants in a stock market agree to observe certain formal norms, for instance, a prohibition on insider trading, because experience shows that these norms function to increase the efficiency of the market, making for greater profit for greater numbers of participants.

Third, instrumental rationality is "polytheistic." Modern societies, characterized by the advance of instrumental rationality, are organized into spheres, each having its own formal norms and modes of measuring results, its "gods." There is no way, rationally speaking, of resolving conflicts between the spheres and their diverse norms. Conflicts between the spheres of law and of economics, or between the market and family life, for example, are inevitable. Where persons or groups stand with respect to these reflects, not a universally valid and rationally established norm, but their own, arbitrary choices.

Fourth, instrumental rationality is deliberately impersonal. That is, in fact, its genius. In politics, for example, the modern magistrate

> performs his duty best when he acts without regard to the person in question, *sine ira et studio,* without hate and without love, without personal predilection and therefore without grace, but sheerly in accordance with the factual, material responsibility imposed by his

calling, and not as the result of any personal relationship. (Weber, 1978:1, 600)

As Weber had it, the same would be true of an economic planner, an employee of a state bureaucracy, or a military officer. Instrumental rationality demands adherence to formal norms, for the sake of results measured in terms of increased efficiency and (especially) material gain for society as a whole.

As this last suggests, instrumental rationality is "this-worldly." With this fifth (and final) characteristic of instrumental rationality, we understand Weber to point to the way that "modernity" signifies the assignment of priority to material, as opposed to spiritual, well-being.

For Weber, the association of instrumental rationality and modern society was a descriptive reality or a fact of life. As is well known, his insight into this aspect of modernity is premised on the notion that things were not always so. *The Protestant Ethic and the Spirit of Capitalism* makes the point that the development of a society governed by instrumental rationality is related to a breakthrough in religious ethics, signaled in particular by the teaching of Reformed Christianity. Without rehearsing the details of Weber's argument, we may simply summarize his view along these lines: the world of instrumental rationality came into existence on the wings of a particular tradition of religious ethics. Once set in motion, however, instrumental rationality does not need that tradition. Ironically, instrumental rationality pushes its religious-moral base into the background, declaring it, in a sense, to be irrelevant.

In certain contexts, Weber could speak of this phenomenon in melancholy terms. The form of rationality legitimized by Reformed Christianity "needs its support no longer. The rosy blush of [Calvinism's] laughing heir, the Enlightenment, seems also to be irretrievably fading, and the idea of duty in one's calling prowls about in our lives like the ghost of dead religious beliefs." (Weber, 1958: 182) Or, in another place: "The fate of our times is characterized by . . . the disenchantment of the world. . . . Culture becomes even more senseless . . . the world has to appear even more fragmented and devalued. . . . The result is a 'housing hard as steel' and all that is left is the darkness inside an iron cage." (Weber, 1981: xxvi–xxvii) Weber's evaluation of the advance of instrumental rationality was ambiguous. For him, the development of modern social forms enables human beings to attain certain goods. However, the gains come at a large price, and in some ways, those who participate in the project of modernity gain the world while losing their souls. As some have put it, the society governed by instrumental rationality yields "technical humanity." Modernity encourages the type of character whose normative orientation has to do with the "tyranny of the numbers" rather than the sustenance of the soul.

From Talcott Parsons, let us take the notion that modernity is characterized by the phenomenon of "differentiation." Writing on "Christianity and Modern Industrial Society," Parsons argued that the development of spiritual and moral life in the West should be described in terms of this phenomenon in a "double sense." In the first, one speaks of differentiation "within religious systems themselves." Here, Parsons points to the development of alternative notions of religious practice within Christianity, understood as the civilizational or cultural religion of Europe and North America. In the second (and for our purposes more significant) sense, differentiation refers to the process of distinguishing "the religious element from nonreligious elements in the more general system of action." This leads Parsons to conclude that "the general developmental trend may be said to be from fusions of religious and nonreligious components in the same action structures," resulting in the "increasingly clear differentiation between multiple spheres of action." (Parsons, 1972: 37)

Here, Parsons is describing the institutional aspect of Weber's instrumental rationality. As we have seen, the project of modernity, understood in terms of *zweckrationalität*, lends itself to an increasing distinction between various "spheres" of human activity. In every case, the recognition and validation of a particular sphere (law, economy, politics, religious life) is enhanced by the development of a clear set of formal norms that are thought to increase efficiency, measured in terms of progress toward the fulfillment of a given set of interests. "Modernity," in this respect, stands for a type of society in which diverse human interests stand increasingly "on their own feet." Correlatively, we may speak of modernity as a way of organizing society that enhances the ability of persons, as individual agents, to pursue a variety of legitimate interests, and to organize the relations between those in terms of a freely chosen life plan.

With respect to religious ethics, there is no greater symbol of the progress of differentiation than the separation of church and state, or more precisely, the distinction of the authority of religious institutions from that of political, economic, and legal institutions. As Parsons sees it, this insight draws into focus at least one aspect of modernity that Weber did not see. That is, modernity is not simply a matter of the march of instrumental rationality, particularly insofar as that phrase signals the priority of spiritual over material interests. The differentiation of religious and nonreligious institutions is itself a spiritual value, signaling a process of "upgrading" whereby the institutional practice of Christianity comes to adhere more closely to its original ideal. (Parsons, 1972: 49) Christianity, as Parsons sees it, speaks of the relations of individual persons to God. Insofar as the process of differentiation is joined with those notions that moderns speak of in terms of "freedom of conscience" and "religious liberty," there can be no question that modernity, for Parsons, signifies an enhancement of the spiritual life of human beings.

There are certainly ways to minimize the differences between Weber's and Parsons' analyses. As Parsons himself understood, Weber's focus on economic activity influenced him more in the direction of the material values of modernity, and less toward the discussion of modernity's spiritual gains. And, as we shall see, the Muslim critique of modernity rests on connections between the two: the progress of instrumental rationality, and the differentiation between religious and nonreligious spheres of activity, go hand in hand to create a society with peculiar weaknesses. Some of these begin to emerge when we take up a third depiction of modernity, drawn from the work of Richard L. Rubenstein.

From Rubenstein let us draw the depiction of modernity as an "age of triage." In the work that bears that title, Rubenstein understands himself to develop Weber's analysis by connecting the progress of instrumental rationality with concerns about population growth. (Rubenstein, 1981; see also Rubenstein 1975 and 1992) Given that the former indicates a way of thinking about social life that grants sovereignty to various spheres of activity, and that legitimates this arrangement in terms of estimates of increased efficiency and return for society as a whole, one might ask: Just how far can "society" stretch, in terms of disseminating the returns from increased efficiency to actual human beings?

Rubenstein's analysis is haunted by the specter of millions upon millions of people who, for a host of reasons, have been excluded from participation in the modernization of specific societies. The argument is stated in a variety of ways; for our purposes, the following will suffice. If modernity has to do with modes of organizing life legitimated in terms of instrumental rationality's concern for increased efficiency and return for society as a whole, we must expect that modernity will involve attempts to control the range of populations understood as legitimate participants in particular societies. Efficiency and return are not always well served by conceptions of an unbounded or universal society. At least under certain circumstances, the project of modernity will involve "triage" decisions concerning who has a legitimate claim upon the resources of a particular society and who does not. For a variety of reasons, certain persons and groups come to be defined as "surplus people," unnecessary and/or undesirable in terms of the progress of instrumental rationality within a given social unit. In certain cases, the canons of instrumental rationality will legitimate attempts to limit and/or eliminate such persons and groups, and thus to deal with the problem of an "overdemand" for the goods produced by modernization in specific social contexts.

Rubenstein's work suggests a wide range of instances in which "triage mentality" is at work: the enclosures controversy, the Armenian genocide, the Holocaust, and the Soviet Gulags are only a few of the relevant cases. For our purposes, however, the contribution of Rubenstein lies in his depiction of the "dark side" of modernity. If, following Parsons in particular, we might understand modernity to advance a certain spiritual claim concerning the freedom of individuals, particularly in religious affairs, we may at the same time note that modernity involves a tightening of the boundaries within which such freedom is exercised. As Rubenstein has it, when societies find the progress of modernity stalled, particularly in times of economic duress, they seek ways to increase efficiency and return that involve limiting the numbers of those with legitimate claims to a share of social goods. This task is accomplished, in certain cases, by defining persons and groups as "outside the universe of moral obligation." Considerations of race, ethnicity, and religious identity prove convenient in drawing the boundaries between those with legitimate claims to share in the progress of modernity, and those whose claims are not legitimate.

Rubenstein himself interprets the conflict in Bosnia through the lens of the "triage" thesis. In effect, the United Nations, the European Community, and NATO all function as "silent partners" in the efforts of the Serbians to create an "ethnically pure" region for themselves in Bosnia-Herzegovina. The question, from Rubenstein's perspective, is why the UN, E.C., and NATO failed in taking decisive action to deter the Serbian forces. As Rubenstein has it, persons and groups struggling to define themselves and secure their place in post–Cold War Europe strive to establish boundaries of legitimate participation. Who will have a say, and hence a share in the fruits of modern society? The supposition is that everyone and every group cannot be included; lines must be drawn. One convenient way to accomplish this, given the background of European culture, is to draw on the fact of religious difference. For Rubenstein, Islam now occupies the unenviable position once belonging to Judaism within Europe. And there is nothing strange about this; indeed, there is a certain inevitability about the project to delimit the influence of Muslims in the project of defining the post–Cold War European reality. (cf. Rubenstein, 1993)

Whether Rubenstein's analysis is correct is not the point at issue in this essay. More significant is the interpretation of the Bosnian conflict in terms of the "dark side" of modernity, and its relation to a certain line of Muslim thought developed over the last century. As we shall see, Muslim writers have responded to each aspect of modernity outlined above, thus developing a comprehensive critique of European and North American society.

With respect to instrumental rationality, for example, it is instructive to consider the writing of the "father" of Islamic revivalism, Jamal al-Din, known as al-Afghani. Particularly in "The Truth about the Neicheri Sect and an Explanation of the Neicheris," (1880–81) al-Afghani is concerned to criticize the Western fascination with material progress, and in doing so to forestall attempts by Muslims to reform Islam along lines intended to stress its agreement with modern, especially scientific rationality. (Keddie, 1983: 130–174) The term "neicher" is an adaptation into Arabic of the English "nature"; its use in al-Afghani's text is occasioned by the way that the great Indian Muslim, Ahmad Khan (among others), employed the word to signify a reform of Islamic tradition.

Do not be deceived, al-Afghani writes to his Muslim audience, there is nothing new about this so-called reform. The essential ideas of the "Neicheri Sect" were promulgated in Ancient Greece. "Neicheri" is a philosophy of materialism. It sees existence as a matter of chance; with respect to human beings, the "neicheriyya" see the world as a closed horizon. Life, that is, has no telos. There is no overarching destiny for Creation. Indeed, to speak of Creation, with its connotations of the purpose and providence of a Divine Lord, is prima facie a mistake, on the materialist view.

Even so in the modern versions of this "philosophy." In the interests of material progress, the neicheriyya downplay the spiritual and moral aspects of human beings. They push for the formation of a society focused entirely on technical knowledge. In doing so, they undermine the possibility of true civilization, which finds the basis of its science (and, by extension, its economy, politics, and law) in the special nature of humanity, as understood by all legitimate religious traditions, especially Islam.

Al-Afghani's focus, in this as other texts, is on the ways that Islam provides an enduring foundation for human progress. To this end, Islam sets forth three beliefs and three qualities, each set interdependent with the other "six-sided castle of human happiness." (Keddie, 1983: 148) With respect to beliefs, al-Afghani writes, three things are essential: first, "that there is a terrestrial angel (man), and that he is the noblest of creatures"; second, "the certainty that his community is the noblest one"—a kind of group feeling that provides a sense of identity and "place" in orienting persons toward the world; and third, "the firm belief that man has come into the world in order to acquire accomplishments worthy of transferring him to a world more excellent," in other words, a notion of Divine Judgment. (Keddie, 1983: 141)

Correlatively, three qualities have overriding significance. First, a sense of shame—through this, persons are deterred from engaging in ignoble acts; second, trustworthiness, especially understood to include fairness and integrity on the part of those holding power—a kind of public trust, as it were; third, truthfulness and honesty—in some sense, the "private" or "personal" aspect of trustworthiness. In another sense, truthfulness seems related to a notion of humility, in that it involves a recognition that "each man, to secure his interests and repel evils, needs to appeal for the help of his fellow men and must seek their guidance." The limits of personal ability and the quality of truthfulness interact with one another, since the help one is moved or required to seek is only useful from "those who have the quality of truthfulness." (Keddie, 1983: 147)

In any case, al-Afghani's advice to the Muslims of his day involves a warning about and criticism of the rationality associated with modernity. In assigning priority to material welfare, instrumental rationality breaks the link between human nature as this-worldly and human nature as tied to notions of eternal destiny. In classical Islamic terminology, the problem is the relations between this world—

dunya—and the "other" world—*akhira*. The unity of the two lies in religion—*din*—which "binds" or "links," or in this case, "holds together" humanity as a unified being.

The notion that instrumental rationality fails to unify the various aspects or interests of the human being leads us on to Parsons's refinement of instrumental rationality. Modernity involves social "differentiation," in which religious interests, in particular, are distinguished from nonreligious interests, the better to serve the diversity of human agents by providing space for autonomous action. Consider these lines from an influential Muslim critic of modernity, the Ayatollah Khomeini:

> There is a great difference between all the man-made forms of government in the world, on the one hand—whatever their precise nature—and a divine government, on the other hand, which follows divine law. Governments that do not base themselves on divine law conceive of justice only in the natural realm; you will find them concerned only with the prevention of disorder and not with the moral refinement of the people. Whatever a person does in his own home is of no importance, so long as he causes no disorder in the street. In other words, people are free to do as they please at home. (Khomeini, 1981: 330)

To the man-made he contrasts "divine governments," which

> set themselves the task of making man into what he should be. In his unredeemed state, man is like an animal, even worse than the other animals. Left to his own devices, he will always be inferior to the animals, for he surpasses them in passion, evil, and rapacity. As originally created, man is superior to all other beings, but at the same time, his capacities for passion, anger, and other forms of evil are virtually boundless. For example, if a person acquires a house, he will begin to desire another house. If a person conquers a country, he will begin plotting to conquer another country. And if a person were to conquer the entire globe, he would begin planning the conquest of the moon or Mars. Men's passions and covetousness, then, are unlimited, and it was in order to limit men, to tame them, that the prophets were sent. (Khomeini, 1981: 331)

As Khomeini concludes: the aim of Islam, as of the prophets, is "to fashion true and complete human beings." (1981: 332)

It takes little reflection to understand the relation of Khomeini's statements to Parsons's depiction of modernity as a process of differentiation. Left to their own devices, that is, to act autonomously, human beings will sink to the lowest common denominator. Without the guidance of (true) religion, there will be little impetus toward the attainment of nobility in character. Indeed, the differentiated society is actually self-undermining. It limits its interest in morality to a minimalist ethic, by which certain absolutely basic norms are enforced. It lacks, however, any way to encourage the development of persons characterized by a willingness to sacrifice self in the name of a higher good. Can a society that allows maximum freedom for the pursuit of material welfare, as a personal and autonomous life plan, find within itself sufficient resources to survive the challenges of political life? How will its citizens perform under duress—say, in times of war? And what sort of leaders will arise out of the "free" life of a differentiated society? Will political leadership, for example, be about devotion to the public good? Or will it be simply another way of securing material welfare?

One could go on in this regard. Let us turn, however, to another aspect of Parsons's depiction of modernity. The differentiation between religious and nonreligious spheres of activity involves a kind of "upgrading," Parsons argues. The autonomy of the spheres, and thus of individual agents, is a better approximation of central ideals of the Christian tradition. With its separation of church and state, and its correlative affirmation of freedom of conscience and religious liberty, modernity represents a real advance in the spiritual life of humanity.

It is clear what Khomeini might say to this line of thought. It involves a false estimation of what humanity is likely to do with its freedom. While the late Ayatollah, in line with most of the Islamic tradition, would eschew Christian notions of the fallen nature of humanity, he has his own way of estimating the spiritual and moral laxity of men and women. From this point of view, Parsons's analysis suggests naïvete. So far as Parsons's characterization of Christianity goes, Khomeini's general line would be that the religion of Jesus, no less than the religion of Muhammad, was *al-islam,* the active submission to the will of the one God, and involved notions of struggle against all forces that would corrupt and belittle the dignity of humanity. (Khomeini, 1981: 341; Kelsay, 1993: 29–42)

More interesting in some respects is a line of thought from Muhammad Iqbal. Writing in the 1920s, Iqbal's understanding of

Christianity was set by his experience as a student in Germany. Thinking primarily of Lutheran practice, Iqbal speaks in terms that suggest that Parsons may be correct about Christianity—that is, that from a Christian point of view a society that separates religious and nonreligious forms of authority may constitute "upgrading." (Iqbal, 1968) That only proves, however, how far short Christianity falls with respect to the true needs of humanity. "Modern" (or Western) humanity, writes Iqbal, is technical humanity. Or, if we like, we might say "humanity governed by instrumental rationality." As such, those societies characterized as "modern" are destined to fall; they do not and cannot meet the needs of humanity for a holistic existence. The human creature requires and accordingly seeks a way to integrate the various aspects of the self. At its simplest, this involves a search for unity between the soul and body. And this is precisely what Christianity denies. Iqbal cites, among other texts, the passage at Luke 20:27ff., which ends with the saying that those who attain to the resurrection from the dead "neither marry, nor are given in marriage . . . for they are like angels." From its insistence that the spheres of "law" and "religion" are distinct, to its gospel traditions that stress the otherworldly nature of human destiny, Christianity is a religion ill-suited to integrate the social and political needs of human beings with notions of spiritual value.[4] In this regard, Islam is uniquely suitable, provided it can answer its own, central question: Is the law of Islam capable of development? Does Islam, as Iqbal put it, include a principle of dynamism along with a principle of stability, so that it can grow along with the development of humanity?

Following Iqbal, then, one might agree with Parsons' analysis that modern civilization is in a sense the closest approximation in history to Christian civilization. Such agreement is hardly a comfort, however, since it implies the connection of Christian tradition to a form of society that lacks the integrity essential for human flourishing.

It is this line from Iqbal's writing that we find developed in the thought of Alija Ali Izetbegovic, President of the Bosnian Republic and our final example of an Islamic critique of modernity. The very title of Izetbegovic's treatise, *Islam Between East and West,* is inspired, as he indicates, by Iqbal's poetry. Simply put, Izetbegovic's argument is this: human beings are bipolar entities. They are body and soul, matter and spirit. They experience themselves as bound to this world, yet they are able to transcend its particulars through their imagination. The great pillars of modern society, scientific or technical rationality and Christian faith, in themselves reflect the bipolarity of humanity. The former is, like Weber's instrumental rationality, characteristically occupied with the workings of the material world, and is dedicated to improving the material welfare of human beings. The latter is oriented to the realm of the spirit, in particular as that realm stands for concerns about humanity's ultimate destiny in relation to a sacred, otherworldly reality.

One might say that Parsons's depiction of the differentiation between spheres of activity reflects this bipolarity, and thus that Parsons's further judgment that modernity constitutes a significant advance in the moral and spiritual life of humanity is founded on a critical aspect of human nature itself. That is not what Izetbegovic says, however. For him, bipolarity is not finally constitutive of human nature; it is, rather, a way of characterizing human experience. Matter and spirit, body and soul, material and spiritual welfare are ultimately held together as distinctive aspects of the experience of the one, human being. But to be human is to seek integrity in one's experience. Thus the differentiation of modernity, however suggestive as a way of understanding the diverse needs and interests of human beings, should only be considered as a prelude, an opportunity or challenge to achieve integrity. Human nature, and ultimately all reality, is one, characterized by unity or, more precisely, by the integration of particular aspects of existence into a whole. This, one might say, is the import of the affirmation of divine unity, *tawhid,* the most basic aspect of the message of Islam.

For Izetbegovic, Islam's contribution to human beings, particularly in the context of modernity, is the affirmation of this oneness with the divine. One need not become a Muslim, or even hear the message proclaimed in connection with the tradition of the Islamic community to understand this. With all Islamic tradition, Izetbegovic holds that *al-islam,* active submission to the will of the one God, is the natural religion of humanity. Its basic tenets can be grasped by all thinking beings.[5]

Despite the "natural" aspect of Islam, however, the consciousness of human integrity proves difficult to sustain. And thus, there is an advantage, even a necessity, about the mission of a particular community equipped with scriptural and other resources that enable the proclamation of *tawhid.* This describes the Islamic community; writing prior to the collapse of Yugoslavia and the subsequent struggles of his community, Izetbegovic sees the presence of Muslims in Europe as an especially fortuitous occurrence. From this vantage point, the historic mission of the Islamic community can be carried to the heart of modern society. Through its practice of prayer, by the very mode of its common life, and through its perspective on issues ranging from the relationship of scientific and artistic reason, to questions of the use of force, the Islamic community is destined to proclaim the unity or integrity of the human creature, and thus to play its part in the building of a culture dedicated to this ideal. "Islam suits man," as Izetbegovic puts it,

> because it recognizes the duality of his nature. Any different answer would stress only one side of human nature, thereby hindering the full sweep of human forces or bringing about their inner conflicts. That is why man is the most obvious argument of Islam. (1989: 228)

As *Islam Between East and West* clearly indicates, "Islam" is first and foremost a way for Izetbegovic to speak about the integration of various human interests. The community of Muslims bears witness to the necessity of and possibility for such integration, particularly in the context of forms of social order that explicitly separate material from spiritual welfare, and (as most Muslims would have seen it, in the case of communist regimes) make a systematic attempt to exclude concerns with the latter from public discourse.[6]

As Izetbegovic envisioned it in *Islam Between East and West,* the Muslims of Bosnia had before them a great cultural mission. Their task, like that of the Muslims in previous generations, was to serve as an "intermediary nation." In earlier times (Izetbegovic is thinking of the medieval period), Islam served as a bridge between "the ancient cultures and the West." Now, it must serve as a bridge enabling human beings to integrate the bipolar reality within which they live. The Islamic community, especially in Europe, has an historic opportunity to present humanity with a

> call to create a man harmonious in his soul and body and a society whose laws and socio-political institutions will maintain—and not violate—this harmony. Islam is, and should be, a permanent searching through history for a state of inward and outward balance. This is the aim of Islam today, and it is its specific historical duty in the future. (1989: xxxii)

For Izetbegovic, the mission of Bosnia's Muslims was to contribute an Islamic perspective in the search of human beings to find meaning and integrity in the context of modernity—to write, to speak, to participate as citizens in the institutions and associations characteristic of European and North American society. Persuasion and education were the means to be employed in speaking to an open and inquiring culture about the possibilities for a more secure spiritual and moral base.

One can read Izetbegovic only with a sense of sad irony in light of the role that Bosnia plays in the Muslim response to modernity, what Rubenstein depicted as an "age of triage." For Muslims, Bosnia illustrates the failure of modernity to fulfill its universal aspirations. Indeed, the claims of modernity to support freedom of conscience and human rights are a deception, covering over a deep unwillingness to deal with an Islamic "other." Early in the conflict, the Islamic press was warning that European Muslims should have "no doubt that all evidence points to the existence of an organized and well-planned drive by Christian Serbs to dislodge, disperse, destroy and massacre the Muslim population of Bosnia-Herzegovina." The author goes on to insist:

> It is also palpably clear that practically all European Governments . . . have connived at the horrendous crimes against humanity being committed by the Serbs. European governments are using delaying tactics and the U.N. and the E.C. as Trojan horses to hold attention and headlines, thereby giving the Serbs time to eliminate Islam from European soil. What is happening in Bosnia is an action replay of what happened in Spain some five hundred years ago. The 30 million Muslims now living in Europe must take note of this European/ Christian crusade in Bosnia-Herzegovina, which is ultimately an assault on all of us. (*Crescent International*, 1992: 1)

This statement, presented as a motion for consideration by the British Muslim Parliament, is echoed in a variety of Muslim media throughout the world. Thus the fate of Bosnian Muslims is seen as the "Muslim Holocaust." Together with the conflict in Chechnya, the Bosnian tragedy provides evidence of a "Western crusade" against Islam. Most recently, a commentary on Western responses to increased efforts at self-defense by the Bosnian Muslims concludes:

All this diplomatic activity is designed to prevent the Bosnian army from achieving a military breakthrough which would naturally demoralise the already overstretched Serbs. The West's role as co-conspirators with the Serbian war criminals becomes clearer with every passing day. (*Crescent International*, 1995, 1)

In such media, Bosnia is understood as important evidence of the dark side of modernity.

At one level, European and North American societies speak of human rights and hold forth a vision of universal tolerance and respect. The advance of instrumental rationality and the accompanying differentiation between religious and nonreligious spheres of activity are advertised as therapy for a world weary of fighting between groups competing for dominance in the developing countries. Modernity represents technical and spiritual progress, and taps into long-standing hopes on the part of human beings everywhere.

At another level, Europe and North America serve to illustrate the never-ceasing demands of instrumental rationality for efficiency in the name of ever-increasing returns. Under certain conditions, such demands can only be met by reducing the numbers of those with legitimate claims to a share in the goods of modern social life. Modernity's tolerance, its respect for difference, its aspirations to universality have limits. Modernity falls short of its promises, yielding a flawed society capable of, indeed resting upon the phenomena of genocide, ethnic cleansing, and mass death.

How does Islam experience modernity? As the material presented here indicates, ambiguously. Yet running through an important set of Muslim writers over the last century, one finds this theme: despite its technical, especially scientific advances, modernity is lacking in an important sense. That sense can be summarized in the notion that the society characterized by instrumental rationality and social differentiation lacks a way to integrate the varied experience characteristic of the human creature. More tersely put, modernity lacks a spiritual-moral vision of the nature and destiny of human beings.

Given the history of European and North American culture, one might expect those societies most central to the project of modernity to seek for and to find resources for such a vision in Christianity. In the Muslim critique outlined here, however, we are given to understand that this cannot be. Parsons' analysis is correct. Christianity, with its focus on the distinction between the spiritual and material destinies of humanity, does lend itself to a differentiated society. Christianity is, then, a contributor to the peculiar genius of modern society. But that genius is a flawed guide. It fails to set forth the unity implicit in the notion "human being." Correlatively, it fails to honor the aspiration built into human beings everywhere to strive for and attain an integrated life. Even conceived in Christian terms, modernity can never set forth more than a partial vision of humanity. Humanity needs Islam; indeed, the human creature "is the most obvious argument of Islam." (Izetbegovic, 1989: 228)

Islamic Tradition, Justice, and War

Contemporary discussions of justice in war are generally framed in terms of norms derived from or at least similar to those of the just war tradition. The key questions are associated with conduct; as James Turner Johnson argues, one of the decisive tendencies in the development of a modern just war tradition lies in moving debate from a focus on *jus ad bellum* concerns—right authority, just cause, and the like—to *jus in bello* norms of proportionality and, in particular, discrimination or respect for noncombatant immunity. (Johnson, 1981; 1991) As I stated at the outset of this essay, when it comes to such discussions, Islam is typically in the dock. Insofar as various Islamic groups are associated with hostage-taking, airline bombings, suicidal attacks on buses, and the like, they are held to violate ordinary canons governing the conduct of war. In particular, the distinction between combatants and noncombatants makes problematic certain activities associated with (some) contemporary Islamic groups. That is not to say that other concerns are unimportant. Insofar as many of the groups in question are "irregular" units, lacking the sanction of a government recognized as sovereign by the international community, there are problems with the *jus ad bellum* norms as well. Generally speaking, however, this concern collapses into worries about noncombatant immunity. As some might put it, the claims of the groups in question to fight in a just cause would be easier to accept if they would conduct themselves according to justice, that is, by respecting noncombatant immunity.

Islamic tradition is not without its ways of raising and addressing these issues. (cf. Kelsay, 1993: ch. 4–5) That is so whether one is thinking of the classical jurists and their development of an "Islamic law of nations," or of contemporary fighters associated with the label "militant" or "fundamentalist" Islam. The Islamic tradition, in short, can engage in discussions of the norms governing wartime conduct. In a moment, I shall undertake a brief summary of the Islamic version of the rules of war. One should understand, however, that the momentum of Islamic discourse on justice and war takes us in a somewhat different direction from that posed by contemporary just war discussion. In line with the criticisms of modernity outlined above, the Islamic tradition turns us back toward a version of the *jus ad bellum* discussion. What, it asks, are the appropriate purposes of war? What aims does it serve? Its focus, however, is on the way war fits into an overall conception of political life. In contemporary discussions of *jus in bello* restraints, a typical concern for one "thinking Islamically" might be framed thusly: Who or what secures adherence to such norms as respect for noncombatant immunity? In its broad outlines, the Islamic tradition leads us less in the direction of rules for the conduct of war, and more toward a discussion of theories of statecraft as the larger context within which discussions of justice and war take place. (cf. Kelsay, 1993: 115–122)

Nonetheless, war must be carried out with restraint. If we turn, for example, to statements of classical jurists pertaining to the rules of war, we find judgments crafted in an attempt to follow certain standards attributed to the Prophet. The treatise of al-Shaybani (d. 804/5), for example, attempts to implement the following texts:

> He [of the enemy] who has reached puberty should be killed, but he who has not should be spared. The Apostle of God prohibited the killing of women. The Apostle of God said: "You may kill the adults of the unbelievers, but spare their minors—the youth." Whenever the Apostle of God sent forth a detachment he said to it: "Do not cheat or commit treachery, nor should you mutilate or kill children, women, or old men." (Khadduri, 1966: 87, 91–92, 101)

If such norms are not identical with those of the just war tradition, they at least suggest the possibility of a conversation. At least some persons on the enemy side are not to be the targets of direct military attack. Which ones? And why?

More directly parallel to the just war tradition is the statement of the late Ayatollah Mutahhari. Commenting on Qur'an 2:190, "Fight in the path of God with those who are fighting with you and do not transgress," Mutahhari states. "Fight," he continues, "those who are fighting you—i.e., fight them because they are fighting you—but do not violate the limit." The Shaykh goes on to ask what it means to observe the limit. "Its obvious meaning," he says, "is that it is those who are fighting us that we are to fight and not anyone else, and that it is on the battlefield that we are to fight." This places immediate limits on the objects of attack, for "we are to fight with a certain group of people and that group is the soldiers that the other side have sent, the men of war whom they prepared for war with us and who are fighting us." Should this not be clear enough, the Ayatollah insists, "With people who are not men of war, who are not soldiers, who are not in a state of combat, such as old men, old women . . . and children, we must not interfere and we must not do any of the other things that are counted as transgression." (Mutahhari, n.d.: 35) As Mutahhari goes on to indicate, "other things" include damage to property in such a way as to make life more difficult for enemy survivors following the war—a kind of application of the notion of proportionality.

Even Shaykh Fadlallah, the alledged leader of Hezbollah, connected with numerous instances of kidnapping in the Lebanon of the 1980s, speaks in this way:

> Kidnapping people is not excused from a Muslim point of view. In Islam, the Qur'an says, "Do not burden yourself by adding another's to your own," meaning that no person should carry the weight of someone else's crimes. That is why I declare from a responsible, rather than from a defensive position that I am against all kidnappings, and that I do not see any righteousness in any acts of kidnapping, be they of Frenchmen or Americans, of airliners or ships.

He acknowledges that he "might sympathize with the cause of the hijackers"; nonetheless, he cannot "endorse the means they use, because I believe that the Americans they are seizing are participants in cultural, medical, and social institutions, and cannot be held responsible for the actions of their governments." (Fadlallah, 1986: C5)

If we conduct the debate at the level of normative teaching, there is little doubt we will find ample evidence of an Islamic concern with questions of discrimination between legitimate and illegitimate targets in war, or more specifically between combatants and noncombatants. Confronted with the claims of Bernard Lewis and the House Republican Research Committee's "Iran's European Springboard?"

and "The New Islamist Internationale," it is useful and important to note this fact.

At the same time, the criteria governing war conduct are not, as I mentioned, the central issue of the Islamic tradition with respect to war. Shaykh Fadlallah states it well:

> We do not hold in our Islamic belief that violence is the solution to all types of problems; rather, we see violence as a kind of surgical operation that a person should use only after trying all other means, and only when he finds his life imperiled. (1986: C5)

Violence by Muslim "irregulars"

> emanates from given political, economic, and social conditions which have been imposed on reality by a great oppressive power that has intruded in the pursuit of its economic and strategic interests. The violence began as the people, feeling themselves bound by impotence, stirred to shatter some of that enveloping powerlessness for the sake of liberty. (1986: C5)

Again, whether we are thinking of classical or contemporary statements of the tradition, Islamic discussion of the relations between justice and war drives toward broader questions of political life. What are the purposes for which human beings fight? Which are just, and which not? Granted, there are norms governing the conduct of a just warrior. One who fights and violates such norms is unjust and/or ignoble. Even *jus in bello* norms drive one back toward discussion of the larger questions of political life, however. Who, in the end, will see that standards of proportionality and discrimination receive their due? The Islamic answer lies in proposing that political life be connected with, even governed by a religious worldview.

In classical Islamic perspective, such connections were understood in terms of the geographic and political orientation of a great imperial power. The world is divided, the jurists said, into *dar al-islam* and *dar al-harb,* the territory or "house" where Islamic values are acknowledged and the territory where they are not. Because Islam is the closest instantiation of values "natural" to humanity, the House of Islam holds the best hope for human beings to live in peace and justice. In *dar al-islam,* one has hopes of building and maintaining a religiopolitical order in which standards of justice in war might be enforced. In *dar al-harb*, literally "the abode of war," on the other hand, the connections between religion, morality, and political life are less secure. Here, one expects to see the confusion of an unintegrated vision of life played out in numerous social and military conflicts. Under certain circumstances, the jurists said, it is obligatory for Muslims to risk life and limb in the attempt to spread the territory of Islam, and thus to secure the blessings of a just polity for as much of humanity as possible.

In contemporary Islam, the connections are less clear. There is no empire, after all; there is no caliph or head of state to signify the religiopolitical unity of the Islamic community. Indeed, the type of society depicted by Weber, Parsons, and Rubenstein has grown so influential that, if one wishes to speak in imperial terms, he or she adopts language suggestive of the "rule of capitalism" or of "the Western powers." The spread of modernity involves the victory of instrumental rationality and of differentiation as the model for social-political life.

It also involves the spread of the phenomenon of genocide and mass death, even into the heart of the old *dar al-islam*. As a young Iranian, speaking at the United Nations Church Center, once remarked concerning the Turkish perpetration of the Armenian genocide: "That was not Islam; that was secularism." Modernity's failure, according to the Muslim critique, lies in its lack of attention to the integration of humanity's religious-moral interests into economic, political, and military life. Organizing life so as to encourage maximum autonomy, while at the same time actively fostering instrumental rationality, is from this point of view a recipe for disaster.

In Bosnia, in particular, discussions of the rules of war take place in the shadow of the failure of modernity to attend to the connections between justice and political life. What type of social order makes for people who conduct themselves with justice? The model of modernity articulated by Weber, Parsons, and Rubenstein, and instantiated in the modern Christian West, answers this question in terms of instrumental rationality, and the differentiation between religious and nonreligious spheres of activity. It is precisely this priority, and this fact, that much Islamic thinking wants to criticize.

How, then, shall we think about the war in Bosnia? From an Islamic point of view, the tragedy of Bosnia is connected to the shortcomings of modernity as a mode of organizing social and political life. We may and, of course, we should criticize specific violations of the rules of war by all sides in the conflict. Muslims, Serbs, and Croats alike deserve blame whenever they fail to respect the distinction between combatants and noncombatants, or use disproportionate force in the pursuit of a particular objective. From an Islamic point of view, Serbian employment of rape as a weapon, attacks on civilian targets, and interference with UN relief missions as a tactic are obviously significant for thinking about the connections between justice and war.

Such criticism is only part of the picture, however. When groups employ tactics of mass rape; when their war effort is conceived as a means to achieve the end of ethnic cleansing; when, further, those who have sufficient means and, ostensibly, the authority to intervene and deter such behaviors fail to do so; in particular, when the leading violators of standards of justice, the Bosnian Serbs, are legally in the status of irregulars, fighting with outside sponsorship, against a legitimate government, one may well ask whether something other than the criteria governing *jus in bello* is at stake.

This is the direction in which the Islamic tradition takes us, especially as it relates to the war in Bosnia. As such, the development of an Islamic perspective on the war in Bosnia leads us to *jus ad bellum* reflection, and even more to the presuppositions about social and political life that lie behind any substantive instance of such reflection. Justice in war, Islam seems to be saying, is best understood in the context of our suppositions about the justice of war. The latter, in turn, presuppose notions about the frame of human social life. In the largest sense, these notions deal with questions that are the preoccupation of religious traditions, questions dealing with the nature and destiny of the human being.

I do not propose to undertake further discussion of these questions at present. It is interesting to return at this point to the observation made at the outset of this essay, however. When it comes to justice in war, I stated, Islam is in the dock. That is so, whether one is thinking of popular, scholarly, or policy-oriented discussions. The fact that Islam is in this position is not accidental. The modern just war tradition, developed over hundreds of years, has been crafted specifically to deal with the relationship of justice and war in a society characterized by the progress of instrumental rationality and the differentiation of religious and nonreligious spheres of activity. Insofar as contemporary discussion reflects the modern development of just war tradition, with its tendencies toward a relatively narrow focus on *jus in bello* restraints, and its corresponding lack of intensity about *jus ad bellum* concerns, the situation of Islam in the dock is a natural one. With respect to war, as in so many other aspects of life, the genius of modernity lies in deflecting argument about the larger questions of social and political goods that flow from considerations of right authority, just cause, and the like. And these are precisely the questions many Muslim writers want to raise.

If we shift our emphasis, however, so that we think of *jus in bello* criteria as a set of norms that achieve specificity only in connection with a larger view of social life, and thus really of the nature and destiny of human beings, things look different. Is Islam in the dock, from this perspective? Or is it modernity? Perhaps more likely: Is it both?

In discussing the tragedy of Bosnia-Herzegovina, we cannot allow our analyses to be linked to views of Islam that fail to comprehend the depth of Islamic discourse on the relations between religion, society, and justice in war. That discourse raises important questions for just war thinking, particularly in terms of its relations to modernity as a form of social order. From the Muslim point of view, discussions of justice and war require attention to the largest and most difficult issues of religion and culture. For the Muslims of Bosnia, and for ourselves, we are bound to give these issues due consideration.

Notes

Introduction: Interpreting Contemporary Conflicts

1. The volumes I intend to survey were all acquired at local outlets of Barnes & Noble between January and June of 1995; most were available at all three of Richmond's stores. My reason for mentioning this is that most responsible citizens, attempting to inform themselves on an issue of public concern, will not have easy access to an academic library and will thus be thrown on the resources of public libraries and bookstores. At the same time, it would be unreasonable to hold most people responsible for consulting advanced academic works on a topic even when they are available, such as John Fine's two-volume history of the Balkans in the Middle Ages, a key text for dealing with many of the historical issues contested among Bosnians, Croatians, Serbians, and their partisans. But while the ordinary citizen may not be responsible for reading the technical literature, authors who treat these matters are, even if they are writing for a general public.

2. Expelling non-Serbs and expropriating their goods had already been practiced in the Croatian conflict of 1991–1992. The concept of "ethnic cleansing" is, however, much older. Malcolm cites a *chetnik* of the Second World War advocating "the cleansing (*ciscenje*) of the land of all non-Serb elements. The thing to do would be to send the offenders on their way: Croats to Croatia, and Muslims to Turkey or Albania."(Malcolm, 1994: 178) In fact, the intellectual origins of ethnic cleansing, as opposed to the ubiquitous hatreds inspired by local rivalries, may be traced to the "pan-Slavism" of the nineteenth century. "In Serbia and Montenegro," as Aleksa Djilas puts it, "pan-Slavism was primarily anti-Turkish."(Djilas, 1991: 28) The perverse identification of "Muslim" with "Turk" then

leads to the assault by contemporary Serbs on their otherwise indistinguishable neighbors of Muslim heritage.

3. The shape of the war in the Balkans and Eastern Europe is most easily gathered from the various atlases of the Second World War, of which I have found Keegan (1989) and Pitt (1989) most helpful. The nature of bombing in the Second World War is an important but distinct matter. Liddell Hart's chapter is revealing (1970: 589–612). The place of Liddell Hart himself in twentieth-century land and air strategy may be gleaned from essays 20 and 21 of Paret (1986).

4. The question of Muslim fundamentalism and Alija Izetbegovic will be dealt with in a later chapter, but this is another example of Levinsohn's very sketchy history. According to Banac, the young Izetbegovic was a defendant in anti-Muslim trials in the late 1940s (Banac, 1993: 150, n. 19). He was subsequently tried and sentenced to eleven years in 1983 for "hostile and counterrevolutionary acts derived from Muslim nationalism," based in part on his earlier involvements and more importantly on a previously unpublished *Islamic Declaration* written between 1966 and 1970 (Malcolm, 1994: 208; 291, n. 26). Whether Izetbegovic was jailed in the 1970s is unclear, and Levinsohn offers no source for her remark.

5. In the matter of head-taking, Jelavich and Jelavich remark that in 1817, fearing the return of his rival Karadjordje, Milos Obrenovic "had him murdered and sent his head to Marasli [Ali Pasha], who had it stuffed and presented to the sultan."(1977: 37) So much for the perfidy of the Turks.

6. Levinsohn cites Malcolm for the claim that during the Middle Ages Bosnia was a separate nation, but only to cast the claim in doubt, referring to unnamed experts and adding that "the fact that Serbian or Serbo-Croatian, as it was called until the war, has long been the language of the Bosnians . . . seems to offer strong contradictory evidence." (1994: 207) This last, of course, is irrelevant, and the point in general neglects the standard works of Fine (1983, 1987), which Malcolm explicitly acknowledges. To Fine's work can now be added his own summary (Donia & Fine, 1994) and Sedlar (1994) as well.

Chapter 1: Religion, History, and Genocide in Bosnia-Herzegovina

1. In September 1995, the Bosnian army retook the town of Kljuc in Northwest Bosnia. Most of the inhabitants in the formerly 90 percent Muslim-populated town had been killed or expelled by Serb military forces. The few who survived did so through the courage of Serb civilians such as Burka Bakovic and Nedjo Cvaka, who continued to bring them food and keep them sheltered. (Hedges 1995: A12) When the Croat HVO militia "cleansed" the city of Stolac of its Muslim inhabitants and dynamited the town's mosques, courageous Croat civilians shielded their neighbors from HVO atrocities. This essay is dedicated to Burka Bakovic, Nedjo Cvaka, and the thousands of other Bosnian Muslims, Serbs, Croats, Jews, Gypsies, and others who have risked their lives to save the

lives of their neighbors. This writer's earlier exposé of the involvement of significant elements of the Serb church in creating the climate for genocide led to the criticism that such an exposé would contribute to the demonization of Serbs. (cf. Sells 1994) I suggested that, in fact, it is the refusal to tie the crimes to specific individuals and organizations that leads to generic blame against all Serbs. The more specifically and carefully the responsibility is designated, the more Serbs innocent of complicity in these crimes, done in their name, will be freed from generic blame, and the more Serbs who struggled against ethno-religious hate and partition will be honored.

2. The abandonment of Srebrenica and Zepa had been telegraphed by the UN authorities such as UN representative Yasushi Akashi who continually implied that the UN was not prepared to use force to enforce its UN Security Council safe haven resolution. This author predicted that "if war resumes and the 'enclaves' (i.e. ghettos) of Srebrenica, Zepa, Bihac, and Gorazde fall, the events of 1992 leave little doubt as to what will be the fate of the inhabitants. That would happen, as was the case in Zvornik and Foca, away from the media and the TV cameras."(Turkish Times, 3/1/95: 11) See Williams (1995: 16) on the protest resignation of UN Special Rapporteur for Human Rights in the former Yugoslavia, Tadeusz Mazowiecki. It has since been revealed that a Dutch commander deliberately destroyed photographic evidence of Dutch soldiers watching as unarmed boys and men from Srebrenica were being led off for killing. A Dutch commander at the site also signed a document drafted by Serb officers affirming that the boys and men were being taken away according to proper procedures.

3. In the realm of the visual arts, for example, see Petar Palavicini's relief, "The Mother of the Jugovici," and Ljubinka Jovanovic's work of the same title. (Vucinich 1991: 300-301, Figs. 34 and 35) Finally, it should be pointed out that this study focuses solely upon the relationship of religion, Serb nationalism, and the genocide in Bosnia. It is not meant to excuse crimes or acts or aggression by any other group. The behavior of the Croatian militias, particularly in 1993, and the Croatian regular army in 1995, shows a pattern of severe human rights abuses. In many cases, more worldwide outrage might have been generated by the acts of the Croatian army had it not been for the even more brutal and methodical behavior of the Serb armed forces. Thus, while the world was still digesting the horror of the massacre of up to six thousand Bosnian Muslims at Srebrenica, the Croatian army overran the Krajina region, displacing thousands of Serb civilians. At the time of this writing there is evidence of over one hundred civilians murdered by Croatian soldiers or militias.

4. The *Sarajevo Haggadah*, a thirteenth-to-fourteenth-century work brought to Bosnia by Jewish refugees from Spain in the fifteenth century, was saved in the Second World War by a Muslim curator who hid it from the Nazi officer who demanded it be turned over. In 1992 it was saved again during the shelling of the National Museum by an interreligious group of

museum workers, including a Muslim, a Serb, and a Croat. The *Haggadah* is a symbol of cultural resistance to "ethnic cleansing." On Passover 1995, it was ceremonially opened for the third time in Sarajevo in a service conducted by the Jewish religious leaders of Sarajevo and attended by various members of the Bosnian government (Muslim, Jewish, Serb, and Croat).

5. The following depiction is based on the reports of Helsinki Watch (1986–1995), Amnesty International, the United Nations High Commission for Refugees (UNHCR), Doctors without Borders, The Eight U.S. State Department Reports Submitted to the UN War Crimes Commission, the indictments of the UN War Crimes Tribunal, and the detailed articles on war crimes in the journal *Vreme*, written by Serb human rights activists. My own personal interviews with scores of Bosnian refugees have shown the sources above, meticulously gathered by human rights workers with no ties to any government, to be overwhelmingly valid. It should also be pointed out that while Serb government authorities deny such reports, they also deny all access to international human rights workers and war crimes investigators. In contrast to the Croatian and Bosnian governments, the Serb governments also refuse all cooperation with the UN War Crimes Tribunal.

6. See Tribunal Watch 1995 and U.S. Congress 1995. Charged with genocide for activities in Bosnia-Herzegovina are President of the "Republika Srpska," Radovan Karadzic; Serb army General Ratko Mladic; Dusan Sikirica, commander of the Keraterm killing camp near Prijedor, Goran Jelisic, commander of the Brcko-Luka killing camp; Zejlko Meakic (AKA Mejahic), commander of the Omarska killing camp near Prijedor; and Dragan Nikolic, commander of the Susica killing camps near Vlasenica.

7. From this point of view, the religious element in nineteenth-century Serbian nationalism is far more important than works like Benedict Anderson's *Imagined Communities* might lead us to expect. While linguistic purification was also vital to the nineteenth-century construction of the Serb nation, the religious element was also crucial. Greenawalt 1994 has been particularly helpful on this point.

8. Milovan Djilas, one of The *Mountain Wreath*'s admirers, argues that the historical extermination of Montenegrin Muslims was a "process" rather than a single "event," and that Bishop Petar shaped it into a single act for literary and ideological purposes. (Djilas 1966: xx) While there is doubt whether the *Istraga Poturica*, the "extermination of the Slavic Muslims," occurred as a single event in the late eighteenth century, there is none about what happened in 1992.

9. For the revival and nationalistic politicization of the works of Andric and Njegos, see Ramet (1992: 28–29) and Glenny (1993: 22). This brief reading of Njegos and Andric cannot do justice to the range of their work, nor is it meant to explain the genocide in Bosnia. It is meant only to illustrate that religion, despite frequent denials, is indeed a powerful and operative

element in the tragedy and to identify the religious ideologies that are involved.

10. These groups are mentioned in Glenny (1993), but to understand their close cooperation with Yugoslav army and security forces, one needs to consult *Vreme*. A particularly telling example of the cooperation between the regular army and the irregular genocide squads occurred after the Yugoslav army took the city of Vukovar in 1991. Caught on videotape are officers of the Yugoslav army, including the key figure of Colonel Veselin Slivancanin, refusing the International Red Cross access to over two hundred prisoners who had been taken from the hospital at Vukovar. These prisoners included wounded Croat soldiers, orderlies, and other hospital personnel. Also on camera are a group of *chetnik* irregulars, with beards, backpacks, and rifles. According to one of the few survivors, the prisoners were handed over to the irregulars by the Yugoslav army. The irregulars beat them severely, killing some on the spot. The survivors were taken to the Ovcara pig farm, where they were beaten in a gauntlet with clubs and rifle butts. Human rights excavators have uncovered a mass grave with hundreds of victims who had been killed by small-bore rifle shots to the head. The war crime investigation at Ovcara has been slowed by interference from local Serb government and military authorities.

11. The Internet discussion groups show more frankness, with numerous postings (soc.culture.bosna-herzgvna, alt.current-events.bosnia, soc.culture.yugoslavia) angrily questioning why Christians should come to the aid of Muslims who, in effect, deserve what they are getting.

12. For a powerful antidote to such sterotypes see Musanovic (1992), which presents seventeen works of art by internationally known Sarajevan artists of various religious backgrounds, all composed in Sarajevo during the shelling of Sarajevo.

Chapter 2: Nationalism and Self-Determination

1. *Editor's note.* Over the course of the Fall of 1995 it became increasing clear that Bosnian Serb forces carried out mass murders of Muslim men and adolescent boys in and around Srebrenica. Reports suggested that aerial reconnaisance revealed the preparation of mass graves even before the enclave was taken, and the most recent reports, in mid-January of 1996, raise the possibility that mineshafts in other parts of Serb-held Bosnia were used to dump bodies. All of these reports await confirmation, which remains difficult. (cf. *NYT*, 1/28/96)

2. These insights and words are found throughout Havel's works. The reader might want to consult both early and late essays, say, those collected in Havel (1987a) and (1987b), as well as the more recent *Disturbing the Peace* (Havel, 1990).

3. The discussion of Ignatieff is drawn from my review in *Religion and Public Life* (Elshtain, 1994).

4. It is worth noting, by the way, that the most virulent forms of anti-foreign sentiment have broken out, not in the old West Germany, with its nearly half-century of democratic civic life, but in the east, where civic life was not allowed to take root.

5. It is worth a moment's reflection to remember that Oskar Schindler, recently become so prominent in our moral imagination, was a Sudeten German.

Chapter 3: War for Cities and Noncombatant Immunity in the Bosnian Conflict

1. See the following newspaper accounts. For purposes of a manageable sample, these accounts are all from recent phases of the war: *New York Times*, 3/10/95, 4/13/95, 5/3/95, 5/18/95, 5/21/95, 5/25/95, 5/28/95, 5/29/95, 6/1/95, 6/4/95, 6/14/95, 6/15/95, 6/25/95, 6/30/95, 7/13/95, 7/14/95, 7/15/95, 7/16/95b, 7/17/95, 7/20/95, 7/23/95b.

2. For more on Ramsey's place in the development of contemporary just war thinking, see the editor's introduction, particularly pp. 22–25.

3. *Editor's note.* Vitoria's work was published in 1557 by a Lyon book dealer, Jacques Boyer. Boyer's section numbers formed the basis for references for over four centuries. This includes the widely used translation in Scott (1934). The most recent translation, Vitoria (1991), relies on the critical edition of 1981 and reproduces the Thomist structure of the original. To facilitate reference, I give Boyer's title and section, followed by the more recent page number.

4. I have called this the doctrine of "simultaneous ostensible justice" in Vitoria; for further discussion see Johnson, 1975: 185–95.

Chapter 4: Bosnia, the United States, and the Just War Tradition

1. The literature on this is enormous, with the technical materials far exceeding my mathematical abilities, but Morton Davis (1983) is very accessible. An influential presentation of Prisoner's Dilemma in the arena of psychology is Rapoport and Chammah (1965). Contemporary essays comparing game theory to decision theory, along with essays by philosophical critics of both, may be found in Moser (1990). Brams provides a particularly clear introduction to Prisoner's Dilemma, as well as the important game of Chicken, with examples from international conflicts. (1975: 30–47) All of these volumes provide many further references.

2. Brams cites earlier work by Harsanyi in criticizing Schelling for "a rather loose formulation of rational behavior, which incorporates cultural, psychological, and other factors extraneous to the formal structure of game theory; this leads to difficulties in analyzing the bargaining aspects of games."(1975: 46) But is this not exactly the point? Theoretical analysis gets its beauty from its formal precision, and this makes it attractive to the strategist; real-world applications do not conform, the "cultural, psychological, and other factors" get in the way and cannot be ignored.

3. Some evidence for the ongoing rhetorical shift may be gleaned from President Clinton's National Security Advisor, Anthony Lake. While reaffirming the traditional realist emphasis on military force and the defense of our "vital interests," Lake backs away from isolationism and claiming a unique "sphere of influence." To the traditional interests of security and the economy he adds combatting international aggression, protecting human rights, and honoring international agreements. (Lake, 1995: 89–91) Not, perhaps, a full-fledged embrace of justice, but a nod to its basic demands.

4. For obvious reasons the interpretation of all these events is contested. Of the historical overviews Malcolm (1994) seems to me more balanced and precise than Donia and Fine (1994), though their conclusions are much the same. Malcolm closes his narrative in late May of 1993. Djordjevic (1992) provides a clear summary of the history of Yugoslavia, up to March 1991. Banac (1992) gives a very pointed and enlightening account of the rise of Milosevic and particularly his relation with the Yugoslavian National Army. His account also comes from the spring of 1991. Of the ever-increasing number of accounts of the conflict itself, Glenny (1993) is the most distinguished, though in his more recent writings and remarks there is something of the anti-political cynicism emerging in the earlier work.

5. The history and politics of nationalism are contested territory. That nationalism is a volatile and relatively recent invention shows itself in miniature in Benedict Anderson's account of the naming of Vietnam, which reflects the Chinese desire to label the emerging country with a sign of prior conquest; the newly installed ruler named his realm Nam Viet, but the Chinese insisted on Viet Nam, implying it was a province of southern China. Knowingly or not, "today's Vietnamese proudly defend a Viet Nam scornfully invented by a nineteenth-century Manchu dynast." (Anderson, 1991: 158) Hobsbawm (1990) also contains important historical reflections. Banac (1984) is an important account of early Yugoslav nationalism. Denitch (1994) is an insider's analysis of nationalism in the current conflict, while Ignatieff (1993) recounts a journalist's odyssey through half a dozen new nationalisms. See Elshtain's reflections on Ignatieff, above.

Chapter 5: Bosnia and the Muslim Critique of Modernity

1. Both papers were crafted to foster discussion. As such, it is important for the reader to note that these were not "official" papers, and should not be taken as representative of views of members of Congress serving on the Task Force. The interest of the papers here lies in the way they reflect the tendency under discussion; i.e., to view Islam as a specially problematic religious and moral tradition when it comes to issues of politics and war.

2. The discussion of Weber here draws on one section of Feldmann and Kelsay (1995).

3. For al-Afghani's life, cf. Keddie, 1972.

4. Iqbal seems to have in mind Lutheran delimitations of the role of law in the Christian life. The justice of generalizing the distinction between Gospel and Law to the whole of Christianity need not detain us. Iqbal faithfully reflects the post–First World War debate over the nature of the state in Luther's thought, occasioned by Weber's friend and Heidelberg colleague Ernst Troeltsch. Troeltsch's monumental account of Christian social teaching, which appeared in 1912, argued that Lutheranism "fostered the patriarchal attitude and the corporate class spirit," thereby encouraging "the spirit of absolutism."(Troeltsch, 1992: 2, 572) In its Prussian incarnation, Lutheranism "hallowed the realistic sense of power, and the ethical virtues of obedience, reverence, and respect for authority, which are indispensable to Prussian militarism."(2, 575) It is, finally, Troeltsch who concludes that "the main historic forms of the Christian doctrine of society and of social development are today, for various reasons, impotent in face of the tasks by which they are confronted."(2, 1012) The Muslim critic, in this instance, makes one with the Christian critic.

5. Following this line of thought, Izetbegovic's text proceeds in a fascinating digression dedicated to the description of the Anglo-American experience of modernization as "Islamic," in the sense that it involved an attempt to provide integrity for the bipolar (or differentiated) experience of humanity in an industrial age. This, however, is a topic for another occasion.

6. At this point, it is worth noting that "Iran's European Springboard?" (HRRC, 1992) presents Izetbegovic as a kind of "fundamentalist," who in 1970 authored an "Islamic Declaration" expressing the view that "there can be no peace or coexistence between Islamic faith and non-Islamic faith and non-Islamic institutions."(3) One should note that the "Islamic Declaration" served as evidence against Izetbegovic when (in 1983) he was tried, convicted, and imprisoned for subversive activities against the Communist regime. In its depiction of Izetbegovic's views, "Iran's European Springboard?" does not discuss *Islam Between East and West*. I am not prepared at present to undertake a full discussion of the relation between this volume and the "Islamic Declaration" of 1970. One is justified, however, in raising at least two concerns about the earlier document, particularly in terms of its use in "Iran's European Springboard?": (1) does such use indicate proper attention to the context in which the "Declaration" was developed—i.e., life under a communist regime; and (2) connected with this, does the committee's use indicate a full awareness of what Izetbegovic means by "Islamic faith and non-Islamic faith and non-Islamic institutions?" For further background on the "Islamic Declaration" see above, pp. 9–11, and in particular note 4.

References

Aarons, A. and J. Loftus. 1991. *Unholy Trinity: The Vatican, the Nazis, and Soviet Intelligence.* New York: St. Martin's Press.

Abbott, Walter M., S.J. 1966. *The Documents of Vatican II.* New York: Guild Press, America Press, Association Press.

Ali, Rabia and Lawrence Lifschultz. 1993. "In Plain View" in Ali and Lifschultz (1993), pp. xi–iv.

Ali, Rabia and Lawrence Lifschultz, eds. 1993. *Why Bosnia? Writings on the Balkan War.* Stony Creek, CT: Pamphleteer's Press.

Allworth, E. 1994. *Muslim Communities Reemerge: Historical Perspectives on Nationality, Politics, and Opposition in the Former Soviet Union and Yugoslavia.* Durham, NC: Duke University Press.

Amnesty International, U.S.A. 1991. *Yugoslavia: Torture and Deliberate and Arbitrary Killings in War Zones.* New York: Amnesty International.

———. 1992. *Yugoslavia: Further Reports of Torture and Deliberate and Arbitrary Killings in War Zones.* New York: Amnesty International.

———. 1992a. *Yugoslavia: Ethnic Albanian Victims of Torture and Ill-treatment by Police.* New York: Amnesty International.

———. 1992b. *Bosnia-Herzegovina: Gross Abuses of Basic Human Rights.* New York: Amnesty International.

———. 1993. *Bosnia-Herzegovina: Rana u Dust—A Wound to the Soul.* New York: Amnesty International.

Andrejivic, Andrej. 1972. *Aladza Dzamija i Foci.* Belgrade: Dragomir Todorvic.

Andric, Ivo. 1959. *The Bridge on the Drina.* New York: Macmillan.

———. 1990. *The Development of Spiritual Life in Bosnia under the Influence of Turkish Rule.* Durham, NC: Duke University Press.

Anonymous. 1995. "Kosova, the Quiet Siege" *Cultural Survival* 19/2, pp. 35–42.

Anscombe, Elizabeth. 1957. "Mr. Truman's Degree" reprinted in Anscombe

(1981), pp. 62–71. 1981. *Ethics, Religion and Politics: Collected Papers, Volume Three.* Minneapolis: University of Minnesota Press.

Anderson, Benedict. 1991. *Imagined Communities: Reflections on the Origin and Spread of Nationalism,* rev. ed. London: Verso Books.

Apple, R. W. Jr. 1995. "Clinton is Scrambling to Find Way to Help U.N. in Bosnia," *New York Times,* July 14, A4.

Aquinas, St. Thomas. *ST. Summa Theologica,* trans. English Dominicans, 5 vols. Westminster, MD: Christian Classics.

Aristotle. 1984. *EN. Nicomachean Ethics,* trans. Irwin. Indianapolis: Hackett Publishing.

Ash, Timothy Garton. 1989. *The Uses of Adversity: Essays on the Fate of Central Europe.* New York: Random House.

Bakarsic, K. 1994. "The Libaries of Sarajevo and the Book that Saved our Lives," *The New Combat,* Autumn, p. 15.

Banac, Ivo. 1984. *The National Question in Yugoslavia: Origins, History, Politics.* Ithaca: Cornell University Press.

———. 1992. "Post-Communism as Post-Yugoslavism: The Yugoslav Non-Revolutions of 1989–1990" in Banac (1992), pp. 168–187.

———. 1993. "Bosnian Muslims: From Religious Community to Socialist Nationhood and Post-Communist Statehood, 1918–1992" in Pinson ed. (1993), pp. 129–153.

———. 1994. "Serbia's Deadly Fears," *The New Combat* Autumn, pp. 36–43.

Banac, Ivo ed. 1992. *Eastern Europe in Revolution.* Ithaca, NY: Cornell University Press.

Barac, A. 1976. *A History of Yugoslav Literature.* Ann Arbor: Michigan Slavic Publications.

Barraclough, Geoffrey. 1947. *The Origins of Modern Germany,* 2nd ed. New York: Capricorn Books.

Batakovic, D. T. 1992. *The Kosovo Chronicles.* N.pl.: Plato.

Bennett, C. 1995. *Yugoslavia's Bloody Collapse: Causes, Course and Consequences.* New York: New York University Press.

Berlin, Isaiah. 1991. "Two Concepts of Nationalism," *New York Review of Books,* Nov. 21, pp. 19–23.

Best, Geoffrey. 1994. *War and Law since 1945.* Oxford: Oxford University Press.

Binnendijk, Hans and Patrick Claussen. 1995. "New Strategic Priorities," *Washington Quarterly* 18/2, pp. 109–126.

Bollage, B. 1995. "Rebuilding Bosnia's Library," *The Chronicle of Higher Education,* January 13, pp. A35–A37.

Brams, Steven. 1975. *Game Theory and Politics.* New York: The Free Press.

Brams, Steven and Marc Kilgour. 1988. *Game Theory and National Security.* New York: Basil Blackwell.

Brock, P. 1994. "The Partisan Press," *Foreign Policy*, 96, Winter, pp. 152–172.

Bruun, L. L. 1993. "Beyond the 1948 Convention: Emerging Principles of Genocide in Customary International Law," *Maryland Journal of International Law and Trade,* 17/2, pp. 193–226.

Burg, S. 1995. "The International Community and the Yugoslav Crisis" in Esman (1995), pp. 235–271.

Bush, George. 1991. Address of January 16, 1991, reprinted in Sifry and Cerf (1991), pp. 311–314.

Buturovic, A. 1995. "Producing and Annihilating the Ethnos of Bosnian Islam" *Cultural Survival* 19/2, pp. 29–33.

Carnegie Endowment for International Peace. 1993. *The Other Balkan Wars: 1914 Carnegie Endowment Report of the International Commission to Inquire into the Causes and Conduct of the Balkan Wars.* Washington, DC: Carnegie Endowment of International Peace.

Carr, E. H. 1946. *The Twenty Years' Crisis, 1919–1939.* 2d ed., New York: Harper and Row.

Christian Science Monitor (CST). 6/9/95. "End the Bosnia Posturing," p. 20.

Christopher, M. 1992. "The Historical Background of the Contemporary Situation of the Orthodox Church in Yugoslavia." Belleville, Mich: Firebird Video.

Cigar, N. 1995. *Genocide in Bosnia: The Policy of "Ethnic Cleansing."* College Station: Texas AandM University Press.

Congress of the United States. 1995. *Genocide in Bosnia-Herzegovina: Hearing Before the Commission on Security and Cooperation in Europe.* Washington, DC: U.S. Government Printing Office.

Clausewitz, Carl von. 1976. *On War*, trans. Howard and Paret. Princeton: Princeton University Press.

Coles, Robert. 1986. *The Political Life of Children.* Boston: Atlantic Monthly Press.

Crescent International. 1992. "The Muslim Parliament Motion." 21/11 (August 16–31): 1.

———. 1995. "Serbs Promised No More Strikes but Bosnians Warned Not to Lift siege." 24/8 (July 1–15): 1.

Cronkite, Walter. 1991. "What is There to Hide?" *Newsweek*, February 25, reprinted with postscript in Sifrey and Cerf (1991), pp. 381–384.

Davis, G. Scott. 1992. *Warcraft and the Fragility of Virtue: An Essay in Aristotelian Ethics.* Moscow, Idaho: University of Idaho Press.

Davis, Morton. 1983. *Game Theory*, rev. ed. New York: Basic Books.

Debeljak, A. 1994. *Twilight of the Idols: Recollections of a Lost Yugoslavia*. New York: White Pine Press.

Dedijer, Vladimir, et al. 1974. *History of Yugoslavia*, trans. Kveder. New York: McGraw-Hill.

Denitch, Bogdan. 1994. *Ethnic Nationalism: The Tragic Death of Yugoslavia*. Minneapolis: University of Minnesota Press.

Djilas, Aleksa. 1991. *The Contested Country: Yugoslav Unity and the Communist Revolution, 1919–1953*. Cambridge, MA: Harvard University Press.

Djilas, Milovan. 1966. *Njegos: Poet, Prince, Bishop*. New York: Harcourt, Brace and World.

Djordjevic, Dimitrije. 1992. "The Yugoslav Phenomenon" in Held (1992), pp. 307–344.

Donia, Robert J. and John V. A. Fine. 1994. *Bosnia and Hercegovina: A Tradition Betrayed*. New York: Columbia University Press.

Dorich, W., B. Jenkins and A. Dorich. 1992. *Kosovo*. Alhambra, CA: Kosovo Charity Fund.

Dragnich, Alex. 1992. *Serbs and Croats: The Struggle for Yugoslavia*. New York: Harcourt Brace.

———. 1994. *Serbia's Historical Heritage*. New York: Columbia University Press.

———. 1995. "What Serbs Want," letter to the editor, *New York Times*, Sunday, June 4, p. 14E.

Dragnich, A. N. and S. T. 1984. *The Saga of Kosovo: Focus on Serbian-Albanian Relations*. New York: Columbia University Press.

Eliot, Michael. 1995. "Held Hostage by Hypocrisy," *Newsweek*, June 12, p. 27.

Elshtain, Jean Bethke. 1994. "Michael Ignatieff, *Blood and Belonging, Journeys into the New Nationalism*," in *Religion and Public Life* 3/1, pp. 5–6.

Emmert, T. 1990. *Serbian Golgotha: Kosovo, 1389*. New York: East European Monographs.

Esman, M. J. and S. T., eds. 1995. *International Organizations and Ethnic Conflict*. Ithaca: Cornell University Press.

Fadlallah, Muhammad Hussein. 1986. "To Avoid a World War of Terror." *Washington Post*, 6 April, C5.

Feldmann, John, and John Kelsay. 1995. "Economic Reform and Economic Rationality: Understanding the Religio-Political Economy." Unpublished paper.

Filipovic, G. 1989. *Kosovo: Past and Present*. Belgrade: Review of International Affairs.

Filipovic, M., ed. 1987. *The Art in Bosnia-Herzegovina (The Art Treasures of Bosnia and Herzegovina)*. Sarajevo: Svjetlost.

———. 1990. *Yugoslavia*. Sarajevo: Svjetlost.

Fine, John V. A. 1983. *The Early Medieval Balkans: A Critical Survey from the Sixth to the Late Twelfth Century*. Ann Arbor: University of Michigan Press.

———. 1987. *The Late Medieval Balkans: A Critical Survey from the Late Twelfth Century to the Ottoman Conquest*. Ann Arbor: University of Michigan Press.

———. 1993. "The Medieval and Ottoman Roots of Modern Bosnian Society" in Pinson (1993), pp. 1–21.

Ford, John C. 1944. "The Morality of Obliteration Bombing" reprinted in Wasserstrom (1970), pp. 15–41.

Freedman, Lawrence. 1986. "The First Two Generations of Nuclear Strategists" in Paret (1986), pp. 735–778.

———. 1995. "Why the West Failed." *Foreign Policy*, 97, Winter, pp. 53–69.

Friedman, Thomas L. 1995. "Lift, Lift, Contain." *New York Times*, Sunday, June 4, p. 15E.

Gagnon, V. P. J. 1995. "Roots of the Yugoslav Conflict" in Esman (1995), pp. 180–197.

Gjelten, Tom. 1995. *Sarajevo Daily: A City and Its Newspaper Under Siege*. New York: Harper Collins.

Glenny, Misha. 1993. *The Fall of Yugoslavia: The Third Balkan War*, rev. ed. New York: Penguin Books USA.

———. 1995. "Yugoslavia: The Great Fall," *New York Review of Books*, 42/5, March 23, pp. 56–65.

———. 1995a. "The Age of the Para-State," *New Yorker* May 8, pp. 45–53.

Greenawalt, Alexander K. A. 1994. *The Nationalization of Memory: Identity and Ideology in Nineteenth Century Serbia*. Unpublished senior thesis, Princeton University Department of Religion.

Greenfield, Liah. 1992. *Nationalism: Five Roads to Modernity*. Cambridge, MA.: Harvard University Press.

deGruchy, John W. 1994. "Waving the Flag," *Christian Century*, June 5–12, pp. 597–598.

Gutman, Roy. 1993. *A Witness to Genocide*. New York: Macmillan Publishing.

Haass, Richard N. 1994. *Intervention: The Use of American Military Force in the Post–Cold War World*. Washington, DC: Carnegie Endowment for International Peace.

Halleck, Henry Wager. 1863. Letter from Gen. Halleck to Gen. Rosecrans on the Treatment of Disloyal Persons within Our Lines. March 15. Huntington Library, index number LI 176.

Hallen, G. C. and Rajeshwar Prasad, eds. 1972. *Sorokin and Sociology: Essays in Honor of Professor Pitirim A. Sorokin.* Agra: Satish Book Enterprise.

Harsanyi, John C. 1977. "Advances in Understanding Rational Behavior" reprinted in Moser (1990), pp. 271–293.

Havel, Václav. 1987. *Vaclav Havel.* ed. Jan Vladislav. London: Faber and Faber.

———. 1987a. *Living in Truth.* ed. Jan Vladislav. London: Faber and Faber.

———. 1990. *Disturbing the Peace.* New York: Alfred A. Knopf.

———. 1993. "The Post-Communist Nightmare," *New York Review of Books,* May 27, pp. 8–10.

Held, Joseph. ed. 1992. *The Columbia History of Eastern Europe in the Twentieth Century.* New York: Columbia University Press.

Helsinki Watch. 1986. *Violations of the Helsinki Accords: Yugoslavia.* New York: The U.S. Helsinki Watch Committee.

———. 1989. *Increasing Turbulence (As the Federation Disintegrates): Human Rights in Yugoslavia.* New York: Human Rights Watch/Helsinki Watch.

———. 1990. *Yugoslavia: Crisis in Kosovo.* New York: Human Rights Watch/ Helsinki Watch.

———. 1991. *Human Rights in a Dissolving Yugoslavia.* New York: Helsinki Watch/Human Rights Watch.

———. 1991a. *The March 1991 Demonstrations in Belgrade.* New York: Helsinki Watch/Human Rights Watch.

———. 1991b. *Human Rights Abuses in the Croatian Conflict.* New York: Helsinki Watch/Human Rights Watch.

———. 1992. *War Crimes in Bosnia-Hercegovina.* New York: Helsinki Watch/Human Rights Watch.

———. 1992a. *Letter to President of Serbia and JNA Chief of Staff.* New York: Helsinki Watch/Human Rights Watch.

———. 1992b. *War Crimes in Bosnia-Hercegovina: Volume I.* New York: Helsinki Watch/Human Rights Watch.

———. 1992c. *Human Rights Abuses in Kosovo.* New York: Helsinki Watch/Human Rights Watch.

———. 1993. *War Crimes in Bosnia-Hercegovina: Volume II.* New York: Helsinki Watch/Human Rights Watch.

———. 1993a. *Abuses Continue in the Former Yugoslavia: Serbia, Montenegro and Bosnia-Hercegovina.* New York: Helsinki Watch/Human Rights Watch.

———. 1993b. *Prosecute Now!: Helsinki Watch Releases 8 Cases for War Crimes Tribunal on Former Yugoslavia.* New York: Helsinki Watch/Human Rights Watch.

———. 1993c. *Belgrade Demonstrations: Excessive Use of Force and Beatings in Detention.* New York: Helsinki Watch/Human Rights Watch.

———. 1993d. *Procedual and Evidentiary Issues for the Yugoslav War Crimes Tribunal: Resource Allocation, Evidentiary Questions and Protection of Witnesses.* New York: Helsinki Watch/Human Rights Watch.

———. 1993e. *Abuses by Bosnian Croat and Muslim Forces in Central and Southwestern Bosnia-Hercegovina.* New York: Helsinki Watch/Human Rights Watch.

———. 1994. *The War Crimes Tribunal: One Year Later.* New York: Helsinki Watch/Human Rights Watch.

———. 1994a. *War Crimes in Bosnia-Hercegovina: Bosanski Samac.* New York: Helsinki Watch/Human Rights Watch.

———. 1994b. *War Crimes in Bosnia-Hercegovina: U.N. Cease-Fire Won't Help Banja Luka.* New York: Helsinki Watch/Human Rights Watch.

———. 1994c. *Sarajevo.* New York: Helsinki Watch/Human Rights Watch.

———. 1994d. *"Ethnic Cleansing" Continues in Northern Bosnia.* New York: Helsinki Watch/Human Rights Watch.

———. 1995. *War Crimes Trials in Former Yugoslavia.* New York: Helsinki Watch/Human Rights Watch.

Hobsbawm, E. J. 1990. *Nations and Nationalism since 1780: Programme, Myth, Reality.* Cambridge: Cambridge University Press.

House Republican Research Committee (HRRC). 1992. "Iran's European Springboard?" Unpublished report by the Task Force on Terrorism and Unconventional Warfare.

———. 1993. "The New Islamist Internationale" Unpublished report by the Task Force on Terrorism and Unconventional Warfare.

Howard, Michael, George J. Andreopoulos, and Mark R. Shulman, eds. 1994. *The Laws of War: Constraints on Warfare in the Western World.* New Haven: Yale University Press.

Ignatieff, Michael. 1993. *Blood and Belonging, Journeys into the New Nationalism.* New York: Farrar, Straus and Girous.

Iqbal, Muhammad. 1968. *The Reconstruction of Religious Thought in Islam.* Lahore: Sh. Muhammad Ashraf.

Izetbegovic, 'Alija 'Ali. 1989. *Islam Between East and West,* 2nd ed. Indianapolis, IN: American Trust Publications.

Jelavich, Barbara. 1983. *History of the Balkans,* 2 vol. Cambridge: Cambridge University Press.

Jelavich, Charles. 1990. *South Slav Nationalisms—Textbooks and Yugoslav Union before 1914.* Columbus, OH: Ohio State University Press.

Jelavich, Charles and Barbara. 1977. *The Establishment of the Balkan National States, 1804–1920.* Seattle: University of Washington Press.

John XXIII, Pope. nd. "Pacem in Terris," in *The Encyclicals and Other Messages of John XXIII.* Washington, DC: TPS Press.

John Paul II, Pope. 1993. "Pope Sees False Nationalism Tearing at Europe," *The Tablet,* 4 December, p. 1599.

Johnson, James T. 1973. "Ideology and the *Jus ad Bellum.*" *Journal of the American Academy of Religion,* 41/2, 212–228.

———. 1975. *Ideology, Reason, and the Limitation of War: Religious and Secular Concepts, 1200–1740.* Princeton: Princeton University Press.

———. 1981. *Just War Tradition and the Restraint of War.* Princeton: Princeton University Press.

———. 1984. *Can Modern War Be Just?* New Haven: Yale University Press.

———. 1991. "Historical Roots and Sources of the Just War Tradition in Western Culture." In Kelsay and Johnson (1991), pp. 3–30.

Johnson, James Turner and George Weigel. 1991. *Just War and the Gulf War.* Washington, DC: Ethics and Public Policy Center.

Jomini, Antoine Henri Baron de. 1862. *The Art of War.* Philadelphia: Lippincott and Co.

Kahn, Herman. 1960. *On Thermonuclear War,* 2d. ed. Princeton: Princeton University Press.

———. 1984. *Thinking about the Unthinkable in the 1980s.* New York: Simon And Schuster.

Kajan, Ibrahim. 1993. "Is This Not Genocide?" in Ali and Lifschultz (1993), pp. 86–97.

Kann, Robert A. and Zdenek V. David. 1984. *The Peoples of the Eastern Habsburg Lands, 1526–1918.* Seattle: University of Washington Press.

Kaplan, Robert D. 1993. *Balkan Ghosts: A Journey through History.* New York: Vintage Books.

Keane, John. 1992. "Democracy's Poisonous Fruit," *Times Literary Supplement*, August 21, pp. 10–12.

Keddie, Nikki R. 1972. *Sayyid Jamal ad-Din "al-Afghani": A Political Biography*. Berkeley and Los Angeles: University of California Press.

———. 1983. *An Islamic Response to Imperialism: Political and Religious Writings of Sayyid Jamal ad-Din "al-Afghani."* Berkeley and Los Angeles: University of California Press.

Keegan, John ed. 1989. *The Times Atlas of the Second World War*. New York: Harper and Row.

Kelsay, John. 1993. *Islam and War: A Study in Comparative Ethics*. Louisville, Kentucky: Westminster/John Knox Press.

Kelsay, John and James Turner Johnson, eds. 1991. *Just War and Jihad: Historical and Theoretical Perspectives on War and Peace in Western and Islamic Traditions*. Westport, CT: Greenwood Press.

Kennan, George F. 1993. "The Balkan Crises: 1913 and 1993" Introduction to Carnegie Endowment (1993), pp. 1–16.

Kennedy, Paul. 1991. "American Grand Strategy, Today and Tomorrow: Learning from the European Experience" in Kennedy (1991), pp. 167–184.

Kennedy, Paul ed. 1991. *Grand Strategies in War and Peace*. New Haven: Yale University Press.

Kenney, George. 1995. "The Bosnia Calculation" *New York Times Magazine*, April 26, pp. 42–43.

Khadduri, Majid. 1966. *The Islamic Law of Nations: Shaybani's Siyar*. Baltimore: Johns Hopkins University Press.

Kinzer, Stephen. 1995. "Muslims Tell of Atrocities as Safe Town Fell," *New York Times,* July 14, A4.

Khomeini, Ruh Allah. 1981. *Islam and Revolution: Writings and Declarations of Imam Khomeini*, trans. and annotated by Hamid Algar. Berkeley: Mizan Press.

Krauthammer, Charles. 1991. "Bombing Baghdad: No Cause for Guilt," *Washington Post*, February 14, reprinted in Sifry and Cerf (1991), pp. 331–333.

Lake, Anthony. 1995. "American Power and American Diplomacy," *Fletcher Forum of World Affairs*, 19/2, pp. 87–94.

Lane, C. 1994. "Brock Crock," *The New Republic* 9/15, pp. 19–21.

Lemkin, Rafael. 1973. *Axis Rule in Occupied Europe: Laws of Occupation, Analysis of Government, Proposals for Redress*. New York: Howard Fertig.

Levinsohn, Florence Hamish. 1994. *Belgrade: Among the Serbs*. Chicago: Ivan R. Dee.

Lewis, Bernard. 1990. "The Roots of Muslim Rage," *Atlantic Monthly*, September.

Lidell Hart, Basil H. 1971. *History of the Second World War.* New York: G. P. Putnam's Sons.

Lieber, Francis. 1862. *Guerilla Parties, Considered with References to the Laws and Usages of War.* New York: D. van Nostrand.

Lieven, Anatol. 1993. "The Pope's Balancing Act," *The Tablet*, September 18, pp. 1208–1209.

Little, David. 1974. "Max Weber and the Comparative Study of Religious Ethics." *Journal of Religious Ethics* 2/2 (Fall), 5–40.

McDougal, Myres, and Florentino P. Feliciano. 1961. *Law and Minimum World Public Order.* New Haven: Yale University Press.

MacIntyre, Alasdair. 1984. *After Virtue: A Study in Moral Theory.* 2d. ed., South Bend: University of Notre Dame Press.

Magas, Branko. 1993. *The Destruction of Yugoslavia: Tracking the Break-up 1980–92.* London: Verso.

Malcolm, Noel. 1994. *Bosnia: A Short History.* New York: NYU Press.

Mathias, J. 1987. *The Battle of Kosovo.* Athens, OH: Swallow Press.

Milazzo, M. J. 1975. *The Chetnik Movement and The Yugoslav Resistance.* Baltimore: Johns Hopkins University Press.

Mojzes, Paul. 1994. *Yugoslavian Inferno: Ethnoreligious Warfare in the Balkans.* New York: Continuum.

Moser, Paul, ed. 1990. *Rationality in Action: Contemporary Approaches.* Cambridge: Cambridge University Press.

Mutahhari, Murtaza. n.d. *Jihad: The Holy War of Islam and its Legitimacy in the Quran*, trans. Mohammed S. Tawheedi. Albany, CA: Moslem Student Association (Persian Speaking Group).

National Council of Catholic Bishops (NCCB). 1983. *The Challenge of Peace.* Washington, DC: United States Catholic Conference.

———. 1993. "The Harvest of Justice is Sown in Peace," *Origins* 23/26, December 9, p. 453.

The New York Times (NYT).

———. 3/30/95. "Fanatical and Ruthless," p. A29.

———. 4/13/95. "Serb Ex-Police Official Offers Documents Linking Milosevic to War Crimes," pp. A1, A12.

———. 5/3/95. "Rebel Serbs Shell Croatian Capital," pp. A1, A10.

———. 5/18/95. "Battle Rages Around Sarajevo," p. A6.

———. 5/21/95. "In Sarajevo, Victims of a 'Postmodern' War," pp. A1, A12.

———. 5/25/95. "NATO May Be Called On to Silence Guns in Sarajevo," p. A14.

———. 5/28/95. "U.N. Attempt to Retake a Post from Serbs," pp. A1, A12.

———. 5/29/95. "Serbs Kill Bosnian Foreign Minister and Take New Captives," pp. A1, A5.

———. 5/30/95. "Allies Resolve To Bolster U.N. Peacekeeping in Bosnia," pp. A1, A6.

———. 6/1/95. "Bosnian Serbs Call for Talks; U.N. Refuses, Seeing a Ploy," pp. A1, A12.

———. 6/4/95. "Karadzic's Bosnian War: Myth Becomes Madness," p. A14.

———. 6/14/95. "Serbs Free More U.N. Captives," pp. A1, A14.

———. 6/15/95. "With Eye on Sarajevo, Government Bolsters Its Forces," p. A12.

———. 6/25/95. "Hostage-Taking: A Tactic Whose Time Is Now," pp. E1, E3.

———. 6/27/95. "Bosnian Muslim Troops Evade U.N. Force to Raid Serb Village," p. A3.

———. 6/28/95. "As Lull in the War Ends, Sarajevo Is Shellshocked," pp. A1, A8.

———. 6/30/95. "Bosnian Force Gains Slightly Near Sarajevo," p. A3.

———. 7/13/95. "Serbs Start Moving Muslims Out of Captured Territory," pp. A1, A6.

———. 7/14/95. "Muslims Tell of Atrocities in Bosnian Town," pp. A1, A8.

———. 7/15/95. "Serb Forces Shell U.N. Peacekeepers," pp. A1, A4.

———. 7/16/95a. "Bosnia Lets Refugees Leave Camp, but 20,000 Others Are Missing," pp. A1, A9.

———. 7/16/95b. "Bosnian Serbs Push Past U.N. Posts Into Muslim Enclave," p. A8.

———. 7/17/95. "Bosnian Refugees' Accounts Appear to Verify Atrocities," pp. A1, A6.

———. 7/20/95. "Second 'Safe Area' in Eastern Bosnia Overrun by Serbs," pp. A1, A14.

———. 7/23/95a. "Serbs Keeping Up a Heavy Barrage on 3 'Safe Areas'," pp. A1, A9.

———. 7/23/95b. "Survivors tell of Serb Atrocities in Fallen Enclave," p. A8.

———. 1/28/96. "War Crimes Tribunal on Bosnia is Hampered by Basic Problems," p. A1, A6.

Niebuhr, Reinhold. 1957. *Love and Justice: Selections from the Shorter Writings of Reinhold Niebuhr*, ed. Robertson. New York: World Books.

Norris, H. T. 1993. *Islam in the Balkans: Religion and Society between*

Europe and the Arab World. Columbia, SC: University of South Carolina Press.

O'Ballance, E. 1995. *Civil War in Bosnia, 1992–94.* New York: St. Martin's Press.

O'Brien, William V. 1981. *The Conduct of Just and Limited War.* New York: Praeger.

———. 1991. *Law and Morality in Israel's War with the PLO.* New York and London: Routledge.

Orwell, George. "Notes on Nationalism," in Orwell (1968), pp. 361–379.

———. 1968. *The Collected Essays, Journalism, and Letters of George Orwell,* vol. 3, ed. Sonia Orwell and Ian Angus. New York: Harvest, HBJ.

Paret, Peter ed. 1986. *Makers of Modern Strategy: From Machiavelli to the Nuclear Age.* Princeton: Princeton University Press.

Parsons, Talcott. 1972. "Christianity and Modern Industrial Society" in Hallen and Prasad (1972), pp. 33–70.

Perrow, Charles. 1984. *Normal Accidents: Living with High-Risk Technologies.* New York: Basic Books.

Pinson, Mark, ed. 1993. *The Muslims of Bosnia-Herzegovina: Their Historic Development from the Middle Ages to the Dissolution of Yugoslavia.* Cambridge, MA: Harvard University Press.

Pitt, Barrie. 1989. *Month by Month Atlas of World War II.* New York: Summit Books.

Popovic, Alexandar. 1990. *Les Musulmans Yougoslaves, 1945–1989: Mediateurs et Metaphores.* Lausanne: L'Age d'Homme.

Powell, G. C. 1992. "Why Generals Get Nervous," *New York Times* 8/10/92.

Ramet, P. 1992. *Balkan Babel: Politics, Culture, and Religion in Yugoslavia.* Boulder, CO: Westview Press.

Ramsey, Paul. 1961. *War and the Christian Conscience: How Shall Modern War Be Conducted Justly.* Durham, NC: Duke University Press.

———. 1968. *The Just War: Force and Political Responsibility.* New York: Scribner.

———. 1988. *Speak Up for Just War or Pacifism.* University Park, PA: Pennsylvania State University Press.

Rapoport, Anatol and Albert Chammah. 1965. *Prisoner's Dilemma.* Ann Arbor: University of Michigan Press.

Riedlmayer, A. 1994. *Killing Memory: Bosnia's Cultural Heritage and Its Destruction.* Haverford: Community of Bosnia Foundation.

———. 1994a. "The War on People and the War on Culture" *The New Combat.* Autumn, pp. 16–19.

Rieff, David. 1995. *Slaughterhouse: Bosnia and the Failure of the West*. New York: Simon and Schuster.

Roberts, Adam and Richard Guelff, eds. 1989. *Documents on the Laws of War*, 2d ed. Oxford: Clarendon Press.

Rothschild, Joseph. 1974. *East Central Europe between the Two World Wars*. Seattle: University of Washington Press.

Rubenstein, Richard L. 1975. *The Cunning of History: Mass Death and the American Future*. New York: Harper and Row.

———. 1983. *The Age of Triage: Fear and Hope in an Overcrowded World*. Boston: Beacon Press.

———. 1992. *After Auschwitz: History, Theology, and Contemporary Judaism*. 2nd ed. Baltimore and London: Johns Hopkins University Press.

———. 1993. "Silent Partners in Ethnic Cleansing: the UN, the EC, and NATO." *In Depth: A Journal for Values and Public Policy* 3/2 (Spring): 35–58.

Said, Edward. 1978. *Orientalism* New York: Pantheon Books.

Salisbury, Harrison E. 1969. *The 900 Days: The Siege of Leningrad*. New York: Harper and Row.

Schanberg, Sydney H. 1991. "A Muzzle for the Press," *Washington Journalism Review*, March, reprinted in Sifrey and Cerf (1991), pp. 368–375.

Schelling, Thomas. 1960. *The Strategy of Conflict*. Cambridge, MA: Harvard University Press.

Schwarzenberger, Georg. 1962. *The Frontiers of International Law*. London: Stevens and Sons.

Scott, James Brown. 1934. *The Spanish Origin of International Law: Francisco de Vitoria and His Law of Nations*. Oxford: Oxford University Press.

Security Council of the United Nations. 1993. *Annex I: European Community Investigative Mission into the Treatment of Muslim Women in the Former Yugoslavia, Report to the European Community Foreign Ministers*. New York: United Nations.

Sedlar, Jean W. 1994. *East Central Europe in the Middle Ages, 1000–1500*. Seattle: University of Washington Press.

Sells, Michael. 1994. "Bosnia: Some Religious Dimensions of Genocide," *Religious Studies News* 9/2, pp. 4–5.

Sifry, Micah L. and Christopher Cerf, eds. 1991. *The Gulf War Reader: History, Documents, Opinions*. New York: Random House.

Singleton, Fred. 1985. *A Short History of the Yugoslav Peoples*. Cambridge: Cambridge University Press.

Skrivanic, Gavro. 1982. "The Armed Forces in Karadjordje's Serbia" in Vucinich (1982), pp. 303–339.

Smajlovic, Ljiljana. 1995. "From the Heart of the Heart of the Former Yugoslavia," *Wilson Quarterly* 19/3, pp. 100–113.

Stein, Walter ed. 1961. *Nuclear Weapons and Christian Conscience.* London: Merlin Press.

Strange, Susan. 1995. "The Defective State," *Daedalus* 124/2, pp. 55–74.

Sugar, Peter F. 1977. *Southeastern Europe under Ottoman Rule, 1354–1804.* Seattle: University of Washington Press.

Sullivan, A., ed. 1995. *The New Republic: Accomplices to Genocide.* Washington: The New Republic.

Támas, G. M. 1993. "Old Enemies and New: A Philosophic Postscript to Nationalism" in Tamas (1993), pp. 107–126.

Támas, G. M., ed. 1993. *Studies in East European Thought.* Netherlands: Kluwer Academic Publishers.

Taylor, A. J. P. 1954. *The Struggle for Mastery in Europe, 1848–1918.* Oxford: Oxford University Press.

Temperley, Harold W. V. 1919. *History of Serbia.* London: G. Bell and Sons.

Thucydides. 1954. *HPW. History of the Peloponneisian War*, trans. Warner. Harmondsworth, England: Penguin Books.

Troeltsch, Ernst. 1992. *The Social Teachings of the Christian Churches*, trans. Wyon, forward J. L. Adams, 2 vols. Louisville, KY: Westminster/John Knox Press.

Udovicki, J. and J. R. 1995. *Yugoslavia's Ethnic Nightmare: The Inside Story of Europe's Unfolding Ordeal.* New York: Lawrence Hill Books.

U.S. Department of State. 1992–93. "War Crimes in the Former Yugoslavia: Submission of Information to the United States Security Council in Accordance with Paragraph 5 of Resolution 771 (1992)." *U.S. Department of State Dispatch* 8 U.S. State Department War Crimes Commission Reports found in the *U.S. Department of State Dispatch* 3 (1992) 39; 3.44; 3. 46; 3.52; 4 (1993) 6; 4. 15; 4.16; 4.30.

U.S. War Department. 1863. *General Orders No. 100 (1863). Instructions for the Government of Armies of the United States in the Field.* New York: D. van Nostrand.

Vitoria, Francisco de. 1991. *Political Writings*, ed. Pagden, trans. Lawrence. Cambridge: Cambridge University Press.

Vucinich, Wayne, ed. 1982. *The First Serbian Uprising, 1804–1813.* Boulder, CO: Brooklyn College Press.

Vucinich, Wayne and T. Emmert, eds. 1991. *Kosovo: Legacy of a Medieval Battle.* Minneapolis: University of Minnesota.

Vukadinovic, A., ed. 1989. *Kosovo 1939–1989: Special Edition of the Serbian Literary Quarterly on the Occasion of 600 Years since the Battle of Kosovo.* Belgrade: Serbian Literary Quarterly.

Wall Street Journal (WSJ). 7/15/94. "Czech Republic Fields Demands of Germans, Jews for Lost Homes," pp. 1–8.

Walzer, Michael. 1987. *Interpretation and Social Criticism.* Cambridge, MA: Harvard University Press.

———. 1992. *Just and Unjust Wars: A Moral Argument with Historical Illustrations,* 2d. ed. New York: Basic Books.

———. 1995. "The Politics of Rescue" *Dissent,* Winter, pp. 35–41.

Wasserstrom, Richard. 1969. "On the Morality of War: A Preliminary Inquiry" reprinted in Wasserstrom (1970), pp. 78–101.

Wasserstrom, Richard, ed. 1970. *War and Morality.* Belmont, CA: Wadsworth Publishing.

Weber, Max. 1958. *The Protestant Ethic and the Spirit of Capitalism,* trans. Talcott Parsons. New York: Scribner's.

———. 1978. *Economy and Society,* 2 vols, ed. and trans. Roth and Wittich. Berkeley: University of California Press.

———. 1981. *General Economic History.,* trans. Frank H. Knight. New Brunswick, NJ: Transactions Publishers.

West, Rebecca. 1941. *Black Lamb and Grey Falcon: A Journey through Yugoslavia.* New York: Penguin Books.

Will, George F. 1995. "The Last Word," *Newsweek,* June 12, p. 72.

Williams, I. 1995. "Mazowiecki Bucks the Trend" *War Report: Bulletin of the Institute for War and Peace Reporting* 35, July/August, p. 16.

Woodward, Susan. 1995. "Redrawing Borders in a Period of Systemic Transition" in Esman (1995), pp. 198–234.

———. 1995a. *Balkan Tragedy: Chaos and Dissolution After the Cold War.* Washington, DC: The Brookings Institution.

Zimmerman, Warren. 1995. "The Last Ambassador: A Memoir of the Collapse of Yugoslavia," *Foreign Affairs* 74/2, pp. 2–20.

Contributors

G. Scott Davis holds the Lewis T. Booker Chair in Religion and Ethics at the University of Richmond and is the author of *Warcraft and the Fragility of Virtue: An Essay in Aristotelian Ethics*.

Jean Bethke Elshtain is the Laura Spelman Rockefeller Professor of Social and Political Ethics at the University of Chicago. She is the author of many books including, most recently, *Democracy on Trial* and a new edition of *Women and War*.

James Turner Johnson is Professor of Religion and Director of International Programs at Rutgers University. Among his many books are *Can Modern War Be Just?* and *The Quest for Peace: Three Moral Traditions in Western Cultural History*.

John Kelsay teaches in the Department of Religion at Florida State University. He is the author of *Islam and War* and the editor, with Sumner B. Twiss, of *Religion and Human Rights*.

Michael A. Sells is Emily Judson Baugh and John Marshall Gest Professor of Comparative Religions at Haverford College. His most recent book is *Mystical Languages of Unsaying*. Professor Sells is also a founder and president of the *Community of Bosnia Foundation*, dedicated to supporting a multi-religious and culturally pluralistic Bosnia-Herzegovina.

Index